Unlocking the Love-Lock

UNLOCKING THE LOVE-LOCK

The History and Heritage of a Contemporary Custom

Ceri Houlbrook

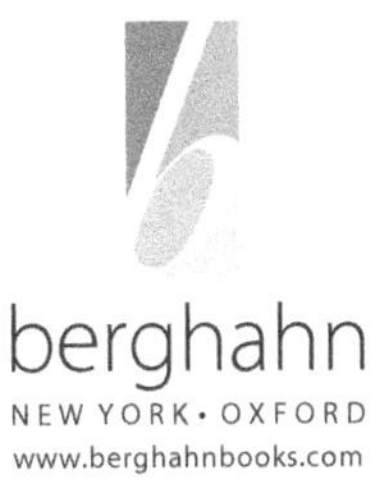

berghahn
NEW YORK · OXFORD
www.berghahnbooks.com

First published in 2021 by
Berghahn Books
www.berghahnbooks.com

Library of Congress Cataloging-in-Publication Data
Names: Houlbrook, Ceri, author.
Title: Unlocking the love-lock : the history and heritage of a contemporary custom /
    Ceri Houlbrook.
Description: New York : Berghahn, 2021. | Includes bibliographical references and index.
Identifiers: LCCN 2020033284 (print) | LCCN 2020033285 (ebook) | ISBN 9781789209228
    (hardback) | ISBN 9781789209853 (paperback) | ISBN 9781789209235 (ebook)
Subjects: LCSH: Dating (Social customs) | Padlocks—History. | Love—Folklore. | Love-lock
Classification: LCC HQ801 .H77 2021 (print) | LCC HQ801 (ebook) | DDC 306.73—dc23
LC record available at https://lccn.loc.gov/2020033284
LC ebook record available at https://lccn.loc.gov/2020033285

British Library Cataloguing in Publication Data
A catalogue record for this book is available from the British Library

ISBN 978-1-78920-922-8 hardback
ISBN 978-1-78920-985-3 paperbook
ISBN 978-1-78920-923-5 ebook

Contents

List of Illustrations and Tables

Illustrations

Tables

Introduction

Inspiration for this introductory chapter struck me while I was browsing the homewares section of a department store in 2018. I was distractedly perusing the photo frame aisle, my eyes skimming the generically sentimental stock pictures of happy families smiling at the camera, pretty landscapes, cute pets and couples walking hand-in-hand, when I came across one that jumped out at me. Bearing the text '5 x 7 Made in Thailand', it was a largely black-and-white image of five padlocks hanging from the cable of a probable bridge, the only splash of colour being a bright red love-heart adorning the one lock that faces the viewer. I recognised the image instantly as a photograph of love-locks: the padlocks that had been appearing en masse on bridges and other public structures on a global scale since the early 2000s. And, having been researching the custom known as love-locking for about five years at that point, it was with a peculiar sense of pride that I realised love-locks had accomplished the status of a stock image.

Stock images, such as those found in advertisements, on billboards and in brochures as well as in photo frames, are so called because they are kept 'in stock'; there are whole catalogues of stock images, often compiled by private companies and sent out to advertising agencies, who select the appropriate images and pay a fee for their use. But they are also known as 'stock images', as Paul Frosh notes, because of 'the predominant appearance of these images: instantly recognizable iconographic combinations which rely upon, and reinforce, "cliched" visual motifs and stereotypes'.[1] Romance is one of the most popular themes of stock photography, and certain objects connote this theme, demarcating the genre of romantic imagery: red roses, wine glasses clinking, lit candles on a table, engagement or wedding rings.[2] Such objects are known as *semes*, as defined by semiotician Umberto Eco as an 'iconic sign' or 'iconographic codes', which bear particular cultural and emotive connotations.[3] As is evident by its presence in a stock photo, the love-lock has become a *seme*: an instantly recognisable icon connoting romance.

The purpose of this monograph is to ask how this happened. How did the image of a padlock hanging from a bridge become an iconic sign of romance? How did it become, to return to Frosh's words, a cliched visual motif? Broadening the perspective, this book uses the love-lock as an exemplar in tracing how a custom and its associated symbolism can become so widespread, firmly established and instantly recognisable in a relatively short space of time. It begins by focusing on the padlock itself, historically contextualising an object that has clearly accrued significance beyond its original purpose.

The History of the Padlock

Vincent Eras, whose work *Locks and Keys throughout the Ages* has been invaluable for this chapter, defines the padlock as a 'detachable lock of which the swinging shackle passes through a hasp and staple or something similar'.[4] Essentially, they are portable locks consisting of a body, a shackle typically in the shape of a U and a locking mechanism. The origins of the lock are unclear, but we know that they predated Christ – the Egyptians, Greeks, Romans and Chinese used variations of them to lock vaults, doors and keep possessions secure.[5] One example of a Roman padlock was 4cm long, made of iron plate and consisted of a metal chain instead of a shackle. The mechanism involved a horizontal metal bolt with a spring, which slid from side to side, opening and closing, with the turn of a key.[6] In the ancient and medieval worlds, padlocks were used primarily for locking chests and securing doors, and remarkably few changes were made to their design and methods of construction between the Roman period and the seventeenth century.[7]

Throughout the Middle Ages, it was the Germans, French and Italians who gained reputations for producing the highest quality locks – in both security and artistic design, for the latter had become an important factor in their manufacture.[8] By the eighteenth century, Britain was also boasting a prosperous lock-making industry, centred on Wolverhampton, and a number of key lock-makers were taking out patents for various designs: Robert Barron, Joseph Bramah, Cotterill and Jeremiah Chubb.[9] In 1857, Linus Yale Jr., an American mechanical engineer, designed the first cylinder lock; taking inspiration from the peg system of ancient Egyptian wooden locks, he designed a pin tumbler mechanism that housed the key-operated mechanism within cylindrically shaped housing, inside the body of a lock [10]

Today, the most common types of padlocks are pin tumbler locks – which require a key to release the shackle – and keyless combination locks, opened when a predetermined sequence of letters or numbers on rotating rings are brought into line. They are still used widely today, both domestically and commercially, and can be purchased on the high street (such as in Wilko and Argos), from DIY retailers and online. Prices on the website for B&Q, a British multinational home improvement retailer, range from £2.68 (roughly €3 or US$3.40) for a 31mm iron cylinder lock to £35 (€39 or US$44) for a 67mm laminated steel closed-shackle lock.[11] Today they are used for a variety of reasons: to secure safe deposit boxes, shed doors, cupboards, luggage, gym lockers, even journals. And now, with the advent of love-locking, they are being attached to bridges and other public structures worldwide for no seemingly practical purpose. A history of the custom of love-locking is the focus of *Chapter One: Dating Love*, but a brief overview is useful here.

As will be demonstrated in the next chapter, our knowledge of the history of love-locks is patchy, with various places worldwide claiming to have birthed the custom. What we do know is that in 2006 Italian writer Federico Moccia published a teenage romance novel entitled *Ho voglia di te* (*I Want You*), in which two young lovers attach a padlock to a lamp post on the Ponte Milvio in Rome and then throw the key into the water below as a statement of their romantic commitment. (Henceforth in this book, padlocks treated in this fashion are referred to as love-locks.) Moccia's novel gained something of a cult following in Italy, and teenagers began to imitate the practice, first on the Ponte Milvio and then elsewhere. Tourists imitated the locals, and soon the custom had spread beyond Italy – and then beyond Europe, with people worldwide inscribing padlocks with their names, initials or messages and attaching them to bridges or other public structures before disposing of the key, in a custom which became dubbed love-locking. The 'tradition' dictates that if a couple wish to go their separate ways, they must retrieve the key from the water and unlock their love-lock.

It is not hyperbolic to claim that love-locking grew into a global custom. Through online research, word-of-mouth and research in the field, I have compiled data of over 500 locations worldwide where people have affixed love-locks to bridges or other public structures, such as railings, fences, gates and sculptures. This is no doubt only the tip of the iceberg, and a network of global researchers would be needed to document the full extent of this custom. However, if the sample of 500 is taken as relatively representative, love-locking seems more prevalent in Europe (granted, this may have more to do with unintentional bias in my research – see below), featuring particularly heavily in Germany, the UK and Italy. The structures can be well-known and in large cities: the Hohenzollern Bridge in Cologne; Tower Bridge in London; the Ponte Vecchio in Florence. They can also be obscure structures in places less known on a global scale, including small towns and rural areas: the railings of the observation deck in Durlach, Karlsruhe; a bridge at Foots Cray Meadows, Bexley; a lamp post in Susa.

Love-locking does feature throughout Europe though, from the Scandinavian countries to the Balkans. It is also popular in North America, particularly in the US, where it stretches from as far east as New York to as far west as Hawaii, with many in between. And large assemblages have grown in the Far East, with particularly well-known love-lock sites on the N Seoul Tower and in the Yellow Mountains in China. Australia is also quite well represented, with most of the large cities and some more rural locations featuring assemblages, including several on fences along coastal walks and at lookout points.

The custom's dissemination has been less successful in Africa and the Middle East, although it has occurred in these areas, in such locations as a bridge in Cape Town, a viewpoint overlooking the Dead Sea in Jordan, a bridge in Basra and along a corniche in Jeddah. Overall, it has appeared in *at least* 65 countries worldwide, on every continent bar the Antarctica (and may well even be there). Love-locks have thus appeared in destinations as geographically distant and culturally diverse as Paris and Vanadzor, New York and Saravejo, and Melbourne and Minsk, also showing up in small towns and rural locations (Illustration 0.1.).

The Love-Lock and Terminology

Throughout this book, various archaeological and anthropological terms are applied to love-locks. Some brief explanations of these key terms are explained here. Firstly, the love-locker as 'depositor' and the love-lock as 'structured deposit'. The latter is an archaeological term coined by Richards and Thomas in their 1984 paper 'Ritual Activity and Structured Deposition in Later Neolithic Wessex', and it is a concept anchored within the archaeology of ritual – of which there will be further consideration in *Chapter Four: Locking Love*.[12] Richards and Thomas describe ritual as 'formalised repetitive actions which may be detected archaeologically through a highly structured mode of deposition'.[13] By 'structured mode', they mean deposited in a way that suggests deliberate placement by the depositor. There is often some cultural or personal significance to objects deposited in such a way, whether prehistoric, historic or contemporary. Harris, writing of axes, animal remains and pottery fragments deposited at Neolithic Etton causewayed enclosure in Cambridgeshire, observed that 'The items deposited were undoubtedly metonymic and mnemonic in quality.'[14] These two qualities will be examined in relation to the love-lock in future pages.

Also writing of prehistoric archaeology, Fontijn observes that some sites become 'multiple-deposition zones', whereby 'people *repeatedly visited specific zones in the land in order to carry out specific types of deposition*' (emphases in original).[15] This description readily applies to love-lock sites. Rarely will you see only one or two love-locks; one becomes two, becomes ten, becomes hundreds, sometimes thousands – sometimes even millions, in the case of the Pont des Arts in Paris. Thus is the nature of accumulation, which archaeologist Clive Gamble describes as having a 'magnetic-like effect'.[16] Deposits attract more deposits, often at an exponential rate. The love-locks cluster and overlap, reaching such high densities that space becomes limited and people begin attaching their love-locks to the shackles of other love-locks (Illustration 0.2.).

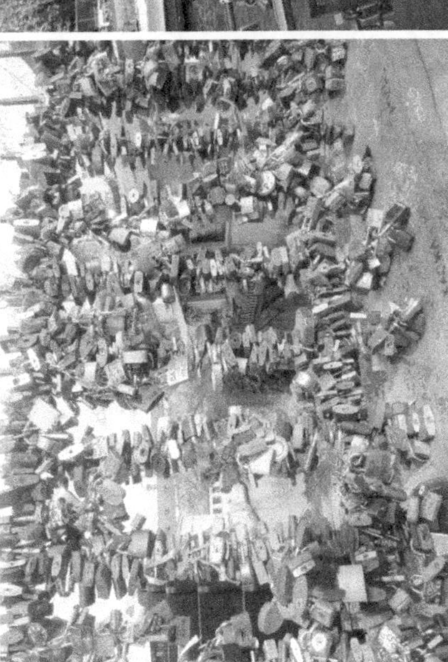

Illustration 0.1. Love-lock assemblages in Prague, Bristol, Lisbon and along the Cinque Terre, Italy. Photographs by the author.

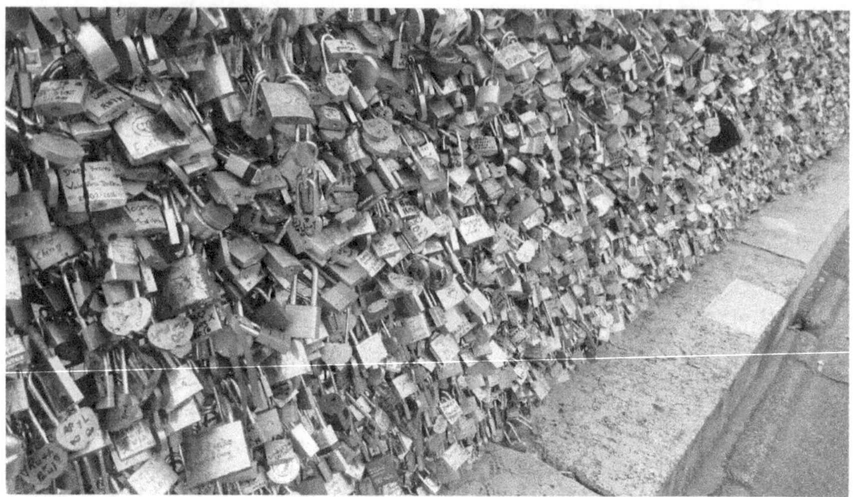

Illustration 0.2. Love-locks overlapping and locked to each other on the Pont Neuf, Paris. Photograph by the author.

The love-locks form what folklorist Jack Santino has termed 'folk assemblages': spontaneous accumulations that invite further participation from others.[17] Cathy Preston, contemporary legends scholar, applies this concept to her work on 'panty trees' and 'shoe trees', claiming that such assemblages evoke the sense of an imagined community:

> that imagined community being the various individuals, usually anonymous, who have responded in kind to the acts of earlier individuals and who frequently envision their responses as linking them to a group of people who, though invisible to them, are made visible by that which they have left behind. Inclusive in this definition is also a sense that, though community-based, the object is not institutionally sanctioned.[18]

In a similar vein, folklorist Lynne McNeill coined the term 'serial collaborative creations'. These creations share four features, all of which can be applied to a love-lock assemblage:

1. People come into contact with objects through geographical movement. Either the objects are passed from person to person (type A) or the people pass by the objects (type B).
2. People involved contribute to the object, either by adding to its physical form or by continuing its journey through some sort of personal effort.
3. Multiple people interact with the object, but they do it one at a time or in small, sequential groups.

4. Those who interact with the object individually (or in small groups) are aware of others' involvement with the object's existence, though they may not interact with them directly. This awareness is expected and necessary; the object, by virtue of being a chain object, implies the presence of past and future participants.[19]

Love-lock assemblages are clearly a type B serial collaborative creation, in that they are encountered through people's movement: as they pass a particular site, as they cross a bridge and so on. People contribute to it by adding to its physical form – that is, by adding their own love-lock – and they do this one couple or group at a time, aware of the fact that others have contributed before them and others will no doubt contribute after.

So, through structured deposition, folk assemblages grow. And through the growth and establishment of folk assemblages, space becomes place. This, too, is an archaeological concept. '[P]eople leave things,' Miles Richardson writes. 'And in their leaving they establish the location as a place.'[20] John Chapman conceptualises 'place' as 'space objectified', as space that has been imbued with meaning and value through human activity and the objects they place or move within it.[21] In the case of the love-lock assemblages, place is established via the custom of love-locking and the structured deposition of the love-locks themselves. A bridge, for example, becomes *the love-lock bridge*; a gate becomes *the love-lock gate* – but not only because of the tangible alterations of a growing assemblage. This process of 'neutral space' transitioning to 'meaningful place', to use Fontijn's wording, is the result of people's connections with it. Deposition fixes a connection between depositor and place by creating a shared history, a shared memory of the depositional event.[22]

Studying the Love-Lock

The vast majority of scholars who have engaged with the above concepts apply them to objects and activities from prehistory and history. Obviously, love-locks are neither. As *Chapter One: Dating Love* will demonstrate, love-locking may date to the early twentieth century but was definitely not a widespread practice until the twenty-first. It is therefore a contemporary custom. The terms outlined above, however, are no less applicable because of this modernity, and this is certainly not the first study of contemporary assemblages. As we will see in *Chapter Three: Excavating Love*, many scholars – archaeologists, anthropologists, folklorists – have engaged with the material culture of modern-day depositional practices, from Jenny Blain and Robert Wallis' examination of Neo-Pagan deposits at prehistoric sites to Tristan Hulse's treatment of handwritten prayers at a holy well in Wales.[23]

Nor is this the first study of love-locking, which is unsurprising considering the extent of the custom's dissemination. Art historian Cynthia Hammond was one of the first scholars to engage with the subject in her 2010 article 'Renegade Ornament and the Image of the Post-Socialist City: The Pécs "Love Locks", Hungary'.[24] In this, she dates a love-lock fence in Janus Pannonius Utca, close to Pécs Cathedral, to the 1980s. Hammond's examination into the history of this early assemblage is discussed in *Chapter One: Dating Love*; what is of significance here is the conceptual framework she applies to the custom. Designating love-locks 'renegade ornaments' because of their unsanctioned nature, particularly at a time when Pécs was still under the hold of Soviet social control, Hammond illustrates how this particular assemblage is representative of layers of control and dissent in the city.

Social scientist Kai-Olaf Maiwald is another scholar who has explored love-locking. He adopts an objective–hermeneutic approach in his 2016 investigation into the symbolic meaning of what he dubs 'padlocking' at the Hohenzollern Bridge, Cologne, entitled 'An Ever-Fixed Mark? On the Symbolic Coping with the Fragility of Partner Relationships by Means of Padlocking'.[25] Maiwald dates the Hohenzollern Bridge assemblage to 2008. He acknowledges the irregularity of focusing on an artefact in sociological research but demonstrates the valuable insight gained into the 'vivid social practice' of love-locking by studying the symbolism of its components: the padlock, the key, the inscriptions and the bridge. These are, he argues, highly appropriate for a custom that he interprets as acknowledging the fragility of romantic relationships. Maiwald's theories will be considered further in *Chapter Five: Symbolising Love*.

In their 2017 article 'Bridges, Locks and Love: Most Tumski in Wroclaw and Thousands of Love Bridges Worldwide: New Secular Sanctuaries in Today's Public Space?', Felix Richter and Verena Pfeiffer-Kloss place the love-lock within the context of the history of signs of romantic love in the public space of the city, alongside symbols carved into trees and benches.[26] Adopting a descriptive-analytical approach, they explore the notion of love-lock bridges as new urban secular sanctuaries, focusing on Most Tumski in Wroclaw, Poland, which they estimate to contain 40,000 love-locks. They also contemplate love-locking as a ritual, dividing the physical act of fixing a love-lock into eleven micro-rituals; these are considered in *Chapter Four: Locking Love*.

Artist Lachlan MacDowell considers love-locks within the context of graffiti and street art, aligning them with other contemporary assemblages of structured deposits, such as shoe trees and chewing gum walls. All of these, she claims, 'provide excellent illustrations of a blunt, quantitative form of stigmergy and the ways in which certain urban practices cluster spatially, without direct coordination'.[27] Central to MacDowell's study is the concept of 'stigmergy', which was originally a biological concept applied to swarm intelligence but now refers more generally to the process whereby one action leaves a trace on the environment, subsequently stimulating another action. This applies to love-locks in respect to the growth of the accumulation; as was stated above, the affixing of one love-lock (one action that leaves a trace on the environment) tends to attract more love-locks, and the assemblage proliferates.

Most recently, consumer culture theorist Stéphane Borraz has published his findings from a five-year (2012–2017) study of love-locking in Paris, which involved empirical fieldwork, interviewing and netnography.[28] Describing the custom as a 'new consumer love ritual' conducted at modern-day 'pilgrimage sites', Borraz maps the sequence of events that form the ritual onto Van Gennep's three-staged rite of passage.[29] The preliminary stage consists of the love-lockers examining the other locks of the assemblage and identifying a suitable place for their own; the liminal stretches from the decoration of the love-lock to the disposing of the key; and the postliminal is the sharing of the experience with others, often via social media. Borraz's valuable findings and discussion of his fieldwork are drawn on throughout this book.

Other scholars have engaged with love-locking more concisely as part of broader studies. Joana Breidenbach and Pál Nyíri briefly refer to love-locks on sale to tourists at the Yellow Mountains and Mt. Emei World Heritage sites in China, in their article on new tourist nations and the globalisation of nature. Their article includes a photograph of tourists affixing love-locks at the summit of Mt. Emei.[30] Oksana Mykytenko considers the rich semiotic status of the padlock and key in Slavic wedding traditions, often understood as erotic symbols, in order to contextualise the love-lock custom; her work is engaged with in *Chapter Five: Symbolising Love*.[31] In 2016, in their work on archaeological approaches to graffiti, Ursula Frederick and Anne Clarke included love-locks in their list of examples of contemporary graffiti, alongside concrete street art and 'knitfitti', which 'transform private and public spaces alike in surprising, subversive and often humorous ways'.[32] And in 2017, Maria Gravari-Barbas and Sébastien Jacquot drew on love-locks in Paris as an example of mobilisation within discourses of tourism-related tensions, exploring how local residents campaigned against the custom, a subject that will be explored in greater detail in *Chapter Seven: Unlocking Love*.[33]

Most scholars engaging with love-locks have done so within the context of urban studies. Urban scenographer Jekaterina Lavrinec considers love-locking an 'urban ritual', one that identifies citizens as active 'interpreters' of urban space and 'reinvents urban places by producing alternative meaning and encouraging alternative scenarios of behaviour'.[34] Engineer Christian Walloth, drawing on Hammond's work on the Pécs assemblage, characterises love-locks as 'emergent [i.e. unplanned and in principle unpredictable] qualities' in a city environment. Walloth explores the influence they have on urban development strategies, considering how Pécs integrated the city's love-locks, which were an unplanned city feature, into its cultural and marketing image.[35] In addition, in 2018, Simon Sleight equated love-lock assemblages with roadside shrines, dubbing them '"vernacular" memorials' and contemplating them within his examination of the city as a palimpsest of memories, which are emotionally inscribed onto the urban landscape.[36]

Undoubtedly, considering the global nature of this custom, there are far more studies of love-locks written in languages other than English. But this serves as a useful overview, demonstrating the various perspectives from which love-locks have been viewed and engaged with, from art history and semiotics to sociology and urban planning. Clearly, the custom is multifaceted enough to be studied from myriad angles, but more than this: it sheds light on those myriad angles. Love-locks can tell us something about art history and semiotics, sociology and urban planning.

Methodology

The interdisciplinarity of the above corpus of studies has been deliberately replicated throughout this monograph, with each chapter taking a different methodological approach to the custom. Throughout, however, participant observation has been the key methodology.[37] I have spent time, ranging from thirty minutes to six hours (one very cold Valentine's Day in Manchester, UK), standing at love-lock assemblages, examining the love-locks and observing members of the public who approach. I often took only mental notes so as to be as unobtrusive as possible and then wrote up my observations immediately after leaving the site. My primary aim in this was to gain insight into how people engage with these assemblages: roughly what proportions of people simply pass them by, stop to examine them or add their own love-lock? If they are in groups, what do they say about the custom? Do they photograph the love-locks? Do they touch them? This method of data collection was conducted at various locations in Australia, Austria, Czech Republic, England, France, Germany, Greece, Holland, Hungary, Iceland, Italy, Northern Ireland, Portugal, Republic of Ireland, Russia, Scotland, Spain and Sweden. A limitation of this method of data collection was its strong European focus, and future studies would undoubtedly benefit from a more global scale.

The Eurocentrism of my observations was slightly offset by the global perspective of another methodology employed: online ethnography (or netnography), which involved viewing videos of participation in the custom globally, uploaded by the participants to video-sharing site YouTube, as well as engagement with posts on Instagram and Twitter.[38] I did not participate in these online communities but simply watched the videos and observed the photographs posted, checking for new material on a weekly basis between 2017 and 2019. As with the participant observations, this method provided valuable insight into how people are engaging with love-lock assemblages, and the significance of the filming, photographing and digital sharing of these engagements is explored in *Chapter Four: Locking Love*.

In addition to observations and netnography, I conducted interviews with people who had participated in the custom. Contact was made with interviewees via word-of-mouth or local authorities. Interviews were often via questionnaires, with the participants writing their responses, sometimes followed by further questions or requests for elaboration. Questions varied depending upon the interviewee but often included the following: When and where did you lock your love-lock? Why did you choose that location? Who were you with? Why did you participate in this custom? When did you become aware of the custom? When and where did you purchase your love-lock? How did you decorate it? Did you photograph/film your participation/love-lock? If so, did you share the picture/video with anyone? Have you visited your love-lock since locking it? In most cases, couples who had deposited a love-lock together answered the questions together.

Contemporary archaeological methods were employed at every location visited. The material culture of the love-locks was examined; assemblages were photographed and individual inscriptions and adornments were recorded. Observations were made on how the assemblages were clustered; whether their deposition had damaged the host structure; what types of padlocks had been used; and whether any keys were visible (only one was ever seen: rusting on a ledge beneath Queen's Park Bridge, Chester, UK). In Manchester, a running inventory was made of love-locks added to the Oxford Road Bridge from 2014–2019; every new addition was photographed, assigned a catalogue number and recorded in detail. This dataset, now containing over 700 love-locks, provides insight into how an assemblage forms and grows over time and is the basis of *Chapter Three: Excavating Love*.[39]

The Following Pages

Chapter One: Dating Love traces the history of love-locking, taking a chronological approach. While acknowledging the futility of seeking origins for a folk custom, and admitting the difficulties faced while researching for this chapter, it attempts to disentangle fact from fiction and determine where contemporary love-locking began, why its popularity grew and how it spread. It examines twentieth-century love-lock assemblages in Serbia, Hungary and Italy, focusing on Moccia's novel *Ho voglia di te* as an impetus in global spread and subsequently contemplating the phenomena of conversion from popular culture to popular custom. The chapter subsequently turns to tourist folklore, identifying tourists (in particular, tourists who are also social media users) as a key group in the perpetuation and dissemination of the custom.

Chapter Two: Consuming Love takes the earlier reference to the transition from popular culture to popular custom as its starting point and delves more deeply into this process. Since Moccia's use of love-locks in his teen romance novel, the custom has appeared in myriad pieces of popular culture: television shows, films, literature and music. This chapter considers the various uses of the love-lock as folk motif in fiction, whether it is employed as incidental backdrop, as a symbolic element adopted to communicate a message or materialise a sentiment, or as integral to the plot itself. Thus through the love-lock, the chapter explores what these uses demonstrate about the relationship – or interrelationship – between folkloric custom and popular culture.

Chapter Three: Excavating Love takes a material culture approach to love-locks, identifying them as ex-votos. The folk assemblages of love-locks, this chapter stresses, are tangible traces of ritual and should be examined archaeologically. Following a review of material culture studies of contemporary ritual, the chapter introduces a primary case study: an assemblage on Oxford Road in Manchester, UK, for which empirical data has been collected since 2014. Drawing on this dataset, this chapter demonstrates the value of recording a folk assemblage during its formation, as opposed to post formation, and the insight this gains us into the pace, the people and the purpose of deposition.

Chapter Four: Locking Love provides an ethnographic examination of love-locking, noting that as useful as a material cultural approach has proven to be, the participants themselves provide the most invaluable insights into the *how* and the *why* of their engagement with the custom. It commences with some storytelling, drawing on interviews with people who have locked their love to outline their experiences with this practice, which is here identified as a 'ritual', one that is often unofficially documented by its participants. Through these interviews and further observations, the love-lock is gleaned as a planned deposit, an object of emotion, a mnemonic device and as an entangled object with a biography that continues beyond its deposition.

Chapter Five: Symbolising Love questions how this one custom appeals to, and has been adopted by, the myriad and myriadly diverse inhabitants of six different continents. While it is wary of claiming universal symbols, it identifies the symbolic potency of the love-lock as a primary factor in its successful establishment and rapid, widespread dissemination. This chapter thus takes a semiotic approach to the custom, exploring both the padlock and the bridge as symbols with global vigour, not claiming such symbolisms as the origins of love-locking but as insight into why such vast numbers of people today have proven so receptive to this contemporary custom.

Chapter Six: Selling Love examines the myriad examples of love-locks being harnessed for tourism and commercial gain worldwide. In some instances, love-locking is encouraged or even deliberately implemented, whether for the revenue it creates – sometimes for charitable causes – or to foster a sense of communal identity. Other examples see the love-locking custom and its symbolism harnessed for advertisements, or love-locks commodified and sold in other forms, from Pandora charms to chocolates. This chapter argues that across the majority of these cases there is a sense that, through commercialisation, the custom has become inherent to the places themselves, through the processes of place-marketing and place-making.

While the majority of this book considers the perspectives of those individuals and groups in favour of love-locking, *Chapter Seven: Unlocking Love* recognises how polarising this custom has proven to be. It therefore adopts the other viewpoint, exploring the love-lock as object of controversy and the love-lock assemblage as contested landscape. Detailing the various methods employed to discourage the deposition of love-locks and contemplating what happens to those assemblages that find themselves removed by local authorities, this chapter questions what the contested nature of the custom reveals about perceptions of heritage 'value'. All of the above themes are drawn together in the conclusion by way of one final case study: a literacy examination sat by secondary school students in Ontario in 2010.

A brief note now about the limitations of this book. There is an undeniable Eurocentrism to many of the case studies used throughout, with a particular focus on Britain due to my geographic base. A lack of non-English sources is also shamefully apparent, testifying to my shortcomings in language abilities. As the global nature of love-locking is so central to my interest in it, every effort was made to broaden the scope of research, with resort to a number of invaluable translators who kindly gave up their time to aid me with Serbian, Italian, German and Portuguese sources.[40] A western bias is still clearly evident though, and so it is with hope that I appeal to fellow researchers worldwide – be you folklorists, archaeologists, ethnographers, anthropologists, historians, geographers or heritage specialists – to either begin or continue metaphorically unlocking love-locks. For both an in-depth *and* culturally broad study of love-locking, we are going to need researchers on every continent to do justice to this global phenomenon.

Notes

1. Frosh, *The Image Factory*, 8.
2. Ibid., 127.
3. Eco, 'Critique of the Image', 35–37.
4. Eras, *Locks and Keys throughout the Ages*, 15.
5. Ibid., 18–20.
6. https://web.archive.org/web/20111008030711/http://www.historicallocks.com/en/site/hl/Articles/The-history-of-padlocks/Roman-Era-500-BC300-AD/ [Accessed 11/07/2019].
7. Eras, *Locks and Keys throughout the Ages*, 91.

8. Ibid., 59.

9. Ibid., 104–9.

10. Ibid., 115.

11. https://www.diy.com/departments/hardware/locks-padlocks/padlocks/DIY580699.cat?sort=rating [Accessed 11/07/2019].

12. Richards and Thomas, 'Ritual Activity and Structured Deposition in Later Neolithic Wessex', 189–218; Garrow, 'Odd Deposits and Average Practice', 85–115.

13. Richards and Thomas, 'Ritual Activity and Structured Deposition', 215.

14. Harris, 'Agents of Identity', 46.

15. Fontijn, *Sacrificial Landscapes*, 260.

16. Gamble, *Origins and Revolutions*, 122.

17. Santino, 'Performative Commemoratives, the Personal, and the Public', 363–72.

18. Preston, 'Panty Trees, Shoe Trees, and Legend', 12.

19. McNeill, 'Portable Places', 285–86.

20. Richardson, 'The Gift of Presence', 260.

21. Chapman, *Fragmentation in Archaeology*, 190.

22. Thomas, *Understanding the Neolithic*, 87; Fontijn, *Sacrificial Landscapes*, 34–35.

23. Blain and Wallis, 'Representing Spirit', 89–108; Hulse, 'A Modern Votive Deposit at a North Welsh Holy Well', 31–42.

24. Hammond, 'Renegade Ornament and the Image of the Post-Socialist City', 181–95.

25. Maiwald, 'An Ever-Fixed Mark?'.

26. Richter and Pfeiffer-Kloss, 'Bridges, Locks and Love', 187–202.

27. MacDowall, 'Graffiti, Street Art and Theories of Stigmergy', 41.

28. Borraz, 'Love and Locks', 7–21.

29. Van Gennep, *The Rites of Passage*.

30. Breidenbach and Nyíri, '"Our Common Heritage"', 322–30.

31. Mykytenko, 'Padlock and Key as Attributes of the Wedding Ceremony', 487–96.

32. Frederick and Clarke, 'Signs of the Times', 54–57.

33. Gravari-Barbas and Jacquot, 'No Conflict?', 44–61.

34. Lavrinec, 'Urban Scenography', 22.

35. Walloth, 'Emergence in Complex Urban Systems?', 121–32.

36. Sleight, 'Memory in the City', 139.

37. See O'Reilly, *Ethnographic Methods*.

38. See Robert Kozinets's 2010 work *Netnography*, which centralises the knowledge that 'Our social worlds are going digital. As a consequence, social scientists around the world are finding that to understand society they must follow people's social activities and encounters onto the Internet and through other technologically-mediated communications' (Kozinets, *Netnography*, 1). As well as 'netnography', Mariann Domokos lists 'cyberethnography', 'virtual ethnography', 'virtual anthropology' and 'e-folklore' as terms that have been applied to online ethnography (Domokos, 'Towards Methodological Issues in Electronic Folklore', 286).

39. An enhanced version of the complete love-locks catalogue is available online through Berghahn Digital Archaeology at https://berghahnbooks.com/digitalarchaeology.

40. Particular thanks to Raško Ramandanski, Marija Maric, Francesca Benetti, Chiara Zuanni, Cait Houlbrook and Ami Houlbrook.

CHAPTER I

DATING LOVE

A History of the Love-Lock Custom

Questing for the origins of a contemporary folk custom is an often futile and
fruitless task. It is also not an endeavour favoured by modern-day Folklore Studies, partly because of the difficulties entailed in reaching confident conclusions
but also because focus tends to be less on where a custom comes from and more
on its state today. However, I am as much a historian as a folklorist, and in order to understand the twenty-first-century widespread popularity of the love-lock
custom, I maintain that it must be placed within its historical context. After
all, no custom emerges entirely out of the blue. Customs are nearly always (one
might go so far as to say always) adaptations or borrowings from other periods,
cultures or communities. Where, then, did the custom of attaching padlocks to
public structures begin? And how did it spread to over 500 locations worldwide?
This chapter attempts to answer these questions.

However, compiling a history of love-locking has proved no easy feat. There
are two primary reasons for this. Firstly, the custom's international spread, which
sees numerous narratives and networks of dissemination, rather than a single,
linear thread. The origins of one assemblage are not necessarily the same as the
origins of another, neither are the rates of growth, and with at least 500 (but
probably thousands of) assemblages worldwide, the establishment of a chronol-
ogy poses difficulties. Secondly, in light of these difficulties, a range of fictions
have been created, adapted and adopted in order to contextualise the custom,
most notably by the tourist industry and the media. Rumours are presented as
reality, and it has been a complicated task separating fact from fiction. This chapter traces the solid facts, handling the solid evidence, while the shakier evidence
(such as the frequent attribution of the practice to a tragic pair of Serbian lovers)
and the likely fictions (the casual attribution to an 'ancient Chinese custom')
will be examined in *Chapter Six: Selling Love*.

Love-Locking in the 1980s

The earliest solid evidence for the mass deposition of padlocks on public structures comes from Europe in the 1980s.[1] The best-documented example is in Hungary. In Janus Pannonius Utca in the city of Pécs, close to the historic monuments of Pécs Cathedral and the former mosque Pasha Gázi Kászim, is a fence festooned with love-locks. Art historian Cynthia Hammond, whom we met in the Introduction, confidently dates this assemblage to the 1980s.[2] Hammond argues that in order to understand this custom, it must be set within the context of late twentieth-century Hungarian history, when the hold of Soviet social control over the country began to loosen. This control, she asserts, extended to a repression of public displays of romantic love, and the 1980s saw a gradually growing freedom of expression. By the 1990s, it was far more permissible to express romantic relations publicly.

Love-locks were being deposited prior to this though, at a time when the custom would have been frowned upon or even forbidden. Why would the depositors have risked censure and punishment? Hammond theorises a connection with the Punk music subculture permeating the youth scene of Hungary during this period. During the 1970s, Sid Vicious of the Sex Pistols adopted the padlock as a symbol, wearing one around his neck on a chain. The padlock therefore became, in Hammond's words, 'a forceful symbol of resistance, dissent, and art against convention'.[3] Hammond does not believe it was a coincidence that within a few years of the padlock becoming a symbol of the Punk movement people had begun attaching them to the fence in Pécs. Despite the Pécs love-locks' controversial origins, by 2007 the fence had become part of the city's heritage and repackaged as a tourist destination (see *Chapter Six: Selling Love*).

Another example of the mass deposition of padlocks on a public structure was in Merano, an Alpine town in northern Italy. From the 1980s until 2005, it was a local custom for Italian soldiers undertaking their military conscription in Merano to celebrate the end of their service by locking the padlock from their barracks locker to the Ponte Teatro in the town centre. They would often inscribe the lock with their period of military service and the name of their military company.[4] Local authorities tolerated the practice, removing the locks only when the balustrade began overflowing. The custom died out with the ending of obligatory conscription and the closure of the Merano military complex.[5] Also in Italy, graduates of the San Giorgio hospital academy similarly attached the padlocks from their lockers to a bridge in Florence at the end of their training.[6]

Interestingly, none of these examples appear to have originally been about declaring romantic attachment – in fact, as Richter and Pfeiffer-Kloss observe, the Italian customs celebrated regained freedom[7] – although the Pécs assemblage did develop an amorous element over time. It would take over a decade for other sites to host the custom with an explicitly romantic colour, and again these appear quite isolated. The love-locks on Jade Peak of the Yellow Mountains, China, for example, are believed to have appeared in 1999/2000, possibly leading to dissemination in the Far East (see *Chapter Six: Selling Love*). However, it was not until the 2000s that the custom gained global popularity – spurred by a teenage romance novel.

The Moccia Phenomenon

In 1992, Italian novelist Federico Moccia released his first novel *Tre Metri Sopra il Cielo* (*Three Meters Above Heaven*), paying the publishing costs himself and printing 1,500 copies. A first-person narrated story of teenage angst and love, centred on Roman 'bad boy' Step's ill-fated relationship with 'good girl' Babi, it gained popularity amongst young Italian readers and, soon out of print, circulated by way of photocopies. Twelve years later, in 2004, a heavily-edited *Tre Metri Sopra il Cielo* was reissued by Feltrinelli, one of the biggest publishing houses in Italy. It sold 1,850,000 copies and was subsequently turned into a film directed by Luca Lucini. Riding on its success, Moccia published a sequel in 2006 entitled *Ho voglia di te* (*I Want You*), in which the protagonist Step remains the same but his love interest – now a girl called Gin – does not. In the second half of the novel, Gin and Step, driving through Rome in Step's brother's car, stop near the Milvio Bridge. Gin takes him to the middle of the bridge and points out a street lamp surrounded by padlocks. '"This is the lover's chain",' she explains to him. 'You have to put a padlock on this chain, lock it and throw the key in the Tevere.' 'And then?' 'You never break up.'[8] Gin accuses Step of being 'scared of locking a padlock', to which he responds by retrieving a padlock from his brother's car:

> I hold the key between my thumb and forefinger. I hang it loose for a while, suspended in the air, uncertain. Then suddenly I let it go. And it flies down, fast, rolls in the air and gets lost in the waters of the Tevere.
> "You really did it."[9]

And thus the love-lock phenomenon was born.

In an interview with *USA Today*, Moccia – who may have already been familiar with the custom in Florence – admitted to placing a padlock on the third lamp post of the Ponte Milvio the night before *Ho voglia di te* was published, for the benefit of any curious readers who may visit the site to check if the love-lock custom was real. 'I thought only someone particularly engrossed by the story would have wanted to check,' Moccia is reported to have recalled in 2015, bemused by what happened next. 'I went there a week later and there were already 300 locks. They haven't stopped since.'[10] It certainly did not take long for the custom to establish itself on the Ponte Milvio. One year later, an article in the

'Travel' section of the *Telegraph* reported that, following Moccia's novel, the lamp post on the Ponte Milvio has become:

> . . . bedecked with hundreds of padlocks. Like characters in the book, lovers come here to add a chain inscribed with their names – and then throw the key into the river. But hurry if you want to follow suit. The weight of the locks is bending the post, and there are now calls for the custom to be banned.[11]

It is unsurprising that such quantities of people visited the site from the book. It was a remarkably successful novel, with a million copies sold in Italy alone, and translations also proving popular; 600,000 copies were sold in Spain, for example.[12] Moccia's work has been published in fifteen languages worldwide, with an English translation planned for 2021.[13] Films followed the books, with *Ho voglia di te*, directed by Luis Prieto, hitting the screens in Italy in 2007 (a Spanish version – as *Tengo ganas de ti* – was released in 2012). The film is evidence of the love-lock custom on the Ponte Milvio, for the scene with Step and Gin on the bridge features the real assemblage. So, in the short amount of time between the book's publication in February 2006 and the release of the film in March 2007, the love-lock lamp post had become an established feature.

Connected to the film was singer-songwriter Tiziano Ferro's *Ti scatterò una foto* (*I will take a photo of you*). The lyrics of this love song speak of 'memory', 'always', 'remember forever' and the fear of being forgotten. The music video for this featured Ferro standing on the Ponte Milvio with actress Laura Chiatti, who played Gin in *Ho voglia di te*. Throughout the video, which is regularly interspersed with shots of the bridge's assemblage, both Ferro and Chiatti melancholically touch and study the love-locks. The song was released in February 2007 and was in the Italian music charts for 20 weeks.[14] The popularity of the novel, films and song has been dubbed the 'Moccia phenomenon' in popular media;[15] the love-lock custom – which sprang from this popularity in such a short space of time – was soon being dubbed the same.

From Popular Culture to Popular Custom

This conversion from popular culture to popular custom is not uncommon. Literature, film and television are well-known travel inducements, attracting fans to the sites that feature in the fiction. Fans of *The Lord of the Rings* visit New Zealand in their search for Middle Earth; for the *Twilight Saga* they travel to Forks (Washington) and Volterra (Tuscany); for *Gladiator*, the Roman Coliseum.[16] Similar to the Moccia phenomenon is what Amy Sargent terms the 'Darcy Effect', which saw immense increases in visits to historic homes following the hugely successful 1995 BBC adaptation of *Pride and Prejudice*.[17] Visitor numbers at the National

Trust property of Lyme Park – BBC's Pemberley and of Colin Firth's wet-shirt-scene fame – rose from 32,000 to 91,000 the year of the miniseries' release.[18]

What compels such visits? Ashley Orr writes that fans seek connections with fictional 'characters through a sense of shared geographical, if not temporal, space', and such trips 'offer the possibility of inhabiting a beloved narrative'.[19] This form of visit, known as literary tourism and film tourism, can sometimes offer more than habitation in a narrative; it can offer the opportunity for imaginative and embodied play through the re-enactment of character actions. This is what is happening when, as Nick Couldry writes, visitors to the Manchester set of British soap opera *Coronation Street* 'pretend for a moment they live on the Street, posing with door knocker in hand or calling upstairs to a Street character'.[20]

This is what is happening in Transylvania when fans of Bram Stoker's *Dracula* retrace the journey made by the character Jonathan Harker, and when they pay a fee to lie in – and rise dramatically from – a coffin in the basement of Hotel Castle Dracula.[21] And this is what is happening in London King's Cross train station, when fans of *Harry Potter* queue up at the staged 'Platform 9 ¾', don a Hogwarts scarf, grasp hold of the handlebars of a half-disappeared luggage trolley and pose for photographs.[22] To use a folkloric term, these are examples of ostensive action. Folklorists Linda Dégh and Andrew Vázsonyi borrowed the word 'ostension' (from the Latin *ostendere*, 'to show') from semiotics to make sense of this relationship between folklore and popular culture. Communication through ostension is, they explained, 'essentially the showing of actions'; the physical enactment of folk narrative and legend.[23] And like folk narratives and legends, popular culture, Chieko Iwashita observes, 'is very good at turning people's dreams and curiosity into action'.[24]

Such re-enactments even precipitate adaptations of belief systems and lifestyles. For example, Helen Berger and Douglas Ezzy explore how modern witchcraft has been impacted by popular culture, with the number of teen witchcraft practitioners seeing a significant increase during the 1990s. This was, Berger and Ezzy argue, accelerated or even triggered by the popular 1996 film *The Craft*, which centred on a group of teenage witches, and television shows *Sabrina the Teenage Witch* (which ran 1996–2003) and *Charmed* (1998–2006).[25] The same process is evident in what Markus Davidsen identifies as 'fiction-based religions', such as those based on *The Lord of the Rings* and *Star Wars*; while the 'Jedi Census Phenomenon', which in 2001 saw more than 500,000 people claim 'Jedi' as their religion, was largely a prank, there are groups who earnestly identify themselves as Jedi Knights.[26]

Often, however, re-enactments are transient, consisting of a single action that lasts no longer than a few moments. They also often, like Moccia's love-locks, have a romantic element. Visitors to the Casa di Giulietta in Verona, for instance, queue for their brief moment on 'Juliet's balcony' to re-enact that most famous of love scenes: 'Romeo, Romeo, wherefore art thou Romeo?' Likewise,

Kim explores couples' fan play at sites from South Korean television show *Winter Sonata*, where they re-enact romantic scenes of bicycle rides through a specific redwood-lined road, as the show's characters did before them. 'By this performance', Kim writes, '. . . it is presumed that the tourists would then become true lovers in their own context and love story.'[27]

These romantic re-enactments, or ostensive actions, while transient, can sometimes leave tangible traces, physically altering the landscapes and creating something real that only previously existed in fiction. Love-locks are one example of this. Another example is a bench in Oxford's Botanic Gardens carved with the names 'Lyra + Will' or initials 'L and W'. This is the bench from Philip Pullman's popular fantasy trilogy *His Dark Materials*, on which the parted protagonists, unable to reunite, promise to sit once a year and think of each other. Despite the bench bearing no marker officially identifying it as 'Lyra and Will's' bench, fans have come to share the spot with Pullman's fictional characters and carve their names into the wood.

Melissa Beattie details another example of imaginative play tangibly transforming the environment in her paper on the Ianto Jones memorial in Cardiff. Ianto Jones was a fictional character from BBC science-fiction television series *Torchwood*. Following the character's death in the third season of the show, an impromptu memorial was set up by fans at Mermaid Quay, close to the fictional Torchwood headquarters, containing the same assemblage of objects you would find at the memorial of a non-fictional character: flowers, notes, photographs, and personal items.[28] A similar impromptu memorial was formed following the death of actor Alan Rickman in 2016. The actor, having played Severus Snape in Warner Brothers' film adaptations of *Harry Potter* since 2001, had become so synonymous with the character that fans set up a memorial for him at London King's Cross station, identified above as a site of *Harry Potter* imaginative play. Although it was the actor rather than the character who had sadly passed in this case, many of the notes left at the memorial made explicit reference to Severus Snape and the world of *Harry Potter*, as did the location of the memorial: by Platform 9 ¾.

Imaginative play has therefore engendered folk assemblages, popular culture thus begetting a popular custom.[29] This is the process that popularised the love-lock custom in Italy. Fans of Moccia's novels and the subsequent films participated in ostensive actions, re-enacting the locking of a padlock on the Ponte Milvio and creating a folk custom by drawing a fictional action into reality. Fans who could not visit Rome initiated the custom elsewhere, such as Venice's Rialto Bridge, forming further folk assemblages and cementing the custom as a ritual declaration of romantic commitment. And so, by the 2000s, love-locks had become an established feature in some European cities, but what followed was a rapid and geographically unbound growth – and as popular as Moccia's novels were, his fans cannot wholly account for it.

Tourist Folklore

Many of the perpetuators and disseminators of the custom were tourists (see *Chapter Four: Locking Love*). The articles that describe the custom in Italy as a symptom of the 'Moccia phenomenon' go on to observe that by the late 2000s tourists had begun imitating the local fans by adding their own love-locks. One written in 2007 for *The New York Times* notes, 'tossing a key off Ponte Milvio, some Italians complain, may soon be as touristy as flipping a coin into the Trevi Fountain' and 'Some young Roman said that . . . the ritual had lost its appeal and gotten touristy.'[30] Two years later, in Cologne, the custom is described as one practised by local lovers, but the author of the article observes that 'The tokens have also become an attraction for tourists, who stop to take a closer look at the messages inscribed on them.'[31] From this point on, the myriad newspaper and magazine articles that refer to the love-lock custom describe it as a tourist practice – in many cases actually having been initiated by tourists.

It is no coincidence that many of the world's tourist attractions also feature love-locks: New York's Brooklyn Bridge, Paris's Pont des Arts, Florence's Ponte Vecchio, Sydney's Harbour Bridge, Prague's Charles Bridge, Seoul's Namsan Tower. Tourists brought the custom to these sites and took them onwards from there, seeing them whilst on one holiday (or encountering them less directly through, for example, social media – see below) and then disseminating the practice on their next trip or back home. 'The idea of hanging locks originated from local tourists a few years ago who saw the same thing at Tokyo Tower,' wrote Yu-jin in his article on love-locks on Seoul Tower in 2008.[32] Even in the more obscure locations, once enough locks are added to a structure, that structure becomes culturally and aesthetically interesting, consequently attracting tourists. Love-lock assemblages thus became something more than features of tourist attractions; they became tourist attractions in and of themselves.

Mass international tourism has been growing since the introduction of commercial air travel in the twentieth century and has become one of, if not *the* largest industries in the world.[33] The ease and popularity of international travel (together with the dawning of our digital age, see below) has led to a worldwide interconnectedness and consequently a convergence of the local and the global. This has resulted in what is commonly referred to as the 'global village' or 'global ecumene', with the population of any given site or city becoming both more transnational and more transient.[34] Hannerz suggests that what we are seeing through such globalisation is the rise of a 'new civilization': one that is not bound by geography or even nationality.[35] Such dramatic changes in the social fabric of our planet inevitably impact the 'locality' of a people and their customs.

Love-locking on the Ponte Milvio is no longer a 'local' custom practised by resident teenagers but a tourist one, perpetuated by Rome's many domestic and international visitors. Debates surrounding the 'authenticity' of tourist culture are explored in *Chapter Seven: Unlocking Love*; what this chapter is concerned with is the existence of tourist culture. Much past literature has focused on the creation or performance of culture *for* tourists, rather than *by* tourists,[36] and Bruner notes the ethnographer's tendency to omit tourists from their studies altogether: 'a purposeful ignoring of that which is present but that ethnography finds embarrassing'.[37] However, some research has shifted focus to the culture of tourists themselves, such as MacCannell's seminal *The Tourist: A New Theory of the Leisure Class*, and Urry's *The Tourist Gaze*.[38]

Defining tourists as 'sightseers . . . who are at this moment deployed throughout the entire world in search of experience', MacCannell views them as a distinct 'group' from a sociological perspective.[39] They can also be recognised as a 'folk' group. This is apparent if we use folklorist Alan Dundes's oft-cited definition: 'The term "folk" can refer to *any group of people whatsoever* who share at least one common factor' (emphases in the original).[40] Tourists share a common factor in that they are all non-residents of the country, city or site they currently occupy and have travelled there for pleasure. They may have little else in common: a person of any nationality, race, class, occupation and gender can be a tourist, but through their shared status as leisure travellers, they constitute a folk group. And as a folk group, the customs they practise are folk customs, and the lore they share is folklore.

Equations between the tourist and the pilgrim, the holiday and the ritual, have frequently been made.[41] Anthropologists Victor and Edith Turner famously observed, 'a tourist is half a pilgrim, if a pilgrim is half a tourist', whilst Singh notes that pilgrimages have been identified in sociology and anthropology as the earliest form of tourism.[42] The festivals that tourists participate in today are viewed by Cooley as tourist 'rituals'.[43] Tourists' engagement with attractions is described by MacCannell as 'a twofold process of *sight sacralization* that is met with a corresponding *ritual attitude* on the part of tourists' (emphases in the original).[44] And the stories heard, shared and perpetuated by tourists are deemed 'tourist folklore' by Joyce Hammond. An example given by Hammond is that of the 'curse of Pele'. From at least the 1940s, visitors to Hawai'i and Maui shared the belief that Pele, the 'goddess of volcanoes', would punish any tourist who removed rocks from the island. This inevitably led to many rocks being posted back to the national parks by tourists having suffered some bad luck upon returning home with them. This notion, Hammond asserts, has no apparent precedent in early Hawaiian beliefs and is an example of pure 'tourist folklore'.[45]

Tourists therefore not only co-consume; they also co-produce.[46] Love-lock assemblages are possibly the most notable example of this. These structures are both tourist attractions and attractions created largely *by* tourists. MacCannell describes the tourist attraction as 'the locus of a human relationship between un-like-minded individuals, the locus of an urgent desire to share – an intimate connection between one stranger and another, through the local object'.[47] In the case of love-lock assemblages, this sharing has become physical – tourists contribute their own piece to the local object – and this notion overlays neatly onto McNeill's concept of serial collaborative creations[48] (see *Introduction*) and Preston's definition of folk assemblages:

> Such objects are the evolving product of a series of private acts . . . that cumulatively form an object that itself evokes the sense of an imagined community – that imagined community being the various individuals, usually anonymous, who have responded in kind to the acts of earlier individuals and who frequently envision their responses as linking them to a group of people who, though invisible to them, are made visible by that which they have left behind.[49]

The Love-Lock as Marked Attraction

MacCannell defines the tourist attraction as 'an empirical relationship between a *tourist*, a *sight* and a *marker* (a piece of information about a sight)' (emphases in the original).[50] There is, according to this definition, more to the process of love-locks becoming established attractions than tourists simply seeing an assemblage (the *sight*). Also needed is the marker. For many world attractions, this marker takes the form of official signage: plaques or information boards erected at a site/structure, providing some details and clearly demarcating it as a sight of interest. However, although there are some exceptions to this (see *Chapter Six: Selling Love*), this is not usually the case at love-lock assemblages. For these sites, such markers tend to be unofficial: they are not demarcated by land managers or local authorities. And they are less *present* than other markers, rarely tangibly at the site itself.

Most love-lock assemblage markers are forms of written or visual material produced by other tourists or interest groups, often encountered beyond the context of the site. For instance, in January 2019 a Twitter marketing campaign for Viking Cruises advertised their cruise to Paris with a photograph of a Parisian love-lock bridge and the words: 'Feel the love as you stroll across Love Lock Bridge in #Paris. Every day, couples attach a padlock to the bridge & throw the key into the Seine River as a sign of eternal love.'[51] Such markers provide information (both directly and indirectly) about love-locks, increasing knowledge and thus the dissemination of the custom. The media is the most obvious example of this. As Iwashita observes, 'More and more people are being exposed to representations provided by "global" popular culture and they are used to seeing places through the media. Popular cultural forms of the media can create tourism geographies in a strong sense . . . actively shaping interactions in and with places.'[52]

Since the late 2000s, love-locks have been a popular feature of newspaper and magazine articles: 'In Rome, a New Ritual on an Old Bridge' in the *New York*

Times, 2007; 'Seoul Tower Locked in Everlasting Love' in *Korea Times*, 2008; 'Japan's Young Couples Risking Death in "Love Padlock" Ritual' in *The Telegraph*, 2009; 'That's Amore! But Lovers' Locks are Littering the Brooklyn Bridge' in the *Brooklyn Paper*, 2010.[53] Love-locks gained greater popularity in the media as the custom grew more contested (see *Chapter Seven: Unlocking Love*). 'Paris to Remove Love Padlocks from Pont des Arts Bridge' in *The Telegraph*, May 2010, and 'Love Padlocks Vanish from Paris Bridge' in quick succession, less than two weeks later; 'Rome's Ponte Milvio Bridge: "Padlocks of Love" removed' in *BBC News*, 2012; '"Love Locks" to be Removed from Ha'penny Bridge'; '"Love locks" Banned on Ky. Bridge', and so on.[54] Even when the articles are wholly negative about the custom – Jonathan Jones's 2015 *Guardian* article: 'Love Locks are the Shallowest, Stupidest, Phoniest Expression of Love Ever' comes to mind – they are still disseminating knowledge and perhaps, unwittingly, perpetuating it.[55]

The Internet, particularly user-generated content, has also played a significant role in disseminating knowledge of the love-lock custom. This is despite past predictions that folklore would not survive the rise of mass culture and technology, with folklorist Trevor Blank asserting instead that 'folklore flourishes on the Internet.'[56] He believes that new media technology – from laptops and tablets to mobile telephones – is now so deeply integrated into our communication practices that it has become an instrumental 'conduit of folkloric transmission'.[57] Even as early as 1996, Kirshenblatt-Gimblett was noting the Internet's efficacy for transmitting folklore, and in 2005 Dundes asserted that 'folklore continues to be alive and well in the modern world, due in part to increased transmission via e-mail and the Internet.' Tok Thompson, who describes online folklore as 'Folklore 2.0', likewise states that 'folklore is enjoying a tremendous renaissance online', while Mariann Domokos asserts that with the Internet now being the main means of communication, folklorists can neither ignore it nor overestimate its centrality in the mediation of folklore.[58] Love-locks attest to this, most especially with regards to social media.

Love-locks feature widely on Instagram, a photo and video-sharing social networking service that launched in 2010. As of August 2018, 183,224 Instagram posts contained '#lovelocks' in their tagging. Most of these posts are images of love-locks, either close-up shots of the locks and their inscriptions, or photographs of people posing on or beside a love-lock structure. Love-locks are also a popular feature on the video-sharing website YouTube, founded in 2005. Thousands of videos have been uploaded, primarily by tourists as part of their travelling vlogs (video blogs), many featuring couples attaching love-locks themselves. This form of documented participation will be further explored in *Chapter Four: Locking Love*; what is pertinent here are the amounts of people who are encountering love-locks through social media. Significantly, a random selection of 100 YouTube love-lock videos was examined for this study, ranging in date from 2010 to 2018, and these reported a total of 494,966 views. This number will have increased, and those 100 videos are only a small sample of the vast and growing number online.

This posting of photographs and videos of love-locks online demonstrates the significance of another contemporary innovation: the mobile camera phone. First introduced in 2000, camera phones have become a staple product of everyday life. In 2017, 85% of adults in the UK owned smartphones; many of these use the camera applications on their devices, with 39% of teenagers taking photographs and/or videos every day.[59] The ubiquity of this device, now partnered with the 'selfie stick', not only means that most people, regardless of age or camera literacy, are able – and inclined – to spontaneously photograph or record their encounters with tourist attractions without having to pre-plan or spend money on films,[60] but they are also able to share them instantaneously even when abroad, via multimedia messaging and social media platforms.[61] 'Camera phones', observes sociologist Penny Tinkler, 'are heralded as shifting photographic practices.'[62] It seems they are also shifting ritual practices – a process that will be explored in more depth in *Chapter Four: Locking Love*.

What we are seeing here is 'Digital Age Tourism': social media has become central to how people share travel knowledge – electronic word-of-mouth – and thus learn about new places and attractions, with Elisa Giaccardi observing that our sense of place is rearticulated through social media.[63] Videos are particularly important to this process, and Tussyadiah and Fesenmaier note the role they play as MacCannell's *markers*, as discussed above, demarcating a site as a tourist attraction: 'Being perceived as sources of information, the shared videos act as the markers; they provide meanings and structures to different sights that can be visited and activities that can be done . . . The videos can signify that a particular sight is worth viewing, as it is portrayed to be gazed at by other tourists.'[64] Social media, however, does more than mark a love-lock assemblage as a tourist attraction; it perpetuates the custom.

The Internet provides ideal conditions for the transmission and dissemination of folklore and customs for two primary reasons. Firstly, it offers a rapid and effective 'distribution mechanism', computer-mediated communication allowing for the quick (indeed, instant), widespread and easy exchange of information. Secondly, it is not restricted geographically. The Internet has altered not only how the 'folk' communicate and transmit folklore but also what constitutes the 'folk'. As with mass tourism, because of the global discourse of the Internet, cultural identity is no longer necessarily equated with geography, and therefore a 'folk group' has no need for a geographical base. And, as Tussyadiah and Fesenmaier observe, 'An important need of tourists is to share their experiences with others'; a person can share images and information about the love-lock custom with thousands of people from across the globe.[65]

And so, if the 'folk' of the twenty-first century are no longer restricted by geography, then the dissemination of twenty-first-century folklore is not either, and the love-lock custom has been able to spread rapidly and widely across the planet via computer-mediated communication.[66] Digital Age Tourism, therefore, provides more than markers for love-lock assemblages; it *enables* the custom. Tracing the Internet-mediated dissemination of information about 'flash mobs', folklorist Lynne McNeill demonstrates that 'technologically mediated communication affects cultural expression', and Munar et al. note that social media has 'led to the emergence of new tourism cultures and practices'. As will be further explored in *Chapter Four: Locking Love*, the love-locks are a prime example of this.[67]

Conclusion

Compiling a history of love-locking has been no simple task. The custom's origins remain obscure, and we only have any real evidence of it from the 1980s, when it was documented in Pécs and in Italian Alpine towns. This is not to claim that the practice originated then and there, only that no solid proof has yet been identified giving an earlier date. Of course, an absence of evidence is not evidence of absence, but this chapter promised to handle the facts. The difficulties in separating fact from fiction stem from the custom's international spread, which sees numerous narratives and networks of dissemination, rather than a single, linear thread, and from the many rumours circulating and presented as fact by the media. However, while this has complicated the task of contextualising the practice, it is also central to it because internationality and obscure origins are what make the love-lock custom so interesting.

This chapter has demonstrated how rapidly a custom of unknown provenance can become established at one site and then can disseminate to hundreds, probably thousands, of locations around the globe, without any official driving force – and often without the approval of landowners and site managers. Through popular culture and embodied play, tourist folklore, and the geographically unbound distribution mechanism of the Internet, the custom of love-locking has spread like wildfire, and assemblages have become marked attractions worldwide, culturally consumed by the millions who visit them. The following chapter further explores this notion of consumption by considering the love-lock's place within popular culture.

Notes

1. Solid evidence has proved difficult to attain regarding the history of this custom, and I am not confident that these are the earliest examples of love-locking. International researchers proficient in a range of languages would be required to ascertain with any certainty when and where the earliest love-lock assemblage emerged.

2. Hammond, 'Renegade Ornament and the Image of the Post-Socialist City'.

3. Ibid., 187.

4. There are unsubstantiated claims that soldiers practised the same custom on the Ponte Vecchio in Florence during the 1960s.

5. Pers. comm. 23/01/2019 Julia Sanin, Tourist office Merano; Pers. comm. Elmar Gobbi, Palais Mamming Museum, Merano, 25/01/2019. With many thanks to Roberto Labanti for tracking this information down.

6. Richter and Pfeiffer-Kloss, 'Bridges, Locks and Love', 189.

7. Ibid., 189.

8. Moccia, *Ho voglia di te* [*I Want You*], 274–76. Translation from Italian by Francesca Benetti, with much appreciation.

9. Ibid.

10. Berton, '"Love Locks" Scourge of Bridges Worldwide'.

11. Owen, 'Rome: City of Love'.

12. Pers. comm. Maria Cardona Serra, Pontas Literary Agency, 23/11/2018.

13. Pontas Literary Agency, 'Grand Central Publishing to Publish the #1 Italian Bestselling Author Federico Moccia'.

14. Italian Charts, 'Tiziano Ferro – Ti scatterò una foto (Song)'. *Italiancharts.com*: https://italiancharts.com/showitem.asp?interpret=Tiziano+Ferro&titel=Ti+scatter%F2+una+foto&cat=s [Accessed 23/11/2018].

15. Italian Film Festival, *Love 14* (2010): https://www.italianfilmfestival.com.au/2010/films/love14/ [Accessed 23/11/2018]; Anonymous, 'The Moccia Phenomenon, Italian Love Boom!'; Waterfall, 'The Padlocks of Paris'; Anonymous, 'The Triumph of Love Novels that Desperate Critics'.

16. Buchmann, Moore and Fisher, 'Experiencing Film Tourism', 229–48; Lexhagen, Larson and Lundberg, 'The Virtual Fan(G) Community', 133–57; Frost, 'Braveheart-ed Ned Kelly', 247–54.

17. Sargent, 'The Darcy Effect', 177–86.

18. Orr, 'Plotting Jane Austen', 248.

19. Ibid., 247–48.

20. Couldry, 'The View from Inside the "Simulacrum"', 97.

21. Light, 'Performing Transylvania', 248–50.

22. Iwashita, 'Media Representation of the UK as a Destination for Japanese Tourists', 66; Gymnich and Sheunemann, 'The *Harry Potter* Phenomenon', 30.

23. Dégh and Vázsonyi, 'Does the Word "Dog" Bite?', 7–8.

24. Iwashita, 'Media Representation of the UK as a Destination for Japanese Tourists', 70.

25. Berger and Ezzy, *Teenage Witches*, 32.

26. Davidsen, 'Fiction-Based Religion', 378–95.

27. Kim, 'Extraordinary Experience', 67.

28. Beattie, 'A Most Peculiar Memorial', 215–24.

29. Coffey, 'Lyra's Oxford'.

30. Fisher, 'In Rome, a New Ritual on an Old Bridge'.

31. Stolarz, 'Cologne Gets a Lock on Love'.

32. Ji-yun, 'Seoul Tower Locked in Everlasting Love'.

33. MacCannell, *The Tourist*; Lanfant, Allcock and Bruner, *International Tourism*; Fritsch and Johannsen, *Ecotourism in Appalachia*.

34. Storey, *Inventing Popular Culture*; Picard and Robinson, *Festivals, Tourism and Social Change*.

35. Hannerz, *Transnational Connections*.

36. Muri, '"The World's Smallest Village"', 53–64; Creighton, 'Consuming Rural Japan', 239–54; Silverman, 'Touring Ancient Times', 881–902.

37. Bruner, *Culture on Tour*, 8.

38. MacCannell, *The Tourist*; Urry, *The Tourist Gaze*.

39. MacCannell, *The Tourist*, 1.

40. Dundes, *The Study of Folklore*, 2.

41. See Crouch and Lübbern, *Visual Culture and Tourism*; Badon and Roseman, *Intersecting Journeys*; Tuchman-Rosta, 'From Ritual Form to Tourist Attraction', 524–44; Borraz, 'Love and Locks', 7–21.

42. Turner and Turner, *Image and Pilgrimage in Christian Culture*, 20; Singh, 'Secular Pilgrimages and Sacred Tourism in the Indian Himalayas', 215.

43. Cooley, 'Folk Festival as Modern Ritual in the Polish Tatra Mountains', 31. See also Picard and Robinson, 'Remaking Worlds', 1–31.

44. MacCannell, *The Tourist*, 42.

45. Hammond, 'The Tourist Folklore of Pele', 159–79.

46. Crouch and Lübbern, *Visual Culture and Tourism*, 12.

47. MacCannell, *The Tourist*, 203.

48. McNeill, 'Portable Places', 281–99.

49. Preston, 'Panty Trees, Shoe Trees, and Legend', 12.

50. MacCannell, *The Tourist*, 41.

51. VikingCruises [Twitter post]: https://twitter.com/VikingCruises/status/1083092769466249217 [Accessed 22/07/2019].

52. Iwashita, 'Media Representation of the UK as a Destination for Japanese Tourists', 76.

53. Fisher, 'In Rome'; Ji-yun, 'Seoul Tower Locked in Everlasting Love'; Ryall, 'Japan's Young Couples Risking Death in "Love Padlock" Ritual'; Campbell, 'That's Amore!'.

54. Samuel, 'Paris to Remove Love Padlocks from Pont des Arts Bridge'; Samuel, 'Love Padlocks Vanish from Paris Bridge'; Anonymous, 'Rome's Ponte Milvio Bridge'; Hilliard, '"Love Locks" to be Removed from Ha'penny Bridge'; Shafer, '"Love Locks" Banned on Ky. Bridge'.

55. Jones, 'Love Locks are the Shallowest, Stupidest, Phoniest Expression of Love Ever – Time to Put a Stop to It'.

56. Bascom, 'Four Functions of Folklore', 296; Blank, 'Introduction', 13.

57. Blank, 'Introduction', 4.

58. Kirshenblatt-Gimblett, 'The Electronic Vernacular', 21–65; Dundes, 'Folkloristics in the Twenty-First Century', 406; Thompson, 'Netizens, Revolutionaries, and the Inalienable Right to the Internet', 53; Domokos, 'Towards Methodological Issues in Electronic Folklore', 284.

59. Deloitte, *Global Mobile Consumer Survey 2017: UK Cut*.

60. See Schwartz, 'Praying with a Camera Phone', 180.

61. See Kindberg et al., 'The Ubiquitous Camera', 42–50; Gye, 'Picture This', 279–388; David, 'Camera Phone Images, Videos and Live Streaming', 89–98.

62. Tinkler, 'A Fragmented Picture', 262.

63. Giaccardi, 'Introduction', 1–10; Munar, Gyimothy and Liping, *Tourism Social Media*; Sotiriadis and Van Zyl, 'Electronic Word-of-Mouth and Online Reviews in Tourism Services', 104; Edwards et al., 'Ambassadors of Knowledge Sharing', 690–708.

64. Tussyadiah and Fesenmaier, 'Mediating Tourist Experiences', 35.

65. Ibid., 25.

66. Sheenagh Pietrobruno demonstrates how cultural performances shared online, such as via YouTube, cause the spread of global knowledge and the migration of the practices themselves. See *Chapter Seven: Unlocking Love* (Pietrobruno, 'Scale and the Digital', 102).

67. McNeill, 'Real Virtuality', 85; Munar, Gyimothy and Liping, *Tourism Social Media*, 2.

CHAPTER 2

CONSUMING LOVE

Folk Custom and Popular Culture

Ben takes his wife Leslie to Paris for a romantic trip; while there, they buy a padlock and attach it to a love-lock bridge. Dylan and Alma, more recently romantically attached, do the same, while young lovers Lindsey and Jack accidentally drop their love-lock into the Seine and wonder if it's a sign. Long-married couple Meg and Nick simply stand by the love-locks; they don't suggest adding their own. Over in the US, Brody takes his daughter Dana to a love-lock fence to show her the lock he and Dana's mother placed there years before, while Alec and Magnus, having seen the custom in Paris, find a love-lock assemblage in New York and add their own. In Seoul, friends Winter and Jesse sit at the top of Namsan Tower and contemplate whether padlocks are the best way of symbolising romantic commitment. Sonya attaches herself to a love-lock assemblage in Australia, to protest the local council's removal of them, and in Italy, Mara travels to the Cinque Terre to find the lock her ancestor placed there in 1545 in order to break a 500-year-old family curse. And back in Paris, Princess Fragrance kidnaps the prince and attempts to use a love-lock to magically seal their love, before hero Ladybug saves the day . . .

Since Federico Moccia's use of love-locks in *Ho voglia di te*, the custom has appeared in myriad pieces of fiction, from Hollywood to Hallmark, from international drama to Korean soap opera, from teen thriller books to children's superhero cartoons. In some examples, love-locks act as incidental backdrop; in others, they are drawn on to communicate a message or materialise a sentiment; while in yet others, they are integral to the plot itself. This chapter considers the various uses of the love-lock as folk motif in fiction, as a symbolic element within a narrative that draws on a folkloric custom. It subsequently explores what these uses demonstrate about the relationship – or interrelationship – between folkloric custom and popular culture. Please note, popular culture is not used pejoratively. Here it is considered, along with mass media, as mass-produced cultural products – including but not limited to television, film, literature and music – accessible to and consumed by large groups of a given society.

A Brief History of Scholarship

The love-lock phenomenon is certainly not the first folk custom to appear on screen or in the pages of popular fiction; as such, this is certainly not the first study to consider the relationship between folklore and popular culture. As early as 1946, folklorist Stith Thompson was declaring cinema 'perhaps the most successful of all mediums for the presentation of the fairy tale'.[1] Making particular reference to Disney's 1937 *Snow White and the Seven Dwarves*, Thompson noted the animated cartoon's unprecedented scope for constructing the creatures and characters of the folk imagination.

Not only does popular culture provide effective media for the representation of folk narratives and customs, but folk narratives and customs are deemed suitable foundations and focuses of popular media. They thus appear frequently, with folk motifs and popular customs and beliefs common features in films, televisions, songs and popular literature. The decade following Thompson, Richard Dorson noted tentatively that 'The folk can on occasion feed the mass media, and equally the media can feed back into oral lore, but a selective process is at work on both sides; folk and mass culture coexist peaceably and on friendly terms.'[2] Nearly fifty years later, and more assuredly, Paul Smith was claiming 'That a relationship exists between folklore and popular culture is not in doubt.'[3] This has been the general consensus amongst folklorists since the latter half of the twentieth century. However, folklorists have judged and treated this relationship differently over the years.

On 15 May 1969, folklorist Tom Burns watched 19 hours of American television, taking notes on any examples of folklore or 'traditional material' alluded to.[4] He observed examples of traditional music and song, beliefs, gestures, narratives, proverbs and customs, the latter including such practices as throwing the bouquet at a wedding, playing 'pitch penny', square dancing, and the unwritten rules of how to smoke 'like a lady'. In Burns's opinion, though, not all folklore on the television can be treated equal. He judges whether an example is 'true' folklore based on four criteria: 1) a traditional verbal or non-verbal text, 2) a traditional performance of that type, 3) a traditional situation for the performance, and 4) a traditional audience. Burns contends that 'the appearance of a folkloric item in the mass media can be evaluated for its traditionality according to each of the four factors and placed in a continuum as more or less "true" folklore.'[5]

Priscilla Denby, writing on 'Folklore in the Mass Media' in 1971, adopted Burns's criteria for 'true' folklore. She divided the three months' worth of examples she had recorded from books, newspapers, television, and so on, into three categories: Folklore qua folklore (which included articles about folklore, folklore as foundation, and mimetic folklore); folklore as folklure (examples for selling and decorative purposes); and folklore as an aside. The first category, she noted, best met the criteria for 'true' folklore. Of most relevance here is the sub-category 'folklore as foundation', which Denby details:

> The folklore contained within these articles serves as a basis for making a point or creating an effect, but it is not concerned with perpetuating, explaining, or discussing folklore per se ... the greatest bulk of the folklore found in the media is not folklore for its own sake, but for something else's, i.e., folklore is used as a most dependable communication vehicle. This is a logical development inasmuch as anything founded in folk tradition is by nature not esoteric and is likely to be understood by most of the masses.[6]

Over a decade later, as discussed in *Chapter One: Dating Love*, Linda Dégh and Andrew Vázsonyi employed the term ostension – 'to show' – to elucidate this relationship between folklore and popular culture, explaining that communication through ostension is 'essentially the showing of actions'. It is the moment in which folk narrative and legend enter reality through physical re-enactment.[7] Mikel Koven adopted this term in his exploration into 'mass-mediated ostension', with films such as *Candyman* and television shows such as *Most Haunted*, in which folk narratives are not told to us in narration but are shown to us through actions. Folklore in popular culture is less commonly represented than it is presented to us.[8]

Various other terms have been employed to conceptualise folklore's relationship to popular culture. Peter Narváez and Martin Laba identified a 'folklore-popular culture continuum', viewing folklore and popular culture as polar types because of the contrasts in how they are transmitted (folklore via small group encounters and popular culture via technological media in mass societies). Between the two is a continuum of different sized groups and various forms of transmission.[9] More often than not today, though, folklorists draw on comparisons rather than contrasts between the two. Juliette Wood, in her work on fairies in popular film, observes the ways in which folklore and mass culture have converged, structuring each other; James Hornby describes the two as having a 'symbiotic relationship'; Elizabeth Bird argues that while they may not be identical, they are 'closely intertwined'; and Pauline Greenhill writes of the many ways folklore and film intersect.[10]

Cristina Bacchilega, in her analysis of 'folklore *in* literature, folklore *as* literature, and folklore *and* literature', believes we should be aiming to undo the folklore vs. popular culture dichotomy altogether.[11] John Storey maintains that the folklore collections of the eighteenth and nineteenth centuries were not only forms of popular culture but the first examples of it: 'the study of folklore produced not only a concept of popular culture as folk culture, it also helped to establish the tradition of seeing ordinary people as masses, consuming mass culture.'[12]

There is, however, still the recognition that customs and beliefs presented on the screen or on the page are not exactly the same as those encountered in reality, because of differences in motive, environment and audience. Folklore studies have moved beyond Burns's labelling of examples as 'true' folklore and not 'true' folklore, but there remains a certain ambiguity around the narratives and practices we are presented with in popular culture. They may be intertwined, intersecting or converged with folklore, but are they actually folklore? Although the actions may be identical, a person locking a real love-lock to a real bridge in a film or television show is not the same as a person locking a love-lock to a bridge in reality. This is because there is often no earnest emotion or genuine relationship motivating the action in popular culture, but rather the acting of this for entertainment purposes (reality television would be more ambiguous). The folk custom in popular culture is the *imitation* of a folk custom; it is mass-mediated ostension.

Michael Foster and Jeffrey Tolbert have addressed this ambiguity by coining the term 'the folkloresque', which Foster defines as a heuristic tool for identifying 'popular culture's own (emic) perception and performance of folklore. That is, it refers to creative, often commercial products or texts (e.g., films, graphic novels, video games) that give the impression to the consumer (viewer, reader, listener, player) that they derive directly from existing folkloric traditions.'[13] Foster is not interested in whether an example is authentic or 'true' folklore, but is rather concerned with people's perceptions of the folkloric within popular culture.

The frequency with which examples of folklore and folk motifs appear in popular culture cannot be in doubt. However, it is not sufficient to simply catalogue instances or, as Koven disparagingly phrases it, 'motif-spot'.[14] Alan Dundes stressed in the 1960s that folklorists need to do more than simply identify folk motifs.[15] Interpretation and analysis is needed to understand how and why folklore and popular culture converge, and how they structure, adapt to and influence each other. This chapter therefore aims to analyse the various uses of the love-lock as folk motif in popular culture in order to better understand how the love-lock custom is perceived, used and impacted by mass media.

The Love-Lock as Backdrop

In Roger Michell's 2013 film *Le Week-End*, British actors Jim Broadbent and Lindsay Duncan play husband and wife Nick and Meg, visiting Paris to celebrate their 30th wedding anniversary. Taglines for the film included 'Nick & Meg are returning to Paris for a second honeymoon . . . and a last chance' and 'A story about reigniting the spark in the City Of Light.' The spark is not necessarily reignited, but at the end of a dissatisfying trip, the long-time marrieds find some common ground, and towards the end of the film, a 23-second scene has them talking and laughing on a love-lock bridge. There is no discussion or engagement with the love-locks, but part of the scene has the characters as backdrop and the locks in the foreground.[16]

Parisian love-locks also feature briefly in a 2013 Chanel Coco Mademoiselle advert, in which Keira Knightley drives a speedboat down the Seine, passing an admirer – Russian actor Danila Valerievich Kozlovsky – as he walks across a heavily love-locked Pont des Arts, to the theme song of 'She's Not There'.[17] In addition, in 2018, the Paris love-locks made a cameo appearance in an episode of French superhero cartoon *Miraculous: Tales of Ladybug and Cat Noir*, entitled 'Glaciator'. They feature as backdrop in a scene featuring a villainous ice-cream vendor and again are not commented on or looked at by the characters.[18]

These uses of love-locks as backdrop demonstrate two important things. Firstly, they fit one of Denby's categories of folklore in the mass media: 'folklore as an aside', in particular that which is 'used consciously for effects'.[19] The custom of love-locking is incidental within the plot, not directly engaged with, but the love-locks are part of the *mise-en-scène*,[20] consciously chosen to form part of the setting – both for decorative purposes, to make the backdrop more visually interesting, and to locate the scenes within central, popular and romantic locations within Paris. This leads to the second point: love-locks are used in these scenes because, being so popular in Paris, they have become synonymous with the French capital. Therefore, just as stock shots of the Eiffel Tower, Notre-Dame and Sacré-Cœur are employed excessively, almost uniformly, in visual media to set the scene in Paris, now so too are love-lock bridges. The same process has occurred in Seoul, where the vast assemblage of love-locks on Namsan Tower (or N Seoul Tower) features as the romantic backdrop of many Korean dramas (see more details below).

This has happened to a lesser extent at other love-lock locations. For example, the love-locks on Ha'penny Bridge in Dublin featured in a 2012 episode of British soap opera *Hollyoaks*, in which the characters Ste and Brendan are reunited and declare their love for each other on the bridge itself.[21] Likewise in *Coronation Street*, when character Phelan travels to Liverpool's Albert Docks, the love-locks adorning the chain-link fences act as backdrop, and the extent of engagement with them is Phelan briefly and absently looking down at the locks before he walks away. Myriad love-locks attached to chains are also seen in the main characters' (played by Jaden Smith and Jackie Chan) ascent of the Wudang Mountains, China, in the 2010 remake of *Karate Kid*.[22] The love-locks are not engaged with but again act as backdrop.

For Liverpool, Dublin, the Wudang Mountains and Seoul, as well as Paris, the love-lock assemblage has entered the scene-setting corpus of visual media. In many other cases, however, love-locks are used as more than scenery and act as symbolic objects and plot devices.

The Love-Lock as Folk Motif

Objects are a language that popular culture is fluent in. Films and television in particular know how to use material culture effectively; they know how to squeeze the symbolism out of an object. As Bordwell et al. observe:

> When an object in the setting has a function within the ongoing action, we can call it a prop. Films teem with examples: the snowstorm paperweight that shatters at the beginning of *Citizen Kane*, the little girl's balloon in *M*, the cactus rose in *The Man Who Shot Liberty Valance*, Sarah Connor's hospital bed turned exercise machine in *Terminator 2: Judgment Day*.[23]

Obviously, the selection of props is culturally dependent, but there are some objects that boast near universal symbolic resonance. These are objects that we briefly encountered in the Introduction: the *semes* described by Umberto Eco as instantly recognisable iconic signs bearing particular cultural and emotive connotations.[24] The ring is one such object. Betrothal rings and wedding bands have a long history, possibly dating back to the Ancient Egyptians but certainly to the Romans, and over time they have become the 'quintessential' wedding object.[25] As Otnes and Pleck observe, 'The exchange between the bride and groom of jewelry that is intended to be permanent and worn continuously is a visual statement of commitment, marital identity, and/or sexual exclusivity.'[26]

Drawing on this quintessentiality, the engagement or wedding ring as *seme* has been utilised in abundance in film, television and literature to symbolise romantic commitment, to hold a mirror up to a couple's relationship (and economic) status and to foreshadow future events. Hidden in a pocket or sock drawer indicates future plans; deposited in a champagne flute, imminent proposal; slipped on a finger, engagement or marriage; too small for the finger, bad omen; removed from a finger, thrown away or given back, the end of a relationship; and accidentally lost or broken, future problems or tragedy. The ring is without a doubt the most commonly used material symbol of love within popular culture, but it is not the only one. Love-locks have entered the arena of romantic *semes*. They have become, like the ring, 'objects of endearment', to use a term coined by Victor Margolin, who asserts that love, in its myriad forms, can be 'played out through . . . objects' identities both as possessions and as props in the performative enactments of social rituals'.[27]

Chapter One: Dating Love explored Federico Moccia's use of love-locks in *Ho voglia di te*, in which the central characters attach a love-lock to the Ponte Milvio in Rome. This was a short scene, taking over only two pages in the book and less than two minutes in the film, but the love story became so synonymous with the custom that later editions of the novel featured only an image of the love-lock on the front cover. Likewise, the whole of Tiziano Ferro's 2007 music video for *Ti scatterò una foto* [*I will take a photo of you*], which accompanied the film, centred on the bridge and its love-lock assemblage. This was because the love-lock works so well as a folk motif – Bordwell et al. note that when props enter the narrative action, they can 'weave through a film to create motifs'[28] – no doubt due to the universality of its symbolism, as detailed in *Chapter Five: Symbolising Love*. Because this small and inexpensive object can, like the ring, so readily allegorise love, it has been employed extensively within popular culture.

In 2017, Hallmark released the made-for-TV film *Love Locks*, which – unsurprisingly – centred on the custom.[29] Directed by Martin Wood and starring American actors (and real-life husband and wife) Jerry O'Connell as Jack and Rebecca Romijn as Lindsey, the film opens with the couple cycling through Paris. Cue the typical shots of the Eiffel Tower and the Louvre, and of course they end on the Pont des Arts. They are soon to part ways with Lindsey returning to the US, so she has brought a love-lock to attach to the bridge.

> Lindsey: We'll lock it on the bridge and our love will last forever.
> Jack: Forever?
> Lindsey: Forever. [*They write their names onto the lock*]
> Jack: OK. With this lock I thee –

What follows is a clumsy fumble and they accidentally drop the lock into the Seine; the camera follows it to the bottom of the riverbed. They accuse each other of dropping it, and the scene ends with the unspoken assumption that this did not bode well for their relationship. The next scene takes us to New York, twenty years later, Jack and Lindsey not having seen each other since Paris. Lindsey has since married and divorced and is returning to Paris, with her teenage daughter, where she inevitably reunites with Jack.

Love-locks feature throughout the entire film. The daughter, Alexa, wants to include the love-locks in their sightseeing tour:

> Alexa: Oh we should go to the love-lock bridge. It's supposed to be so romantic.
> Lindsey: It's just a bridge. With locks.
> Alexa: Yeah but those locks are people pledging their love for each other.
> Lindsey: Yeah, and how many of those people are still together today?
> Alexa: All of them, in some way.

Later, when they come across the assemblage on Pont Neuf, Lindsey comments on how 'They're all rusted,' to which Alexa brightly replies, 'It just means they lasted.' Reference is made to the council removing the locks, and this is used to explore the custom through other couples' eyes. Side-character Kathryn, a widow, wants to find the lock on Pont Neuf she and her late husband locked there some years before, before it is removed by the council; her new love interest has retrieved the lock for her by the end of the film. In this specific storyline, the love-lock acts as mnemonic device, recalling a past relationship. Alexa is given a love-lock by her new love interest, and she declares not to care if the council removes it: 'It's still ours.' The film ends with Lindsey and Jack back on the bridge, having rekindled their romance. This time they have brought extra love-locks, just in case.

This film is interesting on a number of levels. It reveals something of the love-lock's real-world status; the daughter's eagerness to see the love-locks indicates that they have become tourist attractions in and of themselves. It reveals how the love-lock has become a strong and familiar enough folk motif to act as the central theme of an entire film. It reveals how the love-lock can be variously used as a plot device; while it brings some couples together throughout the film, it foreshadows the main characters' (temporarily) doomed romance. A failed love-lock here symbolises a failed relationship. The love-locks are also used as a character-building device, for instance demonstrating the contrasts between the perspectives of Lindsey, characterised as middle-aged and cynical, and Alexa, young and idealistic. Finally, it tells us something about the tendency to project age onto this custom (explored in *Chapter Six: Selling Love*). According to this film, love-locks were being attached to the Pont des Arts since 1997, over ten years before they were in reality.

An even greater exaggeration of antiquity is given in A. Scott's 2014 independently published novel *The Cornuta Curse*, which is the first in the *Love Locks* trilogy. The blurb reads: 'One in four men cheat. But what if their betrayal is inevitable? What if the women are cursed? Cursed by a 500-year-old love lock. If you were the one in four, would you try to break the curse?' The story follows Mara, an Australian of Italian heritage, who learns that the women in her family are cursed in love, following her ancestors' failure to throw the key into the sea when they attached a love-lock on the Via Dell'Amore (a real place, today heavily adorned with love-locks) on the Cinque Terre in 1545. According to her grandmother, 500 years ago 'Lovers would go up there with a padlock, and put their initials on it, and lock it before throwing the key into the sea. That way, the love would last forever.' However, 'by not throwing the key into the sea, [Mara's ancestors, Adriana and Tomolsino] had failed to complete the pact so had secured their love but without the "forever" part . . . As a result, Adriana was doomed to suffer Tomolsino's infidelity, as we were, one generation after the next, to be betrayed by our partners.'[30]

Mara's plan when she travels to the Cinque Terre – 'find lock, unlock lock, relock lock, throw the dang key into the sea and live happily ever after'[31] – is thwarted by the sheer number of locks on the Via Dell'Amore and the various factions of local inhabitants who wish to see her fail. When she does finally succeed in finding the lock, her observation that 'Its size mocked its importance'[32] is applicable also to its importance within the plot itself. As with the film *Love Locks*, the small object of the padlock is deemed of enough cultural significance and symbolism to play not only the central plot device but the theme holding the novel together.

Another projection of (less unrealistic) age is evident in the US television series *Homeland*, which sees Marine Sergeant Nicholas Brody reunited with his family after being missing in action since 2003. In an episode that aired in 2011, Brody takes his daughter Dana to see a love-lock assemblage on a chain-link fence in some unnamed, nondescript woods in Virginia. When his daughter asks what they are, Brody responds 'Historical artefacts', and explains that he and his wife attached a love-lock there (at some point that must predate 2003, and that therefore predates the spread of the custom). 'Each padlock put here by a couple who thought they'd stay together forever,' muses Brody, 'I wonder how many did. Not many I bet.' When Dana asks why he brought her to see them, he explains 'I'm kind of struggling for things to hold onto.' In this example, the love-lock represents memory and the past but is also used to demonstrate Brody's struggle in the present.[33]

Love-locks have been employed in various ways over a number of years in the Australian soap opera *Neighbours*. The first episode featuring a love-lock storyline aired 13 February 2014 (the day before Valentine's Day) and involved character Callum Jones creating a love-lock assemblage on the chain-link fences along the fictional Lassiter's Lake. He pitched his idea: 'Couples will be brought here to Lovers Lake to put a lock on this bridge, just like in Paris . . . And then afterwards, they'll drop lots of money at local business.' Throughout the following few episodes, the romantic status of several of the show's couples is reflected in their responses to the love-locks. Young love is cemented through the locking of a lock, secret lovers consider using the custom to make their relationship public, while a marriage is shown to be struggling when a husband is too busy to participate in the custom.[34] Love-locks appear again in June 2014 as a mnemonic device, with one character encountering the lock she had attached on Valentine's Day.

Another love-lock story arc emerges in *Neighbours* two years later in February 2016, when the local council attempt to remove the locks on Lassiter's Lake. Local resident Sonya Mitchell attaches herself to one of the fences in protest and manages to convince the council – not wanting negative publicity – to allow the love-locks to stay. Celebrating Sonya's political win, her husband brings a family love-lock for them to attach, and her success spurs Sonya to run for Mayor.[35] And over a year later, in October 2017, they appear again, when Sonya's husband removes their love-lock and throws it into the lake believing their relationship to be over. Comedy ensues when the couple reunite and he tries to fish the lock out of the lake; fortunately, Sonya has already bought a new one: 'as a symbol of a new phase of our relationship.'[36]

In *Shadowhunters: The Mortal Instruments*, a supernatural drama television series based on Cassandra Clare's popular young adult novels, love-locks again act as a mnemonic device in an episode that aired in 2019. The relationship between two of the main characters, Alec and Magnus, has ended, and Magnus returns to a love-lock assemblage he and Alec visited in a flashback. Although the series is set in New York, it was filmed in Toronto, and the love-lock assemblage featured is the one in Toronto's Distillery District. In the flashback experienced by Magnus, he and Alec had seen love-locks in Paris, and Alec had brought him to this assemblage closer to home. Alec presents Magnus with an uninscribed padlock: 'I know it's silly but I wanted us to have a lock too.' Magnus, a warlock, magically inscribes the padlock with the words 'Aku Cinta Kamu', Indonesian for 'I love you' – and also the title of this particular episode. They attach the lock, and then we are returned to the present, where Magnus uses magic to remove it from the assemblage and obliterate it. In this case, the love-lock is a symbol of the hopeful nature of the characters' relationship in the past and of its dissolution in the present.[37]

Humour is central to other, more far-fetched uses of the love-lock, demonstrating the adaptability of this motif. In a 2015 episode of American supernatural comedy *iZombie*, 'The Hurt Stalker', a love-lock on a bridge in Seattle plays a key role in a murder case when a stalker is found dead.[38] In the 2017 children's animated film *Shopkins: World Vacation*, the main characters – who consist largely of fruit and sweets: the 'Shopkins' – visit Paris, where they come across a love-lock bridge. Informed that 'Shoppies and Shopkins come from all over the world and attach locks on this bridge as permanent symbols of love', the giant strawberry decides to attach an anthropomorphised love-lock for every character she loves. The result is a large bulge of locks that cause a traffic jam.[39] In a different episode of French cartoon *Miraculous: Tales of Ladybug and Cat Noir* than the one mentioned above, villain Princess Fragrance kidnaps a visiting prince, takes him to the Pont des Arts, and attempts to use a love-lock to magically seal their love: 'This will lock our love forever, my prince.'[40]

The love-lock is not always used romantically within popular culture, again demonstrating its adaptability. In the 2013 Hollywood film *Now You See Me*, which centres on a mysterious organisation of magicians, character Alma Dray of Interpol describes the custom as one of magic, wishes and secrets:

> There is a place in Paris, Pont des Arts. Sometimes in the mornings I sit on a bench there and I watch the people make a wish and lock it in a lock on the bridge then throw the key into the Seine. All day they do this. Mothers, lovers, old men. Watching the keys sink into the water and their secret is locked away forever. For real and at the same time magical.

In the final scene of the film, Alma is on the Pont des Arts with FBI agent Dylan Rhodes (who has – spoiler alert – revealed himself to be a member of the secret organisation). He asks Alma to keep the secret of his identity and has brought a padlock: 'One more secret to lock away.' They lock it and throw the key into the Seine; the camera follows it beneath the water to rest on the riverbed, amidst hundreds of keys.[41]

The clear popularity and adaptability of this motif has led to some tokenistic appearances, such as in Barbara Pintoro's 2017 Kindle novel *Love Lock*. Despite the novel's title and the front cover showing a stock image of love-locks in front of the Eiffel Tower (see *Introduction*), this supernatural thriller set in the US has nothing at all to do with the love-lock custom. The only vague reference appears on the final page, when we learn that the protagonist and his new fiancé are going to Paris for their honeymoon: 'She wants to go there so we can put our love locks on the bridge over the River Seine.'[42] Clearly, the love-lock motif has been drawn on here to capture potential readers, indicating that the custom has become familiar and popular enough to be put to commercial use (an aspect that is explored in *Chapter Six: Selling Love*).

Effects of Popular Culture

The love-lock custom has impacted popular culture by providing a familiar and adaptable motif easily employed to symbolise romance and memory, and to hold a mirror up to the status of people's relationships: young love, secret love, long-lost love, rekindled love. However, as was shown in the previous chapter's detailing of the 'Moccia phenomenon', the love-lock custom has also been impacted *by* popular culture. Gin and Step attached a love-lock in *Ho voglia di te*, so Italian teenagers began imitating the practice in a form of embodied play. We witness the same process following the appearance of the custom in other examples of mass media, where audiences become aware of the custom through their exposure to it on the screen or in the pages of a novel, and then perhaps even visit the specific love-lock assemblage referenced. Bruce Jackson would term this 'the folklore of audiences'. Writing his editor's note in a 1989 issue of the *Journal of American Folklore*, he identified a subcategory of this as 'the ways the contents of films enter general consciousness and style.'[43]

This process is behind the popularity of the Namsan Tower love-locks, Seoul. Going to the top of the tower has become the stereotypical Korean date, as shown in Korean dramas (known popularly as K-Drama), and it is often accompanied by the locking of a love-lock. Appearing in such dramas as *Boys Over Flowers*, *Rooftop Prince*, and *My Love from the Star*, it is unsurprising that the site features in many 'K-Drama' sightseeing itineraries.[44] However, references to the site are not limited to K-Drama. An article in *Korea Times* identifies the Namsan

Tower's love-locks' appearance in Korean reality television programme *We've Got Married* in 2008 as another factor behind its popularity.[45] They also feature in Paula Stokes's 2017 young adult thriller *Ferocious*, in which protagonist Winter and love interest Jesse climb to the top of the tower and discuss the locks, observing that there are similar assemblages in the US. 'It's a cool gesture, but I never really understood,' Jesse admits. 'I feel like love is the kind of thing you have to nurture and care for. You can't just lock it up in some faraway place if you want it to last.'[46]

This has occurred to a lesser extent following other popular cultural references. The *Hollyoaks* scene, described above, which features two characters declaring their love on the Ha'penny Bridge, Dublin, is believed to have motivated fans to visit the bridge and attach love-locks themselves.[47] One commenter on travel review website TripAdvisor responded to a complaint about the love-locks on Ha'penny Bridge by noting, 'those locks could be something attracting tourists to Dublin – ever since the same bridge was seen in Hollyoaks with ste and Brendan!' Responding to an online *The Journal* article on the love-locks, another person wrote 'Hollyoaks, the TV show, has a lot to answer for'. Following the episode in 2012, photographs circulated on the Internet of a love-lock with the two characters' names on, despite the fact that no scene aired showing the pair lock one.[48] This was possibly the result of a scene filmed but cut from the show; it may also have been the deposit of a fan, partaking in embodied play.

Another love-lock deposited in direct connection to a television show was one locked during the 100th episode of American sitcom *Parks and Recreation*, when the central character Leslie takes a romantic trip to Paris with husband Ben. One of the final scenes of the 2014 episode shows them locking a love-lock on Pont Neuf. Sean O'Neill, writing for entertainment website *AV News*, observed that 'Fans have since made their own pilgrimages to seek out the lock and take their pictures with it, and it was all incredibly sweet and sentimental and a shared experience until some selfish jerkface cut the fence and stole the lock for themselves.'[49] Actor Adam Scott, who played Ben, shared this news on 5 February 2014 on social media platform Twitter, with the simple message 'This is shitty.'[50]

Another example of fans' engagement with fictional love-locking followed the cancellation of the television series *Shadowhunters* in 2019 after its third season, when fans campaigned for its renewal. One proposal for this campaign, as suggested on Twitter, was for somebody to attach a love-lock to the Toronto assemblage in honour of the 'Aku Cinta Kamu' episode, in which two characters lock their love at this site (interestingly, it is believed that the series producers removed this love-lock immediately after filming to stop fans from flocking to the assemblage and damaging it). Other fans responded to this tweeted suggestion enthusiastically, with further proposals that people could deposit #SaveShadowhunters love-locks to assemblages around the globe: 'Show your passion for

#Shadowhunters with creating your own special love lock for the series. Write a #SaveShadowhunters message on it, hang it up on a public place and show the world some *Aku cinta kamu*', tweeted one fan on 18 April 2019. This tweet received 376 'likes' and 137 'retweets', along with comments from people who had or wanted to deposit a love-lock as part of the campaign.

That the folk custom of love-locking is being transmitted to a wide audience and consequently perpetuated through mass-mediated ostension is not surprising. Larry Danielson, like Stith Thompson above, observed in the 1970s that movies play a major role in legend transmission, an observation also made by Juliette Wood about fairy beliefs and film: 'contemporary audiences are more likely to be exposed to folk legend and belief in the context of mass media than by any other means,' and so, she concluded, traditions 'are transmitted through popular culture'.[51] Leonard Primiano made the same remarks regarding television: 'The nature of television is that it expresses individuals' views while simultaneously influencing them. Television media treatment may often trivialize and sensationalize personal experiences of the supernatural, but it can also inspire and inform them.'[52] And thus has popular culture inspired and informed the love-lock custom.

Mass media has impacted the custom in another way: through the choice of inscriptions on the locks. The vast majority of inscriptions consist of names, initials and sometimes dates, but some include phrases from popular films, books and songs. One love-lock on the Centenary Bridge, Leeds, UK, reads 'MOOMIN TROLL "LOVES" SNORK MAIDEN', referring to the main character and his girlfriend from *The Moomins* book and comic strip series, which have been running since the 1940s and have been adapted for television. Another on the same bridge bore the Beach Boys' quote 'GOD ONLY KNOWS WHAT I'D BE WITHOUT YOU' from the 1966 hit song *God Only Knows*, re-popularised on the soundtrack of the 2003 Christmas romantic comedy *Love Actually*, and another was inscribed with the 'I belong to you You belong to me' quote from The Lumineers 2012 song *Ho Hey*.

Other examples abound elsewhere. The words 'Truly. Madly. Deeply' on one love-lock in York refer to Savage Garden's hugely popular 1997 song of the same title. In Liverpool, 'You'll Never Walk Alone' explicitly links the Gerry and the Pacemakers' 1963 single to Liverpool football club through inclusion of the club's crest. In Manchester, 'OKAY?' may allude to John Green's 2012 popular young adult novel and subsequent film, in which 'Okay? Okay' is the main characters' way of saying 'I love you'. In Stonehaven, Scotland, 'I saw sparks' references Coldplay's 2000 song *Sparks*. In Stockholm, Sweden, 'My heart is, and always will be, yours' is a quote from the 1995 adaptation of Jane Austen's *Sense and Sensibility* (this line was not in the original novel). Lastly, in Budapest, Hungary, 'The greatest gift of all is just to love and be loved in return' is a slightly altered line from Nat King Cole's 1948 *Nature Boy*, re-released in Baz Luhrmann's 2001 musical *Moulin Rouge!*

These references demonstrate the extent to which popular culture is drawn on in our articulation of love. This is unsurprising considering the amount of research undertaken on the social effects of mass media,[53] much of which is concerned with romantic relationships. As Catherine Roach observes, 'The story of romance is the guiding text offered by contemporary American culture and the culture of the modern West on the subject of how women and men (should) relate.'[54] This guiding text of romance, of how those in a relationship should feel towards each other and articulate those emotions, 'is endlessly taught and replayed in a multiplicity of cultural sites: Disney princess movies, the wedding industry, fairytales, Hollywood movies, pop music lyrics, advertising, the diamond jewelry industry, and more'.[55] The quotes from (often romantic) films, songs and novels reproduced on the love-locks as a way of declaring love demonstrate popular culture's propensity for providing social reference for romantic experiences and expressions in reality.[56]

Conclusion

When Moccia used the love-lock custom to make a statement about the romantic commitment between his two main characters, he created a folk motif: a symbolic element within the narrative that draws on a folkloric custom. Having become an established 'object of endearment', one that so succinctly allegorises love, the love-lock's popularity as a folk motif grew. It has appeared in numerous films, television shows and pieces of literature, demonstrating the ease with which folkloric customs and popular culture converge, whether the love-locks act as incidental backdrop, are drawn on to communicate a message or materialise a sentiment, or are integral to the plot. Through a consideration of how the love-lock custom and consequent assemblages are used in mass media, a better insight has been gained into how they are perceived: as familiar landmarks, as romantic settings, and as a ritual of universal but also adaptable symbolism.

This exploration into the love-lock as mass-mediated ostension has also illustrated how popular culture has impacted the custom. Firstly, transmission: through exposure to it on the screen or on the page, audiences become familiar with the symbolism of love-locking and with the assemblages as landmarks. And vice versa, the more familiar audiences become, the more this motif is used. Secondly, dissemination: familiarity leads to the perpetuation of the custom, with fans imitating the practice through embodied play. And thirdly, in a slightly different vein, the referencing of films, novels and songs in the messages inscribed on the love-locks illustrates the extent to which popular culture is drawn on in our articulation of love today. These various strands all serve to demonstrate how interrelated folk custom and popular culture can be.

Notes

1. Thompson, *The Folktale*, 461.

2. Dorson, *American Folklore*, 247.

3. Smith, 'Contemporary Legends and Popular Culture', 318.

4. Burns, 'Folklore in the Mass Media', 90–106.

5. Ibid., 90.

6. Denby, 'Folklore in the Mass Media', 116.

7. Dégh and Vázsonyi, 'Does the Word "Dog" Bite? Ostensive Action', 7–8.

8. Koven, 'Folklore Studies and Popular Film and Television', 176–95; Koven, 'Most Haunted and the Convergence of Traditional Belief and Popular Television', 183–202.

9. Narváez and Laba, 'Introduction', 1–8.

10. Wood, 'Filming Fairies', 279–96; Hornby, 'Rumors of Maggie', 102; Bird, 'Cultural Studies as Confluence', 345; Greenhill, 'Folklore and/on Film', 483–99.

11. Bacchilega, 'Folklore and Literature', 448.

12. Storey, *Inventing Popular Culture*, 15.

13. Foster, 'Introduction', 5.

14. Koven, 'Folklore Studies and Popular Film and Television', 190.

15. Dundes, 'The Study of Folklore in Literature and Culture', 136–43.

16. *Le Week-End* [film], dir. by Roger Michell (UK: Curzon Film World, 2013).

17. 'She's Not There', *Chanel: Coco Mademoiselle* [television advertisement], 2013.

18. 'Glaciator', *Miraculous: Tales of Ladybug and Cat Noir* [television programme] Netflix, Season 2, Episode 9, 14 January 2018.

19. Denby, 'Folklore in the Mass Media', 118.

20. The *mise-en-scène* is defined by John Gibbs as 'the contents of the frame and the way that they are organised': Gibbs, *Mise-en-scène*, 5.

21. *Hollyoaks* [television programme] Channel 4, 19 December 2012.

22. *Karate Kid* [film], dir. by Harald Zwart (US: Sony Pictures, 2010).

23. Bordwell, Thompson and Smith, *Film Art: An Introduction*, 118.

24. Eco, 'Critique of the Image', 35–37.

25. Otnes and Pleck, *Cinderella Dreams*, 61.

26. Ibid., 113.

27. Margolin, 'Introduction: How Do I Love Thee?', 16.

28. Bordwell et al., *Film Art*, 118.

29. *Love Locks* [film], dir. by Martin Woods (US Hallmark, 2017).

30. Scott, *The Cornuta Curse*, 14–15.

31. Ibid., 53.

32. Ibid., 243.

33. 'Clean Skin', *Homeland* [television programme], Showtime, Season 1, Episode 3, 16 October 2011.

34. *Neighbours* [television programme], Channel 5, Episode 6819, 13 February 2014; Episode 6820, 14 February 2014; Episode 6823, 19 February 2014.

35. *Neighbours* [television programme], Channel 5, Episode 7292, 2 February 2016.

36. *Neighbours* [television programme], Channel 5, Episode 7710, 13 October 2017; Episode 7714, 19 October 2017; Episode 7717, 24 October 2017.

37. 'Aku Cinta Kamu', *Shadowhunters: The Mortal Instruments* [television programme] Netflix, Season 3, Episode 19, 22 April 2019.

38. 'The Hurt Stalker', *iZombie* [television programme] Netflix, Season 2, Episode 8, 1 December 2015.

39. *Shopkins: World Vacation* [film], dir. by Richard Bailey (UK/US: Universal, 2017).

40. 'Princess Fragrance', *Miraculous: Tales of Ladybug and Cat Noir* [television programme] Netflix, Season 1, Episode 23, 6 April 2016.

41. *Now You See Me* [film], dir. by Louis Leterrier (US: Summit Entertainment, 2013).

42. Pintoro, *Love Lock*, 257.

43. Jackson, 'A Film Note', 389.

44. Anonymous, 'Namsan Tower AKA Seoul Tower'; Adrian, 'Locks of Love: Why N Seoul Tower is Romantic'.

45. Ji-yun, 'Seoul Tower Locked in Everlasting Love'.

46. Stokes, *Ferocious*, 268–69.

47. Lollymcd, 'SERIOUSLY! The Ha'penny Bridge is not The Love Lock Bridge'; 'Poll: Should "Love Locks" Be Allowed on Bridges?, *The Journal.ie*.

48. 'Emmett Fans', *Tumblr*; Brendan Brady (Emmett J. Scanlan) Fan Thread! *Digital Spy*.

49. O'Neal, 'Some Jerkface Stole the Parks and Recreation "Leslie And Ben" Lock from Paris'.

50. 'Second Chunce', *Parks and Recreation* [television programme] NBC, Season 6, Episode 10, 9 January 2014.

51. Danielson, 'Folklore and Film: Some Thoughts on Baughman Z500-599', 219; Wood, 'Filming Fairies', 281.

52. Primiano, 'Oprah, Phil, Geraldo, Barbara and Things That Go Bump in the Night', 57.

53. See the extensive bibliography of E.M. Perse, *Media Effects and Society*.

54. Roach, *Happily Ever After*, 3.

55. Ibid., 4.

56. Laba, 'Popular Culture and Folklore', 12.

CHAPTER 3

EXCAVATING LOVE

The Material Culture of Love-Locking

As described in the previous chapter, the final scene of the 2013 Hollywood film *Now You See Me*, centred on a group of magicians, shows a padlock being locked to the Pont des Arts and a key thrown into the Seine, which the camera follows as it drifts down to rest on the riverbed amidst hundreds more keys. For the film's writers and average viewers, this is a skilfully shot scene evoking the central themes of the story: secrecy, magic and the question of what lies hidden beneath the surface. Anyone with archaeological training, however, sees something different in that shot. They see the material evidence of ritual. They see the ex-voto, the votive offering, the deposit, the hoard, and are inevitably reminded of the myriad prehistoric and historic ritual assemblages that have been excavated in other landscapes and from other riverbeds the world over.

The archaeologist may also wonder, as I did, how a *future* archaeologist would interpret the masses of padlocks on bridges and the keys in the water beneath them, drawing on the rich history of ritual deposition already on record. And it would not be unreasonable to draw on this history. Love-locks do, after all, qualify as 'ritual deposits' just as much as coins placed in sacred springs or pilgrim tokens left at shrines. Deliberately surrendered with no intention of retrieval in a vow of commitment, they are the epitome of the ex-voto, which is simply defined as an 'offering made in pursuance of a vow'.[1] Archaeologist Ralph Merrifield offers another definition, which applies easily to the love-lock: the ritual deposit is an object 'deliberately deposited for no obviously practical purpose, but rather to the detriment of the depositor, who relinquishes something that is often at least serviceable and perhaps valuable for no apparent reason'.[2]

So, the love-lock is a ritual deposit, and as one becomes two becomes ten becomes a thousand, collectively they form an assemblage; specifically, a 'folk assemblage', to use folklorist Jack Santino's term.[3] These folk assemblages are the physical evidence of the custom; the tangible trace testifying to the ritual long after the depositors have locked their love and departed. And as it is so important to draw on a range of methodologies when contextualising a practice, this chapter will focus on these tangible traces, presenting the custom of love-locking from an archaeological or material culture perspective.

The Material Culture of Contemporary Ritual

Material culture is defined by James Deetz as '*that sector of our physical environment that we modify through culturally determined behavior*. This definition includes all artifacts . . .' (emphases in original).[4] It is an area of study that, according to Christopher Tilley, is centred on the concept that 'persons cannot be understood apart from things'.[5] We influence our physical environments and, in turn, are influenced by them. Culture is inseparable from the objects we use, design, produce, consume, modify, recycle and destroy. It is this notion that stands at the centre of material culture studies, which first entered scholarship in the 1970s and 1980s. Archaeologists had obviously already been using objects and monuments to reconstruct the past, but it was at this point that scholars from a range of other disciplines – history, anthropology, museology, human geography and so on – began recognising the significance of *things* to the social structures they were studying, and thus began actively engaging with material sources.[6]

Material culture studies have proved invaluable to an examination of rituals. This is testified to by the density of Timothy Insoll's 2011 *The Oxford Handbook of the Archaeology of Ritual and Religion*, which contains chapters by 65 scholars on rituals worldwide in prehistory, history and the present day. As Insoll notes:

> today a generally positive situation exists in relation to archaeological approaches to ritual and religions. A 'turn' is also increasingly evident whereby serious consideration is beginning to be given to the materiality of ritual and religions, and what this might tell us about . . . reconstructing rituals and potentially (albeit often elusively) beliefs.[7]

While this is a relatively recent 'turn', some anthropologists and archaeologists have been engaging with the materiality of ritual for some time. After all, prehistorians often only had the material culture with which to reconstruct the past.[8] In archaeology, ritual has frequently been applied to enigmatic material remains – one could argue too frequently. Archaeological specifications designed to distinguish the ritual from the utilitarian have been criticised for identifying dedicated objects by default; as Joanna Brück observes in her paper on ritual and rationality, artefacts 'which cannot be ascribed a practical role often come to be interpreted as evidence for ritual practices'. Brück argues that a deposited artefact with a perceived lack of functionality does not necessarily constitute a votive object.[9] However, many archaeologists have been nuanced in their ritual interpretations, careful not to over-interpret the evidence – and, in many instances, the evidence does strongly suggest ritual deposition.

The materiality of ritual forms a significant part of Richard Bradley's work on prehistoric archaeology, in which he explores hoards and votive deposits, primarily of metallic objects, in northern and western Europe. The centrality of material culture to his work is ironic considering Bradley characterises himself as someone 'with a limited appetite for artefact studies'.[10] Bradley explains this paradox by expressing frustration at artefact studies that record deposits without accounting for the processes of their deposition. He aims, in his *Passage of Arms*, to redress this, concluding that, 'Too often we seem to despair at the limitations of our evidence, but, for once, suitable material is available in abundance; those irreducible objects that will outlast the boldest attempts to explain them.'[11]

This is not just the territory of prehistorians though. Robin Osborne, a classicist, also strongly advocates the material culture study of ritual deposition, arguing that material evidence can provide greater insight into ritual practices than (more partial) literary sources:

> Archaeological analysis of ritual deposits both enables a description of a particular votive choice and votive practice that is very much richer than any participant observer would think it appropriate to give, and enables analysis of variation between deposits which situates the particular deposition into the context of general practice.[12]

In some instances, the material evidence of a practice is all that is available to us, in historical contexts as well as prehistoric. Concealed objects are a case in point. Archaeologist and former Deputy Director of the Museum of London Ralph Merrifield, for example, made much of the material culture of the enigmatic objects found hidden within the fabric of buildings in Britain, from the Roman through to the post-medieval periods. From single shoes up chimney breasts to mummified cats bricked up in walls, Merrifield – and subsequent archaeologists and historians – have had little literary evidence to draw on in exploring the practices and beliefs that led to these domestic concealments, presumed to be ritualistic in nature. The objects are all that remain, and so they stand at the very centre of these studies.[13]

Material culture studies are not only concerned with investigations into prehistoric or historic ritual behaviour. Objects prove just as illuminating in our study of contemporary cultures and social structures. In 1979, archaeologist William Rathje noted that, 'Most of us have played the game, what will an archaeologist learn about us in 1,000 years? A few archaeologists have decided not to wait a millennium for the answer and are taking the question seriously now . . . Archaeologists are now doing the archaeology of us'.[14] These 'few' scholars have been multiplying since the 1970s, and the material culture of the modern world now stands at the centre of many studies.[15]

Rathje advocates the use of contemporary material culture studies in the testing, developing and validating of archaeological principles and practices.[16] This methodology aims to determine how accurately we can interpret the relationships between the cultures and structures and artefacts of past societies employing only the material evidence, by comparing it to the uses of modern-day structures and artefacts. Contemporary settings are thus utilised to evaluate the approaches taken for reconstructing the past.

However, studying the material culture of contemporary ritual is valuable in its own right. Folklorists have been taking that as a given for decades now. In 1880, Walhouse was examining the objects ritually deposited on the rag-trees growing beside holy wells – 'horns, bones, tufts of hair, shreds' – to gain insight into how pilgrims were engaging with the sites.[17] Also in the late nineteenth and early twentieth centuries, Edwin Sidney Hartland and Francis Jones were 'excavating' objects deposited in the holy wells of Wales, while Robert Hope was conducting similar investigations in England.[18] Their examinations of the material offerings elucidated much about the ritual practices that were taking place at these sites.

In 1995, Tristan Hulse was examining the material culture of a more contemporary example of ritual deposition. 'Excavating' the site of St. Trillo's Well, Llandrillo-yn-Rhos, Hulse found that by studying the offerings of written prayers deposited throughout the early 1990s, he was able to gain insight into how people were engaging with the site. The prayers, he found, were a 'spontaneous and imitative gesture', evidenced by the fact that many of them were written on scraps of paper sourced from pockets and bags: pages torn from diaries, receipts, portions of envelopes, train tickets.[19]

In 1997, archaeologist Christine Finn examined how Chaco Canyon, a prehistoric complex in New Mexico, had become a focus for New Age deposition and ceremony. Examining and cataloguing the diverse range of contemporary objects deposited there, from shells and crystals to imitations of native American ritual objects, Finn and LoPiccolo, curator of the site, argued that such deposits should not be considered 'junk' but as 'archaeological objects of meaning and value'. These contemporary ritual deposits were, they demonstrated, 'of value as signifiers of continued use of the Chaco Canyon site'.[20]

Nearly ten years later, Jenny Blain and Robert Wallis were also advocating greater academic attention given to the study of contemporary deposits. Considering Neo-Pagan uses of prehistoric sites in Britain, they concluded that 'Whatever form this material culture takes, it is clearly worthy of serious study . . .

in terms of the construction and performance of identity.'[21] My own work on coin-trees (trees and logs embedded with coins often in exchange for a wish or luck) likewise demonstrates the value of employing a material culture perspective when examining modern-day ritual practices. Combining historic literature and ethnographic testimony with the material evidence of the coin-trees – the coins as convenient offering but also intrinsically associated with exchange; the tree as convenient receptacle with a long history of ritual behind it; the tools used for embedding the coins – proved an effective method for elucidating how the coin-tree custom has changed and adapted over time, from the eighteenth century to the present.[22]

Working on the premise, then, that material culture studies is valuable for gaining insight into contemporary ritual behaviour, this is the perspective adopted by this chapter. This is an updated version of a paper previously published, written in 2017 and based on three years' fieldwork at a love-lock assemblage in Manchester.[23] Following the writing of this paper, two further years of fieldwork have been conducted, amounting to five years' worth of data informing this chapter. The methodology of this data gathering will be outlined below.

Manchester Love-Locks

I have been crossing Manchester's Oxford Road Bridge for many years; situated between home and my former university, traversing it was a weekly occurrence. As bridges go, this one is small and inconspicuous, consisting only of four sculptured metal panels running alongside the pavement of a busy city-centre road. It is actually barely recognisable as a bridge; only by looking through the metal panels would a pedestrian know they were walking over the Rochdale Canal.

It was on 12 February 2014 when I first noticed the padlocks, seven in total, attached to the bridge. Judging by the level of rust on three of them, they had probably been there for a significant amount of time, but it was not until the addition of four more that I first took note of them. Three padlocks were apparently not prominent enough to capture the attention of a casual passer-by; seven padlocks, on the other hand, were fairly conspicuous.

Five of the seven padlocks bore inscriptions and adornment. Thick black marker spelled out what I assumed to be the initials 'D B' on one side of a padlock and a love-heart on the reverse. More probable initials 'J' and 'B' flanked a love-heart on another, whilst initials accompanied the Spanish phrase 'Te Quiero' ('I love you') on the third padlock. The other two inscribed padlocks each bore a pair of names, one a love-heart, and both the number '2013', which may or may not have been the year of deposition (that is, the year that the love-lock had been locked to the bridge); see more in-depth discussion of this below.

Having already researched the practice of love-lock deposition in St. Petersburg, Moscow, Stockholm and Prague, I was naturally excited to find a fledgling assemblage so close to home. I photographed and recorded the seven love-locks, curious to see if, despite their small number, they would attract more. And they did. Less than a week later, on 18 February, another one had appeared; three weeks later, another; three additions in April; three more in May. Thus is the nature of accumulation, as outlined above.

I continued recording additions of love-locks *in situ* as a site-specific investigation into the material culture of contemporary depositional practices. Every addition was photographed and assigned a catalogue number. The plan was to take weekly inventories and photographs of the Oxford Road Bridge, either until the assemblage was removed or it ceased growing. Five years later and neither of these has occurred. The catalogue now contains over 700 love-locks, along with 52 'divergent deposits' (see below), which represent 62 months of deposition (Illustration 3.1, Table 3.1). This chapter will use these data to tackle two primary questions: what insights can be gained into the pace, people and purpose of deposition by studying the ritual's material culture? And what are the benefits of recording a folk assemblage *during* its formation, rather than after?

Table 3.1. A sample of illustrative love-locks (LL) catalogued on Oxford Road Bridge, Manchester, from February 2014 until April 2019, in chronological order. The make of the padlock is provided where visible. Where I can be confident that an inscribed date cannot signify the date of deposition, this is stated. All surnames in inscriptions have been redacted. An enhanced version of the complete love-locks catalogue, including over 700 love-locks and 52 divergent deposits, is available online through Berghahn Digital Archaeology at https://berghahnbooks.com/digitalarchaeology.

Catalogue no.	Date recorded	Bridge panel	Description
LL2	13.02.2014	2	Heavily rusted, steel padlock, unadorned. Re-recorded on 04.03.14. 'Phill + Shaino' written on one side in black marker.
LL3	13.02.2014	2	Rusted steel padlock with a blue plastic base, unadorned. Re-recorded on 03.04.14. 'JIMMY + DAVE' written on one side in red marker. Re-recorded on 28.08.14. '18 July' written on one side in black marker alongside a love-heart. Note: 18 July was not the date of inscription. See LL9 and LL14.
LL6	13.02.2014	3	Brass padlock. 'K + N 28 TQ' written on one side in pen; 'Te Quiero' (Spanish: 'I love you') written on the reverse. Re-recorded on 30.06.2014. It has been removed.
LL11	16.04.2014	3	Brass padlock. 'Sara & Hessa' written on one side in black marker. 'S H <love-heart> 2014 10/4' written on the reverse. Re-recorded on 30.06.2014. Has been removed.

Table 3.1. continued

Catalogue no.	Date recorded	Bridge panel	Description
LL15	11.06.2014	1	Brass padlock: 'RUD JONY' written on one side with white correction fluid. Nothing on the reverse. Make: Jinye Top Security. Re-recorded on 30.06.2014. Has been removed.
LL16	18.06.2014	3	Brass padlock, unadorned. Make: Green Jem Security. Re-recorded 30.06.2014. Has been removed.
LL17	07.07.2017	3	Brass padlock. 'CH + MD 4.10/14' written on both sides in black marker. Make: Cocraft 400B. Re-recorded on 23.07.2014. 'CH + MD' has been scribbled over with silver marker on one side. Re-recorded on 28.08.14. 'MFS RBS 14' along with some possible Farsi or Arabic has been written over the original writing in black marker.
LL18	23.07.2014	3	Brass padlock. 'KR <love-hearts> GD' professionally engraved onto both sides. Make: Hardened. Re-recorded on 28.08.14. Possible Farsi along with '555' have been written over the original inscription in black marker. Re-recorded on 13.10.14. 'RORY + VINCE' written on the reverse in black marker.
LL35	29.09.2014	2	Brass padlock with 'A+B 4.12.13 MOYΣT' on one side, 'B+A 4.12.13 KAΣ' on the other, and 'A' on an edge written in black marker. Make: Colddoor. Note: 4.12.13 cannot be date of deposition.
LL49	25.11.2014	2	Brass padlock. 'xxxx M&S' written on one side in black marker. '20/10/11 xxx 21/11/14' written on the other side. A professionally engraved love-heart on one side. Make: Timpson.
LL60	14.01.2015	1	Brass padlock, unadorned. Loosely attached to the railings, easy to remove. Make: Colddoor. Re-recorded on 02.03.2015. Has been removed.
LL66	09.02.2015	1	Silver padlock. 'John Helen' written on both sides in black marker. Make: Master. Re-recorded on 01.06.2015. Names obscured behind scribbled black marker.
LL82	07.04.2015	3	Purple padlock, unadorned and unlocked. Re-recorded 04.05.2015. Has been removed.
LL83	07.04.2015	3	Brass padlock. 'C + J' written on one side in black marker. 'X + K' written on the other side. Make: Colddoor. Re-recorded on 27.07.2015. Has been removed.

(continued)

Table 3.1. continued

Catalogue no.	Date recorded	Bridge panel	Description
LL98	01.06.2015	3	Brass padlock. 'J <love-heart> A May 15' written on one side in black marker. Nothing on the reverse. Make: Timpson. Re-recorded on 27.07.2015. Has been removed.
LL100	08.06.2015	3	Grey padlock. 'January – June 2015 [AW] It's never goodbye only see you later. Thank you for everything <love-heart>' written on a piece of transparent tape stuck to one side of the padlock. Nothing on the reverse. Make: Tommy Walsh Hardened.
LL152	25.08.2015	1	Red padlock in the shape of two overlapping love-hearts. 'Mr & Mrs [surname redacted] 28.05.15' professionally engraved on one side. Make: Lovelocks. Note: '28.05.15' cannot be the date of deposition. Re-recorded 24.01.2017. 'Broke up sorry' written over the inscription in pink marker.
LL157	02.09.2015	3	Large brass padlock, unadorned. Make: Ifam. Re-recorded 14.09.2015. 'KaNE + Jack <love-heart>' added in pink marker. Re-recorded 14.02.2017. 'Suck Dick' written down one edge in pink marker.
LL166	10.09.2015	2	Brass padlock. '4.10.14 Steve <love-heart> Michelle ALWAYS xxx' written on one side in black marker. '4.10.14 Sunshine x S <love-heart> S x Blue sky + Angels' written on the reverse. Make: Rolson. Note: 4.10.14 cannot be date of deposition.
LL180	08.10.2015	3	Brass padlock. 'LEE & DONNA 1999' scratched into its surface. Nothing on reverse. Note: 1999 cannot be year of deposition.
LL209	14.12.2015	3	Brass padlock. 'Jeannine [surname redacted] 10-4-1951 10-24-2015 Dyersburg Tennessee With Deepest Sympathy' professionally engraved on one side. Nothing on reverse. Make: Hardened.
LL210	14.12.2015	3	Brass padlock. 'Christine [surname redacted] 10-4-1925 11-1-2015 Dyersburg Tennessee With Deepest Sympathy' professionally engraved on one side. Nothing on reverse. Make: Hardened.
LL211	14.12.2015	3	Brass padlock. 'Steven James [surname redacted] 19-3-1986 30-1-2004 Manchester U.K. With Deepest Sympathy' professionally engraved on one side. Nothing on reverse. Make: Hardened.
LL223	19.01.2016	2	Brass padlock. 'NIN 09/1/16 BBF' written on one side in black marker. 'BBLU since 2K8' written on the reverse.

Table 3.1. continued

Catalogue no.	Date recorded	Bridge panel	Description
LL230	15.02.2016	4	Brass padlock. 'Kimberley & Jolyon 12th November 2011' professionally engraved on one side. Nothing on reverse. Note: 12th November 2011 cannot be date of deposition. Re-recorded on 25.04.2016. 'ASYA + ALUA <love-heart>' written over the original inscription in yellow highlighter. Re-recorded on 24.01.2017. 'Samira <love-heart> Lauren' written over the inscription in pink marker.
LL237	25.02.2016	4	Brass padlock. Indecipherable (possibly Mandarin) characters and 'will u marry me?' written on one side in white correction fluid. 'SLF', 'my oath', and 'SYP' alongside a love-heart on the reverse. '22 Feb 2016' written on one edge. '1NTO' alongside a love-heart on the other edge. Make: Timpson.
LL303	10.08.2016	3	Brass padlock. 'SJ <love-heart> BS' written on one side in black marker. 'WILL YOU MARRY ME?' written on the reverse. Three love-hearts drawn one side. Make: Cocraft 500.
LL322	13.09.2016	1	Brass padlock. 'VICKY + LEE' written on one side in black marker. 'HAPPY BIRTHDAY' written on the reverse. '1993' written along one edge. '2016' written on the other.
LL335	03.10.2016	1	Silver and blue padlock. 'CHAZ + JACKIE 4 EVA' written in black marker on one side alongside 'X's and a love-heart. 'KEVIE + JAMES' written on the reverse alongside 'X's and love-hearts. Love-hearts drawn on both sides. '17-9-2016 LOCKED OUR LOVE' written on the bottom.
LL343	18.10.2016	3	Grey padlock. 'Since 16/12/2015' written on one side in black marker. 'Breens + Fri 22/09/16' written on the reverse. Make: Tri-Circle.
LL372	22.11.2016	1	Brass padlock. 'LOVE YOU ALWAYS Victoria xxx' written on one side in black marker. 'JEAN [surname redacted] "Grandma"' written on the reverse. '1930' written down one edge. '2016' written down the other.
LL424	21.02.2017	3	Brass padlock. 'Simon & Beverley' scratched onto one side, alongside two love-hearts and two sets of 'xx'. Make: York. Re-recorded on 09.08.2017. 'AL FAKHROO' has been written on the reverse in pen. Re-recorded on 23.11.2017. Indecipherable writing in pen added. Re-recorded on 20.07.2018. 'FUCK BITHES [sic]' has been added in black marker above a white sticker. Re-recorded on 12.01.2019. Message overlaid with a sticker advertising a dating website.

(continued)

Table 3.1. continued

Catalogue no.	Date recorded	Bridge panel	Description
LL509	13.10.2017	2	Silver padlock. 'Stacey L<love-heart>ves Nadine' professionally engraved on one side. 'I L<love-heart>VE YOU WILL YOU MARRY ME?' engraved onto the reverse.
LL517	13.10.2017	4	Brass padlock. 'Chloe [surname redacted] Will you marry me? Professionally engraved onto one side. 'I will love Chloe forever' engraved onto the reverse.
LL599	23.05.2018	3	Brass padlock. Names associated with Manchester United Football Club: 'Alexis Rashford Lingard Pogba Sir Alex Fergie' written on one side in black marker. 'MAN UTD' written down both sides. '[indecipherable] Scard 14.5.18' written on the reverse. Make: Wilko.
LL600	23.05.2018	3	Brass padlock. 'Paige Georgia Ollie Kian (Scard) 1.5.18-14.5.18' written on one side in black marker. 'MAN UTD' written down both sides. Make: Wilko.
LL601	23.05.2018	3	Brass padlock. Names associated with Manchester United: 'Lingard De gea [indecipherable] Rushford Young MAR-TIAL' written on one side in black marker. 'MAN UTD' written down both sides. 'Kian Scard 11.5.18-14.5.18' written on the reverse. Make: Wilko.
LL602	23.05.2018	3	Brass padlock. 'one love Manchester Ariana' written on one side in black marker alongside a bee and two love-hearts. 'Manchester u rock…Clare xx 11-5-18-14-5-18' written on the reverse. Make: Wilko.
LL613	21.06.2018	4	Brass padlock. 'X MARTIN X WE ALL LOVE + MISS YOU Karen, Dale, Becci, Danni' written on one side in black marker. 'Love u Pop Pop Chloe, Zak, Clayton, Bella, Blake + Bump xxxx' written on the reverse. Make: Yale.
LL635	06.08.2018	3	Silver padlock. 'MAGDA ADRIAN' written on one side in black marker with two love-hearts. 'NA ZAWSZE 26.03.2013' (Polish: 'forever') written on the reverse. '05.08.2018' written down one side. Make: Master. Note: 26.03.13 cannot be date of deposition.
LL720	24.04.2019	1	Brass padlock. 'Y & M <love-heart>' written on one side in black marker. '28/09/09 <love-heart>' written on the reverse. Make: Yale. Note: 28/09/09 cannot be date of deposition.

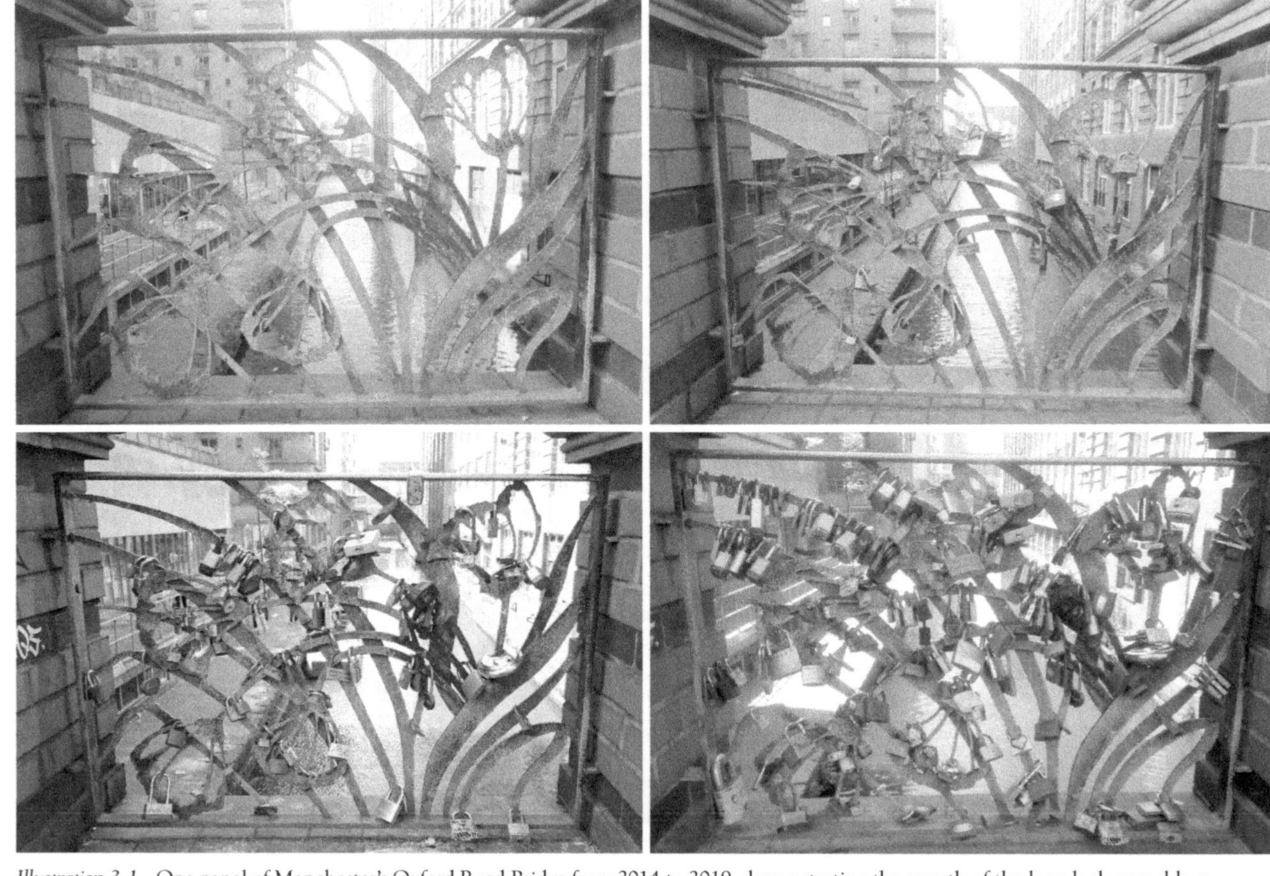

Illustration 3.1. One panel of Manchester's Oxford Road Bridge from 2014 to 2019, demonstrating the growth of the love-lock assemblage. Photographs by the author.

The Pace of Deposition

Before we can consider the pace of deposition, we must first consider the nature of the term 'accumulation'. Laing defines an accumulation as a collection of artefacts deposited over a period of time, rather than at one point.[24] This relates directly to the question of temporality, an element that archaeologists – ironically – can be guilty of overlooking, with Garrow noting that some studies omit 'any serious consideration of the effects of *time* in creating the patterns observed' (emphasis in original).[25] Time, claims Garrow, 'is often flattened significantly, as the deposits plotted two-dimensionally across causewayed enclosures and henges are compared without full consideration of the temporality of their deposition'.[26] Assemblages containing multiple objects are often presumed, rightly or wrongly, to represent single-event depositions, as observed by Bradley.[27]

However, there is compelling evidence to suggest that many assemblages were accrued over long periods of time. Some sites appear to have been repeatedly employed as places of deposition, which Fontijn – citing several Bronze Age examples from the Netherlands – terms 'multiple-deposition zones'.[28] In the case of the love-lock assemblage, the material evidence indicates multiple depositors. The sheer quantities of love-locks and the fact that most bear different names or initials would suggest to any future archaeologist that the assemblages are not the work of one or two individuals but of many. However, how do we determine whether the Oxford Road Bridge is a 'multi-deposition zone'? How can we tell if the Manchester love-locks were deposited by multiple members of a community at one time, as a single-event deposition, or whether they represent an accumulative assemblage, added to by different individuals over a long period?

Employing the methods of contemporary archaeology, this question is easy to answer. By cataloguing the Oxford Road assemblage over a five-year period, observing its growth from a modest seven in February 2014 to a sizeable 723 by April 2019 (Table 3.1), I can testify to the Manchester assemblage being the process of accumulative deposition. This is one particularly notable benefit of diachronic documentation. However, most archaeologists and historians are faced with the evidence of assemblages *post-assemblage*; they encounter it *after* the time period when people were adding to it, rather than during. So, without the ability to record the growth – if, for example, I was to encounter the Oxford Road assemblage for the first time as it currently stands, at 723 – how might I recognise it as an accumulation rather than a hoard? How might I determine a timescale for its deposition?

Archaeologists have employed various methods for ascertaining timescales of prehistoric and historic deposition, usually determined by the date of the deposited artefacts. Coin hoards are useful for this, with coins being particularly valuable finds for the archaeologist because of their ability to offer a relatively accurate means of dating.[29] It is (often) presumed that if the majority of coins in a hoard date to, say, the first century AD, then they were probably deposited in the first century AD. Can love-locks be similarly analysed?

Of the 723 Oxford Road love-locks catalogued, 338 (so nearly half) bore dates. Some were professionally engraved, but most were handwritten, varying in specificity from years (e.g. '2013') to precise dates (e.g. '11/1/19'). I had initially assumed that these dates represented the date of deposition and, in all likelihood, if an archaeologist recorded this accumulation in the future, they would interpret them likewise. A love-lock bearing an inscription of '11/1/19' was deposited on 11 January 2019. However, by cataloguing the love-locks diachronically, I have been able to ascertain that of those 338 dates, 48 per cent could *not* signify the day the love-lock was attached to the bridge.

Some love-locks are dated too early to be consistent with their deposition. For an extreme example, one bears the inscription '1999' – presumed to indicate a year – but cannot have been deposited until 16 years later; it was recorded as having been added between 29 September 2015 and 8 October 2015.[30] Others are less extreme but still clearly demonstrate a time-lag between date inscribed and date deposited. One bore the date '4.12.13' but was first recorded over nine months later, on 29 September 2014, while another, recorded on 24 April 2019, contained the date '28/09/09'. A date on one love-lock actually post-dates its deposition, having been recorded on 7 July 2014 but bearing the date '4.10.14'. Either this was in reference to a future planned event (a wedding perhaps) or it was written in an Americanised sequence (therefore signifying 10 April 2014), in which case it was referring to a date in the past.[31]

A total of 27 love-locks contain two dates, only one of which could indicate the date of deposition, if indeed either of them do. One bears the dates '20/10/11' and '21/11/14' handwritten, one on top of the other; another has '26.03.2013' written on one side and '05.08.2018' written on an edge; and another has '1930' written down one side and '2016' down the other. If one set of numbers signifies the date of deposition, then what does the other refer to? Eleven of the love-locks provide clues. Two appear to pertain to the start of a relationship: 'since 2K8'; 'since 16/12/2015', while another may indicate both the beginning and the end: 'January – June 2015 It's never goodbye only see you later.' Six love-locks possibly denote periods of time, probably visiting Manchester: 'Manchester u rock . . . 11-5-18 – 14-5-18', and another, commemorating a birthday, probably signifies the celebrant's year of birth as well as the year of deposition: '1993 2016'.[32]

These give us an indication of what the dates on other love-locks could refer to: anniversaries, years of birth or the time frame of a trip, and there are a variety of other events they could commemorate. This provides an important lesson; that the date marked on a deposit does not necessarily denote the date it was deposited. This has parallels in the archaeological record.[33] Some hoards, for example, have been found to contain artefacts that were hundreds, possibly even thousands, of years old at the time of their deposition. The 600 items comprising the Salisbury Hoard, for example, date to the Bronze and Iron Ages but are estimated to have been buried c. 200 BC.[34] Perhaps, as has been suggested, the objects' antiquity imbued them with sacredness.[35] Dating a deposit can therefore only proffer a *terminus ante quem*, while its *terminus post quem* remains elusive. The date marked on a love-lock is even less useful for dating because it does not evidence the age of the physical padlock itself or a depositor's engagement with it. As some of the dates precede the time of deposition, they can provide neither a *terminus ante quem* nor a *terminus post quem*.

However, because of the diachronic documentation of the Manchester love-locks, an accurate time frame of deposition can be established. Although it is not known when the first seven deposits were locked in place, I have been able to identify the months of deposition of the subsequent 716. Through this systematic cataloguing, the pace of deposition has been recorded, demonstrating that the Manchester accumulation has continued to grow. Over a five-year period, no month passed without the addition of at least one love-lock, with 11.9 being the mean average quantity added per month. This is unsurprising given the 'magnetic-like effect' of accumulations, with deposits believed to attract more deposits.[36] There have, however, been a few surprises.

The first six full months of recording (March–August 2014) revealed an exponential increase in the rate of deposition. One love-lock was added in March, two in April, three each in May, June and July, and then eleven in August. Following this, I had predicted a continuing exponential escalation, expecting the Manchester assemblage to continue growing until it reached critical mass, at which point there would be marked increase in the numbers of love-locks deposited. However, more than five years since its inception, no such critical mass has been reached. Although there has been a continuous ascending trend, it has been a steady rather than sharp increase. Perhaps in contrast to more established assemblages, such as on the Pont des Arts, the Manchester bridge is too modestly sized or inopportunely located to attract immense quantities.

Another surprise occurred when the data was transferred to a non-cumulative graph, on which the increase appears far less steady. Instead of consistency, there were sharp spikes and slumps in the quantities of love-locks added from one month to the next. December 2014 saw only three love-locks deposited, while January 2015 saw eleven. Only four were deposited in May 2016, while there were fourteen added in June 2016. May 2018 saw 20 added, while the following two months saw only six each. Studying these data demonstrates that there have been periods of intense depositional activity (August 2015 saw the highest quantity with 29) and periods of very little (March 2014 saw the lowest with only one). What might account for these fluctuations?

Garrow, drawing on the patterning of contemporary waste disposal in twenty-first-century Merseyside, UK, considers how an archaeologist might interpret similarly irregular patterns of deposition. 'It would certainly be possible', he writes, 'to interpret patterns such as these as having been intentionally (and meaningfully) constituted in the past'.[37] Might the significant spike in deposition in August 2015 have been deliberately instrumented? Given the casual and unofficial nature of this practice, this seems unlikely, and Garrow certainly advocates considering more 'everyday' explanations for such fluctuations.[38] Analysing quantities of different material types recycled each month in Merseyside, Garrow notes spikes and slumps that are easily attributable to patterns in everyday life, such as the increase of glass disposal over the Christmas period and garden waste during the summer months. As Garrow concludes:

> These patterns of variability were not created intentionally in order to convey a symbolic message. The people making these deposits will not have been aware of the patterns they helped to create. However, that is not to say that those patterns are meaning*less*. They do have something significant to say about the rhythms of everyday practice . . .[39]

If, like Garrow's contemporary waste, deposition was linked to particular seasons or festivals, what might the fluctuations in love-lock deposition reveal? The assumption might be that Valentine's Day would see an increase in love-locks. After all, what better day to ritually declare your love than on the day traditionally associated with romance? However, February witnessed only minor spikes, with February 2018 actually seeing a decline. Perhaps Christmas, another romantic time of year? Again, December saw little increase and one decrease. So, when do we see the spikes?

I am still at a loss to explain the spikes of October 2016 and 2017, January 2017 and May 2018 but can suggest a few possible reasons for the surges in August 2015 and 2017. Firstly, the August summer holidays increase the number of visitors to Manchester, increasing the traffic on Oxford Road, and consequently increasing the amount of potential depositors. Secondly, August Bank Holiday weekend is when Manchester hosts the Gay Pride parade, passing close to the Oxford Road Bridge, which witnesses upwards of 40,000 participants. Not only does the parade further elevate visitor numbers to this particular area of the city, but it also generates a celebratory atmosphere that might inspire depositional activity. The spikes in August 2015 and 2017, therefore, may not have been intentionally created but may nevertheless reveal something significant about the rhythms of city life.

And thirdly, two newspaper articles appeared in *Manchester Evening News* on 4 and 9 August 2015 entitled, respectively, 'Romantic Couples Demonstrate their Love with Specially Designed Padlocks on Manchester City Centre Bridge' and 'Love Locks in Manchester to Get a Special City Centre Location'.[40] Both detail the location of the Oxford Road Bridge and explain the custom: 'Around 100 locks are already attached to the bridge on Oxford Road like they have done in cities around the world, including Paris and New York.' It would not be unreasonable to assume that some of the depositors in August 2015 had been inspired by these articles, hinting at the role the media might play in the perpetuation or dissemination of depositional practices, as discussed in *Chapter Two: Consuming Love*.

The People of Deposition

Love-lock assemblages are generally in visible and publicly accessible spaces. This suggests that they were, to use Needham's term, 'community deposits', in the sense that they are deposited overtly rather than privately, 'in the knowledge . . . of society at large'.[41] As noted above, their sheer quantities also suggest that the assemblages are not the work of one or two individuals but of many. However, in another sense, they are the opposite of Needham's community deposits: they are not attached to bridges 'to the benefit' of society at large.[42] Instead, each love-lock appears to have been employed as a personal deposit, placed to the benefit of the individual depositor(s).

Indeed, there is a certain individuality to these deposits. Granted, their quantities and the general homogeneity and alienability of padlocks contribute to a sense of collective anonymity rather than to conspicuous consumption. Some objects, as Snodgrass observes, are 'too numerous and too cheap to be seen as motivated by competitive ostentation'.[43] However, as I have argued previously in my research on contemporary British coin-trees, by altering context and use, a common and alienable object, whether a coin or a padlock, can become a highly personal and inalienable deposit.[44] Through ritual recycling the padlock becomes a love-lock. The material evidence of the Manchester assemblage demonstrates that the depositors were concerned with distinguishing their love-locks from the masses; with harnessing these padlocks as expressions of their personal identities or relationships, by altering their materiality.

The most popular form of alteration is an inscription, with 98 per cent of the Manchester love-locks bearing some form of writing, either by hand (in marker, pen, correction fluid, nail varnish and so on) or professionally engraved, of which there are significantly fewer. The majority of these inscriptions contain an overt method of personalisation: names or initials, presumably (although not necessarily, see below) of the depositors. This method of personalising otherwise anonymous deposits through the use of initials is certainly not unique to the love-lock custom. In my research on contemporary British coin-trees, I have observed that the coin deposits frequently bear initials and other identifying markers.[45] Far earlier than this though, Josephine Harris was publishing on a twelfth-century Corinthian hoard of thirty gold *nomismata* of Manuel I (1143–1180), excavated in 1938, fourteen of which had graffiti, such as letters, scratched onto their surfaces. Harris suggested that this graffiti may have been used as 'identification marks', a term that aptly applies to the inscriptions on love-locks today (Illustration 3.2.).[46]

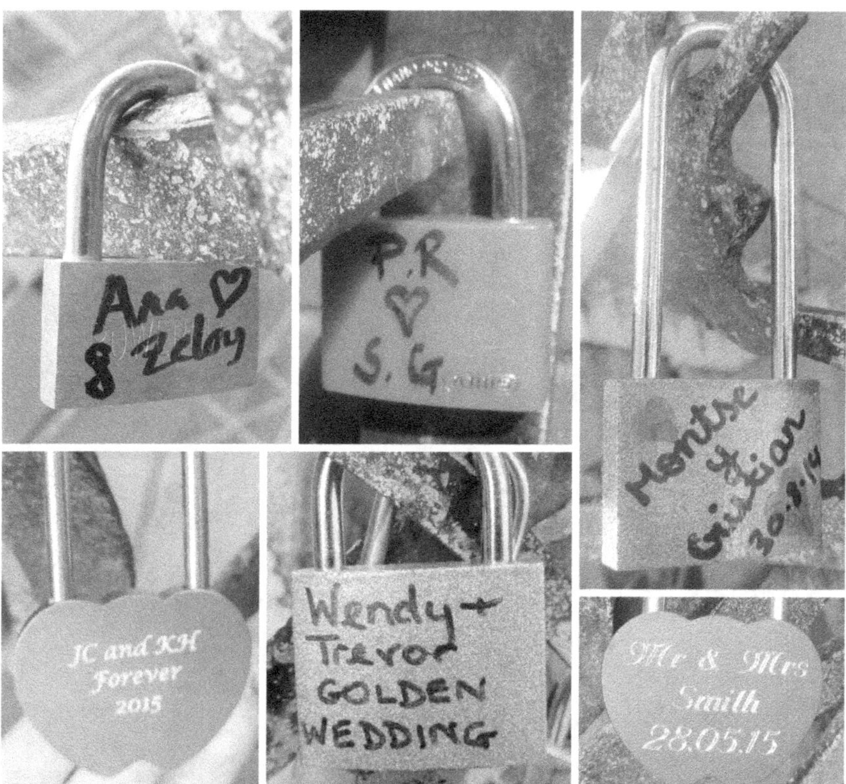

Illustration 3.2. Examples of inscriptions on Manchester's love-locks, from handwritten to professionally engraved. Photographs by the author.

Methods other than the inscription of initials and names have also been employed. Over 400 (over half) of the Manchester love-locks have been distinguished through the adding of adornments using markers, gel pens and nail varnish of various colours, as well as stickers. The majority of these adornments are love-related symbols: love-hearts, crosses, flowers and lemniscates. Three bear images of couples – two hand-drawn and another in photograph form – presumably depicting the depositors. Perhaps a fourth example is a lock adorned with a hand-drawn pig and rabbit. One is embellished with delicate love-hearts, starbursts and a cloud; while another is adorned with white flowers with green stalks. Red love-heart stickers had been added to several locks, with one further distinguished by a piece of silver thread tied to the shackle. A red ribbon had been tied around the shackle of another; a strip of fluffy green material was wrapped around another; decorative, flowery tape covers one; while, interestingly, a plastic skeleton tangled in silver tinsel was attached to another (Illustration 3.3.).

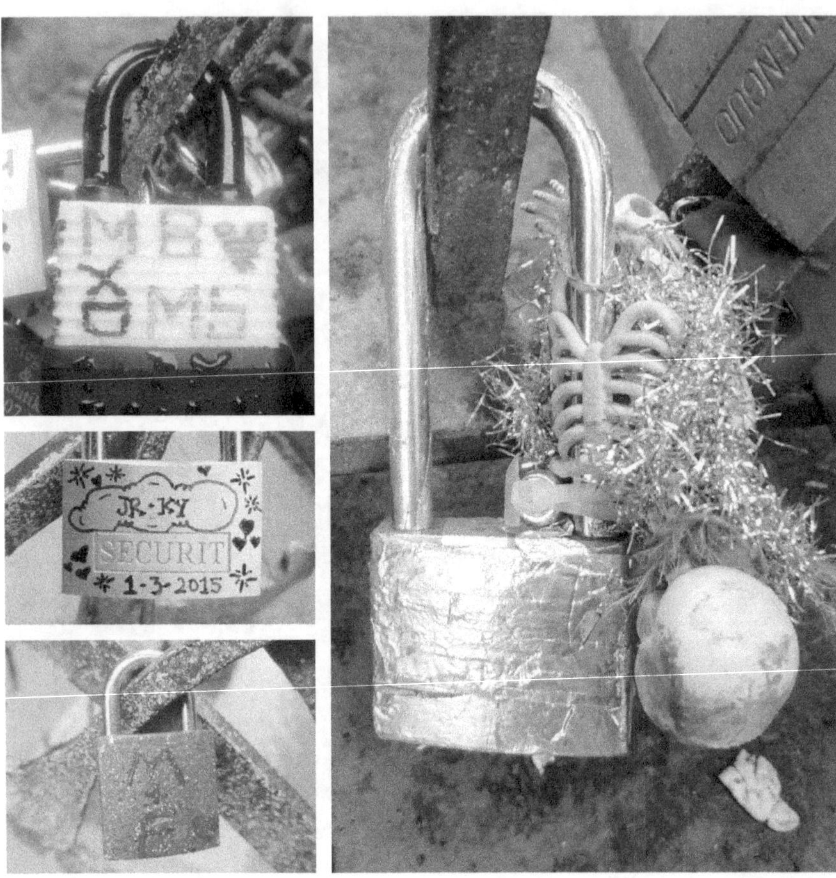

Illustration 3.3. Examples of adornments on Manchester's love-locks. Photographs by the author.

Colour has clearly been employed in distinguishing one love-lock from many. As Jones and MacGregor observe, 'Colour is powerful in the construction of difference.'[47] Bright red, pink and blue nail varnish, glitter paint, and gold marker are just some of the media used to demarcate love-locks. Other padlocks may have been selected for deposition by the virtue of their manufactured colour: with brass being the predominant material of the accumulation, those padlocks that are coloured yellow, purple, green, red, blue, pink, white, gold, glittery and zebra-print stand out from the rest. Further padlocks may have been chosen for their size, some being much larger than others, and the decision to commission a professionally engraved love-lock may have been motivated by a desire to demarcate one from the many. These are examples of conspicuous consumption, which have parallels in other ritual contexts, from prehistory through to the present.[48]

Adorning love-locks creates objects that represent their depositors. By physically associating the love-lock with a couple, the love-lock essentially becomes that couple's 'tag', their expression of identity. Love-locks and depositors become entangled.[49] This entanglement and the desire to associate a ritual deposit with the depositor's identity stretches back to antiquity and probably earlier,[50] but these objects are not designed to only represent the depositor; they are intended to *be* the depositor. As Tilley writes, the 'thing is the person and the person is the thing'.[51] This is a merge that anthropologist Alfred Gell terms the 'objectification of personhood'[52] and subsequently 'distributed personhood', whereby the deposit becomes a detached part – a 'spin-off' – of the depositor.[53] In this way, therefore, each of the love-locks in the Manchester assemblage is intended as a detached part of the person or people who deposited it.

However, by studying this assemblage diachronically, the assumption that each love-lock represents one couple or one depositional event is soon proven erroneous. Interestingly, forty of the love-locks appear to have been 'hijacked', in that they were deposited at one point in time and then were (re)inscribed or (re)adorned (and therefore metaphorically redeposited) weeks, months or years later. Two examples of this are those first recorded on 13 February 2014 as bearing no inscriptions; less than three weeks later, two names had appeared on one; a further month later, two names had appeared on the other, accompanied by a date five months later. Occasionally inscriptions are superimposed over the original messages, with new names obscuring the old ones, creating a palimpsest effect.[54]

Five love-locks actually appear to have been hijacked more than once. One was first recorded in February 2016 with a professional engraving, it was then recorded in April 2016 with handwritten names superimposed over the original inscription, and then again in January 2017 with a different set of names. Another lock was first recorded in February 2017, with names scratched into its surface; by August 2018, a name had been written over the original inscription in pen; more writing was added in November 2017; by July 2018, the obscenities 'FUCK BITHES [sic.]' had been written over the names in black marker; and by January 2019, a sticker advertising a dating website had been stuck over the palimpsest of inscriptions.[55]

However, in most cases, later inscriptions are made (more respectfully?) on bare padlocks or over heavily-faded messages, in a process of 'ritual recycling'.[56] Clearly these are cases of people wishing to make a deposit but being unable or unwilling to source their own padlocks, and so they 'recycle' or 'redeposit' another's, creating a palimpsest of deposition. By adding their names, initials or messages to the love-locks of past depositors, these opportunistic 'recyclers' are still participating in this custom, albeit in a distorted form.

However, this not only distorts the custom; it also skews the material evidence. Looking at the Manchester assemblage in toto, postliminary to the processes of accumulation, might lead the archaeologist to assume that one love-lock represents one set of depositors and one depositional event. For at least forty, however, this is not the case; these love-locks represent the activities of at least two, possibly three or four, sets of participants: the original depositors and also the subsequent recyclers. In the more common case of later inscriptions being added to bare love-locks or over faded messages, though, this process of ritual recycling would not be materially evident and so would be easy to overlook.

The ritual recycling of past deposits is not without precedent within the archaeological record. The Cnip skull is one particularly illuminating comparative example. During excavations of Cnip, a first- to second-century AD settlement on the west coast of Lewis, a cache of structured deposits was discovered beneath the foundations of a building. Included in this cache was the upper part of a human cranium, and Ian Armit notes how easy it would be to interpret this as evidence of a foundation sacrifice – except for the fact that this cranium dates to 1540–1410 BC, nearly a millennium and a half before it was buried beneath the building's foundations.[57] Thunderstones offer another example of this: Stone Age tools such as axes, spearheads and arrowheads buried over time and uncovered by chance millennia later. Unfamiliar with the tools, the later finders believed them to have travelled down from the sky and into the ground through a striking lightning bolt; they thus imbued them with supernatural properties.[58] Believing them to protect against fire or lightning strike, they were concealed within the fabric of buildings – within a wall, in the roof, up the chimney – and there is evidence that some of these objects, already discovered and concealed, were later rediscovered and re-concealed. Sonja Hukantaival offers an example of a Stone Age axe found in a field in Finland at the end of the nineteenth century. Following discovery, it had been concealed in the hearth of the finder's house in Karvoskylä village but was later discovered immured in the hearth of another building before being delivered to the National Museum of Finland in 1974.[59]

These above examples not only illustrate that the date of deposition does not necessarily correspond with the age of the artefact (as observed above) but also that objects previously deposited can be *re*-deposited at a later time by other individuals or groups. This teaches a vital lesson: that an object's biography does not end at its moment of deposition. As Fowler observes, 'Artefacts, like people, are multiply-authored'; and, as Gruner notes, they can 'go beyond the intentionality of the person who originally constructed them'.[60] The structured deposit is a product not necessarily just of its original depositor but of later 'authors', whose engagement can alter the object both tangibly and intangibly: those who add their names or messages to another person's love-lock. It is not, however, only the recycling of love-locks that demonstrates their continued biography. There is evidence suggesting that some love-locks were in fact later altered by their original depositors.

According to the widely known 'tradition', by attaching a love-lock to a bridge and throwing the key into the water below, the depositors are declaring or affirming their commitment to each other. Should they ever wish to separate, the key must be retrieved from the water and the love-lock symbolically unlocked. By studying a love-lock assemblage only after the processes of accumulation, it would be difficult – impossible perhaps – to judge whether or not some love-locks had been removed. However, a diachronic study allows for this assessment, and it has revealed that at least eight love-locks were removed from the Manchester bridge over the course of this 62-month period.[61] Whether they were ritually 'un-deposited' by their original depositors to signify the end of the relationship, or by somebody else for a different reason, is impossible to ascertain, but either way it is doubtful that people would wade into the Rochdale Canal beneath the bridge in order to find the key. Perhaps bolt-cutters were used or the key was retained rather than dropped into the water.

In other cases, a different (easier) method of 'un-deposition' is employed: erasure of the inscription. This has occurred on three love-locks. One was recorded as bearing initials and a date on 7 July 2014, but by 23 July (a short-lived relationship?), silver marker had been used to obscure the initials. Another was recorded as bearing two names on 9 February 2015, but by 1 June the names had been covered by scribbled black marker. And the professional inscription of another, recorded on 25 August 2015, was covered with the words 'Broke up sorry' by 24 January 2017.[62] Clearly, an assemblage does not only grow over time but can experience alteration, ritual recycling and depletion (Illustration 3.4.).

The Purpose of Deposition

At first glance, the purpose of deposition appears obvious. Even without the myriad news features declaring that padlocks are being employed as 'love-locks', deposited to affirm romantic commitment, this function is fairly self-evident in the material record. The symbolism of padlocks as objects of security and steadfast unity, as explored in *Chapter Five: Symbolising Love*, is made explicit by some depositors in their inscriptions. The vast majority of the Manchester love-locks contain the names or initials of two people, as well as the romance-related symbols of love-hearts, crosses and lemniscates. Many more make overt reference to love and commitment: 'forever and always', 'I love you', 'Love Forever', 'for always', '4 EVER', 'FOREVER and a Day', 'Always', 'LOVE YOU ALWAYS', 'Sarah Loves Peter', 'Soul Mates', 'Te Amo' (Italian for 'I love you'), 'NUESTRO AMOR SERA LEYENDA' (Spanish for 'Our love will be legend'), to list only some. One draws on an analogy with the love-lock itself, inscribed with the words 'LOCKED OUR LOVE'.[63]

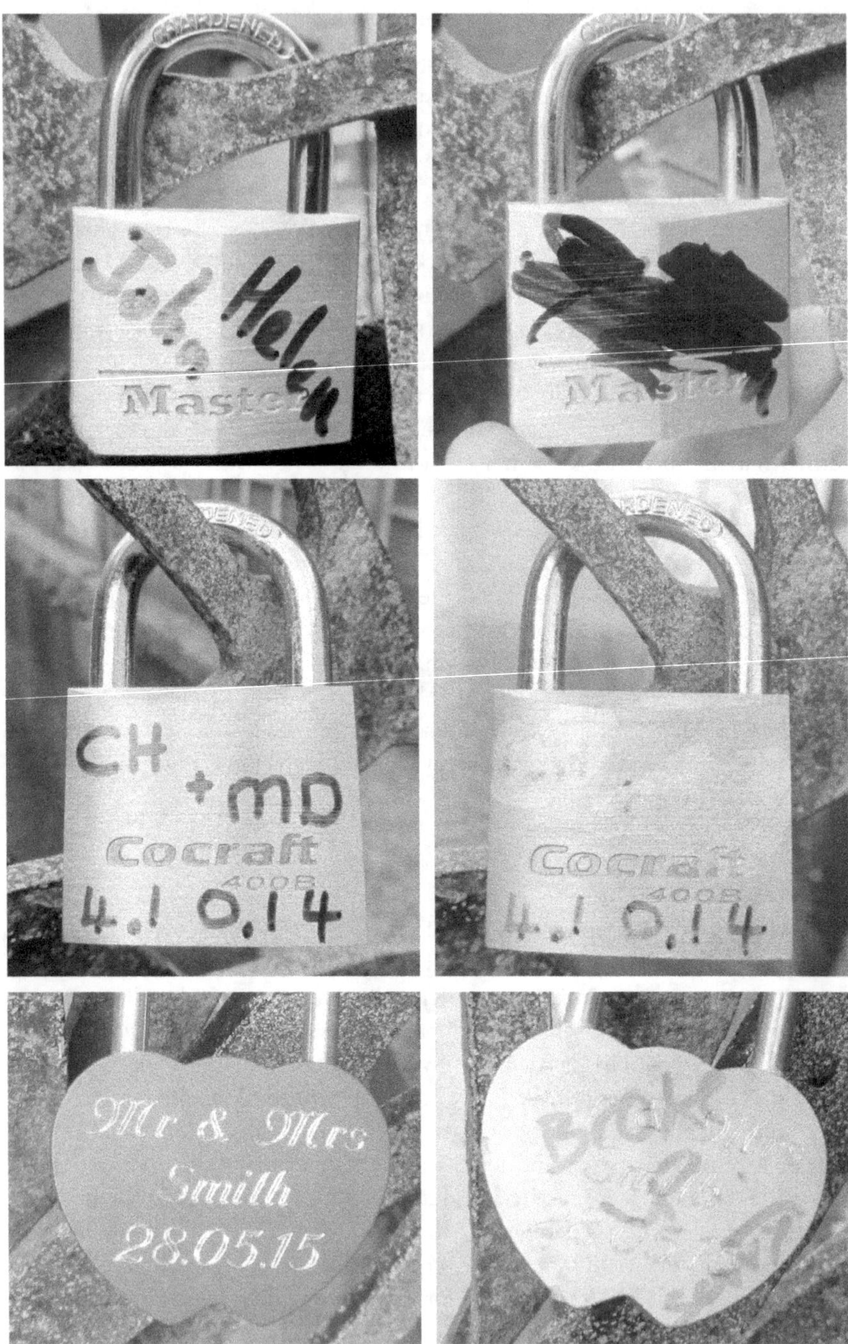

Illustration 3.4. Three examples of erased or obscured inscriptions on Manchester's Oxford Road. Photographs by the author.

It would be easy to conclude, therefore, that all padlocks attached to bridges are declarations of romantic commitment. However, we must be wary of assuming homogeneity. As I have argued previously:

> Scholars may seek to unearth *the* meaning of a custom, but when that custom is observed by multiple practitioners, in numbers that can range from 'several' to several million, how can one single motivation be ascribed to every individual? Humans are distinct, emotionally heterogeneous creatures. Granted, physical actions are widely imitated and homogeneous; participation in folk customs tends to be formulaic and ritualized. However, the reasons behind participation and the 'meanings' ascribed to the custom will be as varied as the practitioners themselves.[64]

Some inscriptions do deviate from the more typical 'I love you' message, as Stéphane Borraz also discovered in his examination of Paris love-locks, and it is these divergent examples that evince the mutable nature of this custom.[65] Some refer to specific events, often anniversaries: 'wedding Anniversary', '1 Year Together', '1ST YEAR', '1 YEAR', 'Happy 1st Anniversary', '7 years', '8 years', '10 Years', '10th Wedding Ann', '12 years', '21 YRS', and 'GOLDEN WEDDING'. The word 'Engaged' is inscribed on another. The custom of love-locking has clearly developed as a form of celebrating romantic milestones; it also appears to have become a method of *creating* them. Four love-locks bear variations of the words 'will you marry me?'.[66] Did their depositors actually employ these objects to propose to their partners, or were they deposited to celebrate an engagement? Either way, they are clearly being used to mark significant moments in relationships.

These relationships, however, are not always romantic. Sometimes it is friendships that appear to be affirmed ('Friends foreveR', 'BFF', 'Best Friends for Life', 'AS FRIENDS'), while others seem to celebrate familial bonds ('sisterly sisters', 'Sisters Forever', 'CHLOE & MUM', 'Grandma', 'Love u Pop Pop', 'DADDY'). A couple clearly celebrate pregnancy or the birth of a child ('two became three', 'It's a Boy'). Others appear to honour individual milestones ('HAPPY BIRTHDAY', '100 YEAR', 'Alex's 40th', '1st Trip Together'), accomplishments ('Study Abroad 2K16'), or events ('We are seeing LANA DEL REY', 'Billy Elliot Manchester', 'Al Star EP tour'). A set of five love-locks from May 2018 are awash with names of people connected with Manchester United Football Club: 'Sir Alex Fergie', 'Rashford', 'Lingard'. Another, deposited at roughly the same time, refers to the 22 May 2017 Manchester Arena bombing at the Ariana Grande concert, inscribed with the words 'one love Manchester Ariana' and a drawing of a bee, the popular symbol of Manchester.[67]

Some love-locks are more commemorative than celebratory: three near-identical love-locks bear the message 'With Deepest Sympathy', each one bearing a different name but undoubtedly deposited by the same person or group. Another one is inscribed with the words 'I'll never forget', another 'WE ALL LOVE +

MISS YOU', whilst another declares 'It's never goodbye only see you later', memorialising relationships if not individuals.[68] As Petts observes, durable items 'serve to crystallize into physical form the dynamic act of remembrance',[69] and it is unsurprising that love-locks have developed memorialising functions alongside romantic ones, with the symbolism of the padlock being particularly appropriate to messages of memory.

The padlocks may be durable, but the inscriptions are relatively ephemeral. Constant exposure to the elements means that even those professionally inscribed or written in permanent marker will become faded or obscured over time. Many inscriptions that were recorded with ease in 2014 and 2015 are now difficult or impossible to decipher. It is likely therefore that, given further years of exposure, the majority of the inscriptions will become illegible. And as the variant messages fade from existence, the variant purposes (celebratory of specific events, commemorative, etc.) may fade from knowledge – hence the importance of current cataloguing attempts in the recognition of the mutability of the love-lock.

It is not, however, only the occasional inscription that proves divergent; some deposits are divergent in themselves. At least 52 objects have been deposited on the Oxford Road Bridge that are not padlocks. These objects, which I term divergent deposits, vary significantly, from nightclub entrance wristbands to disposable lighters; from a half-eaten cupcake to an uncooked rasher of bacon; from pieces of ribbon to a hyperbolic inflatable penis. Some are more clearly personal and functional – if not valuable – than others. A child's dummy (or pacifier) was attached to the railings via a beaded chain that spelled out what was presumably the child's name, while an intact pair of gloves were placed on the wall of the bridge. Whether these were lost (and displayed by finders) or purposefully deposited is impossible to say, but either way they can be classified as structured deposits. They were either displayed by finders in a prominent way to increase the chances of reunion with their owners or placed in lieu of a padlock as a more personal deposit.

The other objects, however, are more obscure: the McDonald's drinking straw; the barcode stickers; the blue latex glove; the rolled-up pages of newspaper; the hair bobbles and clips; the paper napkin; the elastic band; the plastic carrier bag; the ribbons; the plastic cup; the various sweets and pieces of chewing gum. If these items were encountered on the floor they would be unambiguously classified as 'rubbish'; objects of discard rather than structured deposits. Fontijn considers this distinction within the archaeological context: 'The difference between discard and deliberate deposition is that they are steered by different motivations. Discard is defined here as a way of getting rid of an object that is no longer considered to be meaningful and useful.'[70] However, this distinction is not always clear-cut or self-evident.

While the nature of these divergent deposits suggests that they were disposable, alienable objects, not unlikely to have been thrown away, the material evidence of their placements suggests deliberate deposition rather than casual discard. These objects are not dropped to the pavement or tossed in the general direction of the bridge; they are carefully draped over, balanced on top of, tied around, stuck to, or stuffed between the bridge's railings and the love-locks. Why might the depositors of these objects have chosen to place them on the bridge rather than dispose of them in the rubbish bin standing only a few feet away? Perhaps they were deposited by people unwilling or unable to source a padlock (much like the 'recyclers' discussed above), and so they used whatever objects they happened to be carrying. Perhaps, to return to the notion of conspicuous consumption, they were deliberately chosen because of their deviance. Or the depositors may have intended to dispose of these objects in a bin or on the floor but, upon seeing the bridge, chose a more unusual style of discard, in which case the object falls somewhere between rubbish and structured deposit.

Evidently, as Thompson avers, 'rubbish' and 'valuable' are malleable categories, a concept that has been most usefully explored by archaeologist Brück. Writing of 'odd' deposits in Middle Bronze Age settlements, from a smashed bucket to the carcass of a cow, Brück asks, 'how can we draw the line between refuse and ritual? Many of these items were considered "rubbish" but were disposed of in a ritualistic style'.[71] The same applies to Manchester's divergent deposits: items that are considered 'rubbish' but, because of their atypical context, suggest a ritualistic style of discard. Clearly the line between discard and deliberate deposition is a blurred one, the categories of refuse and ritual existing on a scale rather than as polar opposites.

Much like the inscriptions, however, these divergent deposits prove far more ephemeral than the padlocks. With the exception of pieces of thread tightly tied to a railing and the chewing gum, none of the divergent deposits have lasted beyond a few weeks. The inflatable penis, for example, retained its place perched in front of the love-locks for less than 36 hours. This is unsurprising when we contrast their methods of placement with the secure attachment of a padlock. These objects either fall to the pavement or into the canal below or are cleared away by street cleaners or simply taken by passers-by (be they human, bird, or rat). Without a diachronic study of this assemblage it is unlikely that the divergent deposits would be recorded.

Conclusion

This chapter had two primary objectives: to consider what insights can be gained into the pace, people and purpose of deposition by studying the ritual's material culture and what the benefits are of recording a folk assemblage during its formation rather than after. And the answers? Many. A diachronic material culture approach to love-locks has enabled a rich understanding of the custom and has highlighted the value of tracing the development of an accumulation, rather than simply viewing it in temporal isolation. This diachronic form of documentation has revealed much about how we might approach and possibly renegotiate interpretations of ritual deposits. Archaeologists may take from this the lesson that accumulations should not be studied at one static point in time, and this will prompt us to question assumptions about the pace, people and purpose of historic and prehistoric accumulations.

However, as historian Owen Davies attests, 'the archaeological material cannot always be given primacy, because it . . . is partial in what it represents.'[72] This chapter has left many questions unanswered because the material culture of the love-locks gives us only half of the image. It shows us an after-shot of the ritual; it testifies to what the depositors left but not necessarily to *how* they left it. Were certain words spoken as the padlock was locked? Was the key thrown into the murky canal below or taken away? Was it one depositor, two, more? Was it a ritual conducted in the busy hustle of day or quiet lull of evening? The material culture also only gives us a partial glimpse into the *why* of this ritual. The inscriptions tell us something of the motivation behind deposition, but not everything. They don't explain why the depositors had chosen that particular day, that particular bridge, that particular message.

This loss of context has long been lamented a challenge of the ritual archaeologist's craft. Those who research prehistoric ritual frequently encounter difficulties in the interpretation of its often tantalisingly incomplete material record, with many details of deposition beyond reconstruction. As Fontijn observes in his work on the sacrificial and depositional landscapes of the Bronze Age:

> We know something about the treatment of the object deposited as well as its earlier history, but many questions remain. How was the actual depositional procedure carried out? On what occasion was it done, which people were present, what further activities did it involve and so on? All these aspects may contribute to a further understanding of the meaning of depositional practices, but they are practically beyond the limits of archaeological knowledge.[73]

The value of material culture is lauded, but it is also acknowledged that it cannot answer all of our questions. For the prehistorian, many of those answers are beyond reach, so separated by time are the archaeologists from their subjects. Fortunately, in the case of the love-lock, the depositors are actually available to question. Contemporary rituals provide the researcher with the invaluable opportunity to engage with the practitioners, to witness the *how* of participation with their own eyes, and to answer the often elusive question of *why* – which is the focus of the next chapter.

Notes

1. 'ex-voto'. *Oxford English Dictionary*.

2. Merrifield, *The Archaeology of Ritual and Magic*, 22.

3. Santino, 'Performative Commemoratives, the Personal, and the Public', 363–72.

4. Deetz, *In Small Things Forgotten*, 35.

5. Tilley, 'Objectification', 2.

6. It should be noted that 'material culture' has been subject to numerous debates, most thoroughly examined in: Hicks, 'The Material-Cultural Turn', 25–98; Lucas, *Understanding the Archaeological Record*. Criticisms of ambiguity are levelled at the term, and there are arguments over whether a focus on the brute physicality of an object provokes neglect of a consideration of their human significance. While I acknowledge these debates, 'material culture' will continue to be used here, defined simply as the significance of an object's physical properties in a consideration of its social role.

7. Insoll, 'Introduction', 1.

8. Davies, 'The Material Culture of Post-Medieval Domestic Magic in Europe', 379–417.

9. Brück, 'Ritual and Rationality', 284.

10. Bradley, *The Passage of Arms*, xiii.

11. Ibid., 203.

12. Osborne, 'Hoards, Votives, Offerings', 6.

13. Merrifield, *The Archaeology of Ritual and Magic*. See also Hutton, *Physical Evidence for Ritual Acts, Sorcery and Witchcraft in Christian Britain*.

14. Rathje, 'Modern Material Culture Studies', 2.

15. See, for example, Rathje, 'Modern Material Culture Studies'; Shanks and Tilley, *Re-Constructing Archaeology*; Gould and Schiffer, *Modern Material Culture*; Hodder, 'Bow Ties and Pet Foods', 11–19; Graves-Brown, *Matter, Materiality and Modern Culture*; Buchli and Lucas, *Archaeologies of the Contemporary Past*; González-Ruibal, 'The Past is Tomorrow', 110–25; Tilley et al., *Handbook of Material Culture*; González-Ruibal, 'Time to Destroy', 247–79; Harrison and Schofield, *After Modernity*; Harrison, 'Surface Assemblages', 141–61; Holtorf and Piccini, *Contemporary Archaeologies*.

16. Rathje, 'Modern Material Culture Studies'; Rathje, 'A Manifesto for Modern Material Culture Studies', 51–56.

17. Walhouse, 'Rag-Bushes and Kindred Observances', 104.

18. Hartland, 'Pin-Wells and Rag-Bushes', 451–70; Hope, *The Legendary Lore of the Holy Wells of England*; Jones, *The Holy Wells of Wales*.

19. Hulse, 'A Modern Votive Deposit at a North Welsh Holy Well', 33.

20. Finn, 'Leaving More Than Footprints', 169.

21. Blain and Wallis, 'Representing Spirit', 103.

22. Houlbrook, *The Roots of a Ritual*.

23. Houlbrook, 'Lessons from Love-Locks', 214–38.

24. Laing, *Coins and Archaeology*.

25. Garrow, 'Odd Deposits and Average Practice', 90.

26. Ibid.

27. Bradley, *The Passage of Arms*, 6.

28. Fontijn, *Sacrificial Landscapes*, 260.

29. Betlyon, 'Guide to Artifacts', 163. The Hallaton Hoard is one such example. Discovered in 2000 and excavated by the University of Leicester Archaeology Unit, this site, situated on a hilltop in Hallaton, Leicestershire, has yielded the largest assemblage of Iron Age coins recovered under controlled archaeological conditions in Britain. Over 5,000 Iron Age and Roman Republican gold and silver coins were recovered, along with a Roman iron cavalry helmet, which appear to have been deliberately buried in at least fifteen separate hoards at a site that is proposed to have been an

open-air gathering place with possible ceremonial significance. Using the testimony of the coins, archaeologists were able to estimate a relatively short time-period of deposition at this site: late pre-conquest and/or the early Roman period, the majority of the coins having been issued roughly between AD20–50 (Williams, 'The Coins and the Helmet', 361–62; Priest, Clay and Hill, 'Iron Age Gold from Leicestershire', 358–60; Score, 'Ritual, Hoards and Helmets', 197–207; Leins, 'Coins in Context', 39; Score, 'Hallaton', 152–64).

30. Table 3.1, LL180.

31. Table 3.1, LL35, LL720, LL166.

32. Table 3.1, LL49, LL635, LL372, LL223, LL343, LL100, LL602, LL322.

33. See Bradley, *The Passage of Arms*, 186.

34. Stead, *The Salisbury Hoard*, 123.

35. Eckardt and Williams, 'Objects Without a Past?', 142.

36. Gamble, *Origins and Revolutions*, 122.

37. Garrow, 'Odd Deposits and Average Practice', 111–13.

38. Ibid., 113.

39. Ibid., 111.

40. Butler, 'Romantic Couples Demonstrate their Love'; Butler, 'Love Locks in Manchester to Get a Special City Centre Location'.

41. Needham, 'Selective Deposition in the British Early Bronze Age', 246.

42. Ibid., 246.

43. Snodgrass, 'The Economics of Dedication at Greek Sanctuaries', 265.

44. Houlbrook, 'Possession through Deposition', 189–214.

45. Ibid., 203–4.

46. Harris, 'A Gold Hoard from Corinth', 273.

47. Jones and MacGregor, *Colouring the Past*, 12.

48. Bradley, for example, considers the role of prestige – 'the common currency of non-market societies' (1990: 137) – in Late Bronze Age deposits, when opulent ritual offerings were intended to lend themselves to 'the quest for personal prestige' (*The Passage of Arms*, 188). Ritual deposits in Archaic Greece were similarly harnessed, with Day observing that 'competitive self-presentation or social display on the dedicator's part played a major role in dedicatory practice' (Day, *Archaic Greek Epigram and Dedication*, 182). Anthropologists and economists have similarly detailed evidence of conspicuous consumption in contemporary societies (see Douglas, *The World of Goods*; Mason, *The Economics of Conspicuous Consumption*).

49. Hodder, *Entangled*.

50. See Dowden, *European Paganism*, 176.

51. Tilley, 'Objectification', 63.

52. Gell, *Art and Agency*, 74.

53. Ibid., 104.

54. Table 3.1, LL2, LL3.

55. Table 3.1, LL3, LL18, LL157, LL230, LL424.

56. Houlbrook, 'Ritual, Recycling, and Recontextualisation', 99–112.

57. Armit, *Headhunting and the Body in Iron Age Europe*, 225.

58. See Hoggard, 'The Archaeology of Counter-Witchcraft and Popular Magic', 182; Dowd, 'Bewitched by an Elf Dart', 451–73.

59. Hukantaival, '"For a Witch Cannot Cross Such a Threshold!"', 183.

60. Fowler, *The Archaeology of Personhood*, 65; Gruner, 'Replicating Things, Replicating Identity', 57.

61. Table 3.1, LL6, LL11, LL15, LL16, LL60, LL82, LL83, LL98.

62. Table 3.1, LL17, LL66, LL152.

63. Table 3.1, LL335.

64. Houlbrook, 'The Mutability of Meaning', 41.
65. Borraz, 'Love and Locks', 7–21.
66. Table 3.1, LL237, LL303, LL509, LL517.
67. See Table 3.1, LL599–LL602.
68. Table 3.1, LL100, LL209–211, LL613.
69. Petts, 'Memories in Stone', 194–95.
70. Fontijn, *Sacrificial Landscapes*, 33.
71. Thompson, *Rubbish Theory*, 10; Brück, 'Ritual and Rationality', 296.
72. Davies, 'The Material Culture of Post-Medieval Domestic Magic in Europe', 382–83.
73. Fontijn, *Sacrificial Landscapes*, 275.

CHAPTER 4

LOCKING LOVE

An Ethnography of the Love-Locking Custom

The previous chapter demonstrated the value of material culture in gaining insight into ritual depositional activities, but it also acknowledged that the love-locks alone cannot answer all of our questions. Fortunately, as love-locking is a contemporary practice, its participants are available to observe and to question, affording us the invaluable opportunity to witness the how and the why of participation, which are so often unattainable to the researchers of ritual. The aim of this chapter is to present an ethnography of love-locking to understand the ways in which people are engaging with this custom today.

The methodology behind this chapter is three-pronged. Firstly, non-intrusive observations were conducted at 30 different love-lock sites across Europe (and one in Australia) from 2014 to 2019.[1] During these, I observed how people engaged with the assemblages: Did they stop to examine or comment on them? Did they photograph them? Did they add their own? Secondly, I conducted interviews with people who had participated in the custom in the past. These were often via questionnaires, with the participants writing their responses. The interviews are slightly biased, as the participants are all British and Irish. This is offset by the global perspective of the third strategy: online ethnography (or netnography), which involved viewing videos of participation in the custom globally, uploaded by the participants to video-sharing site YouTube, as well as engagement with posts on Instagram and Twitter.[2] A wealth of information was amassed this way and, as will be explored below, the very presence of these videos and images demonstrates something interesting about the nature of the custom itself.

Chapter Three: Excavating Love will be kept in mind throughout. On one hand, this is to consider whether the material culture of the custom aligns with the lived experiences of it. And on the other hand, it is to keep the love-lock itself in our focus; to explore how people interact with its materiality and how depositor and deposit become 'entangled', to use an archaeological term.[3] It is through people that the love-lock is given a life beyond that of a utilitarian padlock, and we will delve into the complex biographies of some of these modern-day deposits. First, though, we will engage with some storytelling, drawn from the interviews conducted.

Andy and Naomi

Andy and Naomi attached a love-lock to the Centenary Bridge back in June 2015 as part of their one-year anniversary.[4] Naomi had seen the love-locks in Paris and wanted to celebrate their anniversary by adding their own love-lock – but in Leeds. As they were in a long-distance relationship, with Andy studying in Leeds and Naomi living in Buckingham, they thought the Centenary Bridge, which they discovered via an online search, was 'a perfect place to put it . . . it was special to us to have something with our names on in Leeds.'

Naomi had ordered the love-lock from eBay, professionally engraved with their initials. They went to the bridge together, attached the lock, took a photo of it and threw the key into the river below. This was not the last time they saw it though; whenever Naomi came to visit they would return to the bridge to seek out their love-lock as 'something special for us to do' – which is why it was such a surprise when they recently made their way back to the Centenary Bridge only to discover all of the love-locks had gone: 'it was a pretty upsetting way to find out.'

In October 2016, Leeds City Council, concerned about structural damage, removed all of the love-locks from the Centenary Bridge (see *Chapter Seven: Unlocking Love*). They did, however, retain them and offer depositors the opportunity to retrieve their locks. This is what Andy and Naomi did, and now they keep it stored in a 'box of memories and keepsakes for things we've done together or places we've been'.

Mandy and Trisha

Mandy and Trisha were the first same-sex couple to marry in the North East, and so in March 2015 they wanted to mark their first wedding anniversary 'as it was an historic event'.[5] They had seen love-locks elsewhere in the world on a travel television show and chose to mark their anniversary with a love-lock of their own. They ordered the lock online with a professionally engraved inscription and decided to attach it to Newcastle's High Level Bridge because Mandy was born on the south side of the river and Trisha on the north: 'The bridge to us is in the middle, and we are both very proud of where we come from and thought it was the perfect place to put our love-lock.' They photographed the lock in place and shared the images on Instagram.

Mandy and Trisha both visited the lock again on their second wedding anniversary and planned to go again on the fifth. However, Network Rail, who manage the bridge, has removed the love-locks amidst safety concerns. As with Leeds City Council, they have offered depositors the chance to retrieve their locks, and Mandy and Trisha plan to. 'We are also both sad that our love-lock has been removed and is probably sitting unceremoniously in a heap . . . Our love-lock is a very sentimental item, and we would like to place it somewhere else. If we cannot do that, we have decided to get it framed in a 3D frame and hang it in our home.'

Clair and Drew

In March 2016, Clair and Drew – who had enjoyed a 'whirlwind romance' in New Orleans the previous summer – were reunited in Leeds.[6] Clair, living beside the River Aire, passed the love-locks on Centenary Bridge often; she 'always liked seeing them – they hold stories and hope and love and that made me smile.' So, when Drew came to Leeds on his first visit to the UK, she suggested that they add their own love-lock. It was a 'last minute decision'; they had purchased the padlock in a hardware shop in Leeds and handwrote their names, the date of deposition and a message.

'Drew was visiting for such a short time, and I wasn't sure I'd ever see him again,' Clair told me, 'so wanted to add my own memory'.

With Drew back in the US, Clair would often check on their love-lock when she crossed the bridge and, a month or two after locking their love, Clair took a photo of it still on the bridge and sent it to Drew as a reminder of their time together; 'with Drew being so far away it was always nice to see it.' So, she was sad, come August, to read the signs that were displayed on the bridge announcing the removal of the locks. Like Andy and Naomi, Clair retrieved her lock from Leeds City Council: 'I didn't like the thought of it just being disposed of,' she explains. 'It marks a special time of my life that I wanted to keep.' And what will she do with it now? 'Keep it somewhere special – or maybe frame it as a gift for Drew.'

Àine and Mark

Àine and Mark, from Co. Dublin, Ireland, were on a three-day trip to Paris in May 2015.[7] When they arrived, Mark presented Àine with a large padlock bearing both of their names in black marker around a red love-heart, surrounded by nine 'X's to signify nine months together, which he had designed at home.

On the edges of the lock were the Irish words 'Grá' and 'mo chroí' ('love of my heart'). Àine had been unfamiliar with the love-lock custom, but Mark had come across it while researching Paris holiday tips online. Locking a love-lock had been flagged as a 'must do' for a romantic break in France's capital.

They photographed the love-lock while still in the hotel and then headed out into Paris, getting off the city bus tour at the Pont des Arts, which was 'full of couples placing the locks on the bridge. It was evening time and getting dark. We both placed the lock on the bridge and threw away the key into the water. It was really nice and we had a moment on the bridge.' They photographed their lock post-deposition and then spent some time reading the messages on the 'thousands and thousands' of other locks. Àine tells me that they would have loved to return to Paris to find their lock, but they had heard that the locks had been removed.

AJ and Emily

AJ and his fiancé Emily were on a weekend trip to Manchester in January 2017 to watch *Billy Elliot* at the Palace Theatre.[8] Across the road from the theatre is the Oxford Road love-lock bridge, as detailed in *Chapter Three: Excavating Love*. To honour this trip, they had ordered a padlock from eBay – 'They have a great variety and are quite cheap' – professionally engraved with their names and 'Billy Elliot – Manchester' (Illustration 4.1.). They attached it to the Oxford Road Bridge and took photographs of it in place.

This was not the first love-lock AJ and Emily had attached. They had been participating in the custom serially since 2016, having read about the custom in articles about love-locks in other countries. Their first love-lock, a plain padlock with their initials on, was locked in Belgium, and they have since locked two others in Liverpool, one to celebrate their anniversary and another to celebrate their son's first birthday, and another on Tower Bridge, London. The Manchester love-lock is their fifth, and they plan to see it

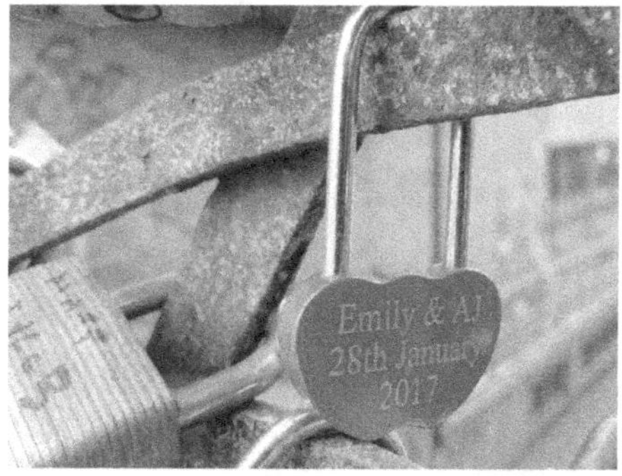

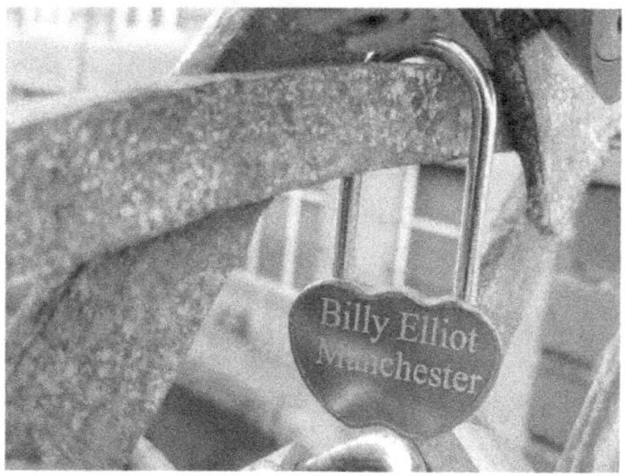

Illustration 4.1. AJ and Emily's love-lock on Manchester's Oxford Road. Photographs by the author.

again: 'They make good memories and are good to visit and find them again . . . Every time we get a chance to visit we will; we go to Manchester & Liverpool regularly.'

Claire

In February 2017, Claire was headed to Paris with her husband to celebrate his 30th birthday.[9] They had seen photographs of love-locks on Instagram and de-cided they wanted to add their own. 'We thought it was a sweet symbol of love,' Claire tells me, and they liked the idea of leaving something of theirs in a city they do not live in. So they bought a love-lock on eBay, had it professionally engraved with their nicknames and the date of Claire's husband's birthday and took it with them to Paris.

The original plan had been to attach it to the Pont des Arts – the 'original love-lock bridge', as Claire terms it – but, seeing that the locks had been cleared away and acrylic glass panels put in place, they made their deposit elsewhere: the Flame of Liberty. They chose this spot because of the 'beautiful view' it offers of the Eiffel Tower and also, being fans of the royal family, because of the monu-ment's status as an unofficial memorial for Princess Diana. They photographed the love-lock in place and hope to search for it if they ever return to Paris.

Kirsty and Andy

In March 2014, Kirsty attached her love-lock to the Centenary Bridge in Leeds.[10] It was on her birthday, and it had been a present from her husband Andy to mark their first pregnancy. Andy had inscribed the lock with 'Andy, Kirsty & baby K, March 2014'. Living in an apartment close to the bridge, they knew about the love-locks and wanted to attach theirs in Leeds rather than somewhere like Paris or Venice because 'the city is important to both our families'. They also liked be-ing able to see their lock afterwards: 'We would periodically look out for the lock when crossing.' When they found out about the removal of the locks by Leeds City Council, they retrieved it. When I asked why, she said 'It is a sentimental item that reminds us of a lovely time.' She has put it in a keepsake box with other sentimental objects for their son to have when he is older.

This story, like the others above, illuminates myriad facets to the love-lock custom. What is most apparent is that every love-lock has a story, and every love-lock can reveal something about the unique people, relationships and events behind its deposition. What is also clearly evident is the amount of thought that goes into all stages of the custom: the purchasing of the lock; the designing of it; the giving of it as a gift; the date on which it is deposited; the place in which it is deposited; and the continued engagement with the lock. Each of these aspects will be explored separately in the following pages, beginning with people's initial decisions to participate in this custom.

The Love-Lock as Planned Deposit

I have argued previously that contemporary folk assemblages tend to be casual and ad hoc.[11] At least in the British Isles (the geographic focus of my previous research), this is evident in the deposits themselves, which are generally low in economic value. It is pennies rather than pounds that people throw into fountains or hammer into coin-trees. And while padlocks cost more than pennies, they are still not particularly expensive or luxurious objects: one can be purchased from popular British homeware chain Wilko for £1.95 (roughly €2.20). This may reflect the (low?) level of belief bestowed on such rituals today. Perhaps they are observed more for the sense of collaboration and 'imagined community' they provide than for any credulity in the efficacy of the ritual.

However, I have also argued previously that convenience is another significant factor in determining which objects are deposited.[12] In Walhouse's nineteenth-century study of rag-trees, he observed that participants do not always come to the rag-tree prepared. By necessity, they often source their deposit from 'any trivial objects ready at hand – horns, bones, tufts of hair, shreds, and the like'.[13] Likewise today, people are depositing objects ready at hand (e.g. coins) or sourced on site (e.g. rocks on cairns) because they have not come to this assemblage with the purpose of making a contribution. For instance, most people usually have some coins in their possession, either carried in a purse or a pocket. Therefore, if they wish to participate in a casual ritual that necessitates the deposition or 'sacrificing' of some object, a coin is the most convenient item for that purpose.

This is evident in historian Tristan Hulse's examination of St. Trillo's Chapel, Llandrillo-yn-Rhos, Wales, referenced in the previous chapter. Visiting the site in the 1990s, Hulse observed a large assemblage of contemporary deposits, primarily handwritten prayers, and found that the majority were written on scraps of paper sourced from pockets and handbags: envelopes, receipts, pages torn from diaries and transport tickets.[14] This indicates spontaneity. However, not all contemporary deposits are spontaneously made. Some are clearly planned; purchased or produced before a visit to an assemblage with the express purpose of being deposited. The love-lock is one such deposit.

While it is true that many people probably pass a love-lock assemblage by chance, the decision to participate in the custom cannot be spontaneous. Unlike coins, people rarely just happen to have a padlock on their person; they do not tend to walk around with them in their pockets. Padlocks do not fit Walhouse's definition of 'trivial objects ready at hand'. Granted, it is usually not difficult to find a padlock for purchase, especially in urban environments. As Clair and Drew explained, in their story above, their decision to attach a love-lock to Leeds Centenary Bridge was 'last minute'; they purchased their padlock from a hardware shop in the city centre. In fact, as will be explored further in *Chapter Six: Selling Love*, there are some love-lock locations that capitalise on the custom by selling padlocks on site: Pont Neuf, Paris; Huangshan, China; the 'Capulet House', Verona; N Seoul Tower, Seoul; Gretna Green, Scotland. Padlocks, often in the shape of love-hearts, are sold alongside markers so that people can write their messages and can make quite a casual decision there and then to participate in the custom. In these cases, therefore, love-locks do possibly constitute spontaneous deposits.

However, in the majority of cases, many depositors pre-plan love-lock deposition, as is demonstrated in the stories above. Naomi had ordered her love-lock from an online retailer, as had Mandy and Trisha, AJ and Emily, and Claire, while Mark had purchased and decorated his love-lock as a gift to Àine prior to their trip to Paris. Similarly, Andy had bought and inscribed his love-lock as a birthday gift to his wife Kirsty. These people had all encountered the love-lock custom before – in person, on television or online – and had planned to participate, deliberately visiting a love-lock assemblage already equipped with an inscribed love-lock.

This forethought is reflected in the material culture of the assemblages. Many love-locks are not average padlocks. Some of them, such as the beautifully ornate locks from the Leeds Centenary Bridge and Erzsébet Square, Budapest, and the impractically oversized ones from the Luzhkov Bridge, Moscow (Illustration 4.2.), were clearly expensive. Many others have been professionally engraved

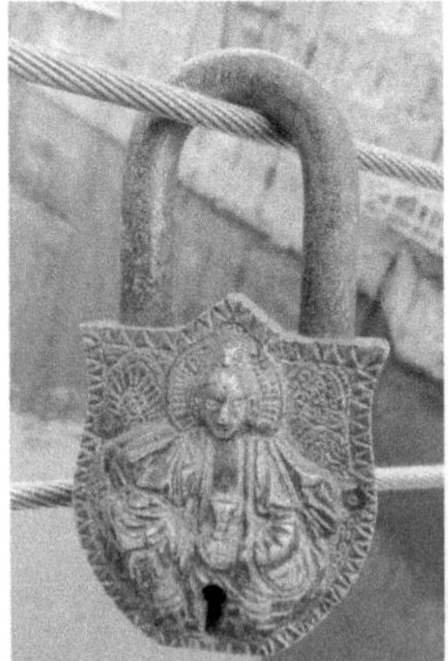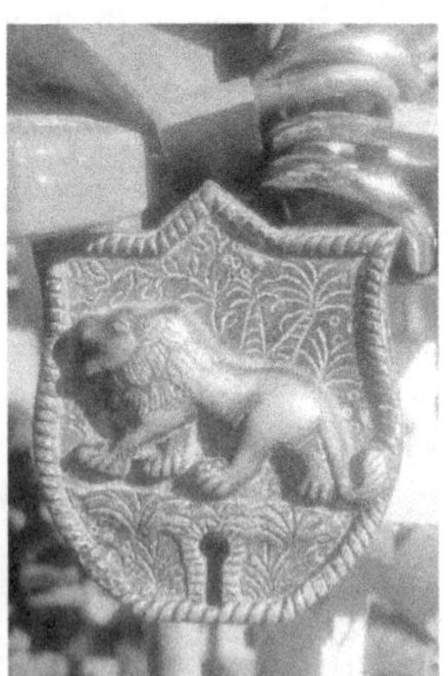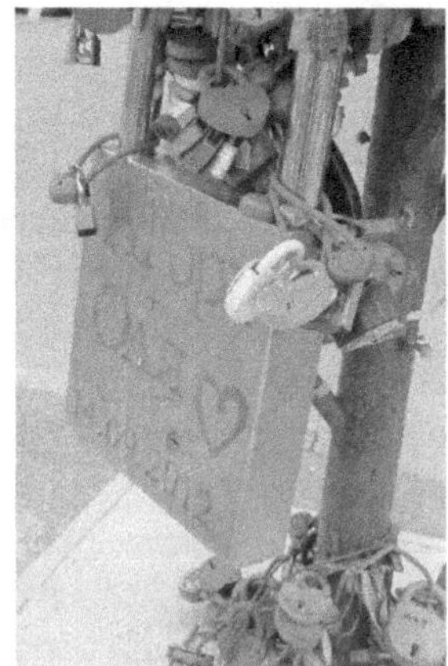

Illustration 4.2. Ornate locks from the Leeds Centenary Bridge and Erzsébet Square, Budapest, and an impractically oversized one from the Luzhkov Bridge, Moscow. Photographs by the author.

with names, messages and even images. Often these will have been commissioned from one of the many websites advertising their engraving services: *Make Love Locks, Beloved Padlocks, Lock-itz*. You can order an engraved love-heart-shaped padlock from *Love Locks UK*, for example, for £19.99, with buyers currently being advised that 'Due to demand there is currently a 7–14 day processing time on orders.'[15] For that price and that length of time, the engraved padlock is certainly not a casual deposit.

Even of those that are basic, utilitarian padlocks, the clear majority of them have been personally decorated; ritually recycled to become love-locks. As was demonstrated in the previous chapter, while most have simply been written on in marker (names, initials, dates, messages), some have been creatively embellished. The bodies of padlocks are covered in drawings, from self-portraits to bumble bees, or adorned with stickers, ribbons or patterned tape. Some have been painted with glitter and nail varnish, while others have been fitted with fabric rosettes and home-knitted jackets. Clearly these are padlocks that have been dressed up prior to the depositor visiting the site; they are planned, premeditated and they indicate that many – if not most – depositors do come upon these assemblages by design.

Indeed, judging by the number of weddings and anniversaries referred to in the love-lock inscriptions, there are specific times in a couple's relationship when it is deemed most appropriate to deposit a love-lock. This may also be the case for those locks where a special event is not explicitly inscribed, as is evident from the stories above. For instance, Andy and Naomi attached their love-lock to Leeds Centenary Bridge to celebrate their one-year anniversary, but this is not indicated in the inscription, which bears only their initials. For Clair and Drew, it was Drew's first visit to the UK that they wished to celebrate; for Claire, it was her husband's 30th birthday; and for Andy, it was Kirsty's birthday – again, not explicitly evident in the inscriptions. An ethnography of love-locking thus reveals the importance of timing.

It also reaffirms what was demonstrated in *Chapter Three: Excavating Love*: that not all love-locks are intended as romantic deposits. Others celebrate or commemorate different types of relationships and milestones. AJ and Emily locked a love-lock in Manchester to honour their trip to watch *Billy Elliot* at the Palace Theatre, and they locked another in Liverpool to celebrate their son's first birthday. Kirsty and Andy locked theirs not only to celebrate Kirsty's birthday but also her first pregnancy. The meaning is mutable, as it is for most – if not all – other rituals and customs.[16]

This ethnography of love-locking also reveals the importance of place. A spontaneous deposit often involves a depositor stumbling upon an assemblage by chance; they do not visit that specific place in order to make their deposit. However, as was evident in the stories above, many depositors deliberately choose a location to leave their love-lock based on place association. About half of the participants observed and interviewed are tourists (the significance of which has been considered in *Chapter One: Dating Love*), and for those who are travelling, the decision to lock a love-lock in one place over another may be due to the popularity of that particular site.

Àine and Mark chose the Pont des Arts because it was a 'must do' for a trip to Paris; the city's association with romance and the fact that it was a well-established assemblage – there were 'thousands and thousands of locks' – were both significant factors here. Claire and her husband chose the Flame of Liberty in Paris, partly for the view of the Eiffel Tower but also because of its unofficial status as a memorial for Princess Diana – 'being a fan of the royal family'. For AJ and Emily, love-locks are more about keeping a record of places they have been: Belgium, Manchester, Liverpool, London, as 'They make good memories'. In this case, the love-lock acts as inverted souvenir, a concept explored more below.

However, many people choose to lock their love closer to home. Andy and Naomi specifically did not want to deposit their love-lock in Paris but preferred to lock it in Leeds: 'We're in a long distance relationship . . . so it was special to us to have something with our names on in Leeds.' A similar reason was given by Kirsty and Andy: 'the city is important to both our families.' Mandy and Trisha chose to lock their love on Newcastle's High Level Bridge because Mandy was born on the south side of the river and Trisha on the north: 'The bridge to us is in the middle, and we are both very proud of where we come from.' Therefore, whether the participants are tourists or local residents, thought goes into location.

The love-lock demonstrates that not all contemporary deposits are casual, ad hoc and spontaneously made. Purchased, commissioned or creatively embellished before a visit to a deliberately chosen love-lock assemblage, many love-locks are clearly planned. This implies greater intentionality and emotional investment in the custom than may be evident in the more casual examples, such as throwing a coin into a fountain or placing a rock on a cairn.

A Contemporary Ritual

Once the love-lock has been purchased, commissioned or personally crafted, and once the decision of location has been made, what happens next? The answer to this is based on observations at 31 different love-lock sites as well as interviews and a sample of 100 YouTube videos featuring love-locks.[17]

Most frequently, a couple (or, less frequently, a group of relatives or friends) will arrive at a love-lock assemblage together with an inscribed love-lock already in their possession. They select a specific place amidst the assemblage, often in a densely populated area but where there is still a vacant space for their deposit. Their spot selected, (if a couple) they then hold the love-lock together, each with a hand touching it, and then lock it in place. This is often at an angle so that the main inscription is on view. Sometimes the couple then kiss – 'sealed with a kiss', as one couple declared. One of them may film the process, sometimes with a 'selfie stick' so that both are in the shot, narrating it as they go along. If they are over a river, they then both clutch the corresponding key, or if there are two keys, then sometimes one key each. Perhaps having kissed the key and perhaps having counted down from three, they then together throw the key(s) off the bridge – the further the better. Occasionally, if only one of them locked the love-lock then the other person will throw the key, and this may be over the shoulder. They watch as it arches away from them and disappears into the water, often amidst whoops of delight and possibly another kiss. 'We are locked for life,' declared one person as they bid farewell to the key; 'locked and sealed', said another. They then turn back to their lock, zooming in on it or photographing it to capture the inscription before departing.

So far this book has largely referred to love-locking as a custom, but in light of this description, I feel that a more specific term may be applied to it: ritual. Granted, many scholars have noted the difficulties involved in applying the term ritual to a practice. Archaeologist Joanna Brück observes that '[i]nstinctively most archaeologists feel they know what ritual is but, on closer inspection, the picture becomes rather less clear', while Don Handelman has proclaimed definitions of 'ritual' proposed by scholars 'unremarkable, noncommittal, and innocuous'.[18] Unsurprisingly, Moore and Myerhoff have remarked that this 'looseness of the concept of ritual . . . is a serious obstacle to investigation of the subject'.[19] Indeed, Asad reveals just how complex and mutable the term 'ritual' actually is, detailing how definitions have altered through the centuries. For example, in the first edition of the *Encyclopaedia Britannica*, published in 1771, the brief entry under 'ritual' reads: 'a book directing the order and manner to be observed in celebrating religious ceremonies and performing divine service in a particular church, diocese, order, or the like.'[20] A 'ritual' was originally a script regulating ceremony; it has now come to mean something far more abstract.

The *Oxford Dictionary of English* may propose a relatively simple definition of 'ritual' as 'a religious or solemn ceremony consisting of a series of actions performed to a prescribed order', but a consideration of popular and scholarly perceptions of the term 'ritual' reveals that the matter is far more complex.[21] Bender et al. write that '[o]nce upon a time there used to be a little black box labelled "ritual". In it the archaeologist put anything that did not have a "sensible" explanation, anything surplus to everyday requirements'.[22] Brück has made a similar observation, remarking that an action that appears irrational or non-functional is often equated with ritual; 'ritual is identified by default'.[23] In attempts to steer clear of this identification by default, numerous scholars have proposed their own definitions of 'ritual' before attempting to apply the term to certain activities.

Some scholars include sacred elements and intended preternatural results as integral to a ritual's identification. Handelman writes that a ritual is an event that 'makes recourse to paranatural, mystical powers', while Shils describes ritual as 'a pattern of symbolic actions for renewing contact with the sacred'.[24] However, most scholars focus on the physical and symbolic aspects of a practice. Rostas has asserted that 'to attain ritualization, a degree of corporeal performativity seems to be necessary', and Bocock has defined the term as *bodily action in relation to symbols* (emphases in original).[25] Other scholars describe repetition and formalism as the inherent aspects of ritual: Myerhoff, for example, defines the term as 'an act or actions intentionally conducted by a group of people employing one or more symbols in a repetitive, formal, precise, highly stylized fashion', while Fernandez defines it as a 'tightly patterned and repetitive form of non-random behavior', and Rappaport uses terms such as 'stylized' and 'repetitive' in his definition.[26] Karin Becker identifies rituals as containing 'peak moments': 'instances that carry particular meaning for the ritual as a whole, serving as symbols that gather and condense the meanings that are dispersed throughout the rest of the event'.[27]

According to many of these definitions, love-locking is an indisputable ritual. Most people participate in this custom by following a series of intentional, very stylised, performative and symbolic actions, repetitive in that many others have participated in such acts in that same spot before and many are likely to in the future. There is a precision and self-conscious choreography to many of the actions, and although at many sites love-locking is an unauthorised or even explicitly prohibited practice, the participants appear to be following a prescribed sequence of actions. There is a definite sense that they are imitating what they have witnessed others doing before them or elsewhere.

Stéphane Borraz, as outlined above, divided the actions of love-locking – what he dubbed a 'new consumer love ritual' – into the preliminal, the liminal and the postliminal,[28] while Felix Richter and Verena Pfeiffer-Kloss have divided love-locking into eleven 'micro-rituals', which are summarised as: 1) The purchase of the lock; 2) Personalising the lock; 3) The choice of where to mount it geographically; 4) The choice of where to mount it on the bridge; 5) Opening the lock; 6) Attaching the lock; 7) Clicking the lock closed; 8) Throwing the key into the river; 9) A kiss; 10) Sometimes an exclamation; 11) Sometimes a moment of silence.[29] Richter and Pfeiffer-Kloss identify the throwing of the key into the river as 'the climax of the action', which Becker would no doubt classify as a 'peak moment' of the ritual, as a moment that condenses the symbolisms and meanings of the overall ritual (see the next chapter for the symbolic significance). However, I would add another peak moment: clicking the shackle closed. These two peak moments tend to be conducted by both members of the couple simultaneously. Perhaps because of the personal nature of the action, the kissing that occurs immediately after the two peak moments appears particularly prescribed, tokenistic (and often quite stiff – perhaps due to the public nature of the ritual), rather than spontaneous and intimate.

This said, the proceedings are rarely formal or solemn. This is an element of the ritual that Richter and Pfeiffer-Kloss, and Borraz, either have not witnessed or do not acknowledge. There is often a lot of talking, laughing, exclamations of delight, joking and clapping. Declarations that the love-lockers are now 'locked for life' and 'locked and sealed' are less earnest affirmations than tongue-in-cheek puns. On a few occasions where couples have had difficulty locking their love-lock or where their keys have landed in the wrong place, they have exhibited amusement rather than anxiety or frustration. And some love-lock inscriptions speak of humour: 'None of This Bullshit! Forever and Always X' declares one lock in Manchester, while another includes names, dates and 'Bumhole forever'.

For many participants, this ritual is above all else about having fun. It is a pleasurable activity; it is recreation. And while I have previously dichotomised recreation and ritual, love-locking has demonstrated that the two are not mutually exclusive.[30] Ritual does not require formal prescription and solemnity; it does not preclude playfulness and fun. In fact, Victor Turner – a cultural anthropologist at the forefront of ritual theory – placed 'play' at the centre of ritual: participants 'play' with symbols, meanings, words and actions.[31]

Selva Raj and Corrine Dempsey have developed the concept of 'ritual levity' in their work on South Asian traditions, defining it as 'playful ritual actions that are at once light-hearted and serious'.[32] This would certainly fit the nature of love-locking, which combines prescriptive actions, performativity and symbolisms with laughter, jesting and a touch of flippant irreverence. This levity is not incidental to the ritual. In the context of love-locks, it is central to it, the sense of play allowing people who may not ordinarily have participated in a ritual to justify participating in *this* ritual. As Raj and Dempsey stress:

> it is the liminal character of ritual and the freedom inherent in liminality that provide the space and stimulus for creative imagination, empowering ritual performers to engage in what ordinarily might be considered 'improper behaviour'. . . . Levity, therefore, is neither an anomaly nor an aberration but an essential, intrinsic part of ritual.[33]

Declaring Love

The purpose of the love-lock ritual is rarely articulated by participants, who largely view it as self-explanatory, with the symbolism being obvious. There is a vocabulary around binding and locking love, which is explored in greater detail in *Chapter Five: Symbolising Love*, and the historian or folklorist may be inclined to ascribe some notion of sympathetic magic to this custom. The couple have crafted (commissioned or decorated) the love-lock, inscribing it with their names or initials to ensure a sympathetic link to them. By locking it in place and disposing of the key, thus rendering it permanently locked, their relationship becomes metaphorically locked, the ritual thus magically ensuring the longevity of their love. And while this interpretation does litter popular literature – and does hold some water in terms of the custom's symbolism – it is likely an example of over-interpretation.

Although some love-lock inscriptions testify to this – 'locked in love', 'I wanna lock your love', 'LOCKED TOGETHER FOREVER', 'as long as this is locked, so will our hearts', 'LOCKED + SEALED' – no interviewee or observed participant has expressed a genuine belief in the power of the love-lock to bind a couple together. Granted, belief is notoriously difficult to articulate, and even more difficult to establish in an interview or through simple observation, but in the case of this ritual, the likelier explanation is that most people adopt the vocabulary of sympathetic magic associated with the love-lock while actually ascribing it a vaguer, more general function of *symbolising* – rather than magically ensuring – their love.

It was already established in *Chapter Three: Excavating Love* that people craft their love-locks to represent themselves; to construct or even perform their relationship. Most commonly, this involves the inscription of names or initials, but various other forms of adornment have been used. The most explicit personalisations are hand-drawn self-portraits and photographs of the couple imposed onto the body of the lock (Illustration 4.3.). But even those locks that bear no inscription represent their depositors simply through the fact that it was they who locked it. The love-lock becomes the couple's 'tag', an expression of their

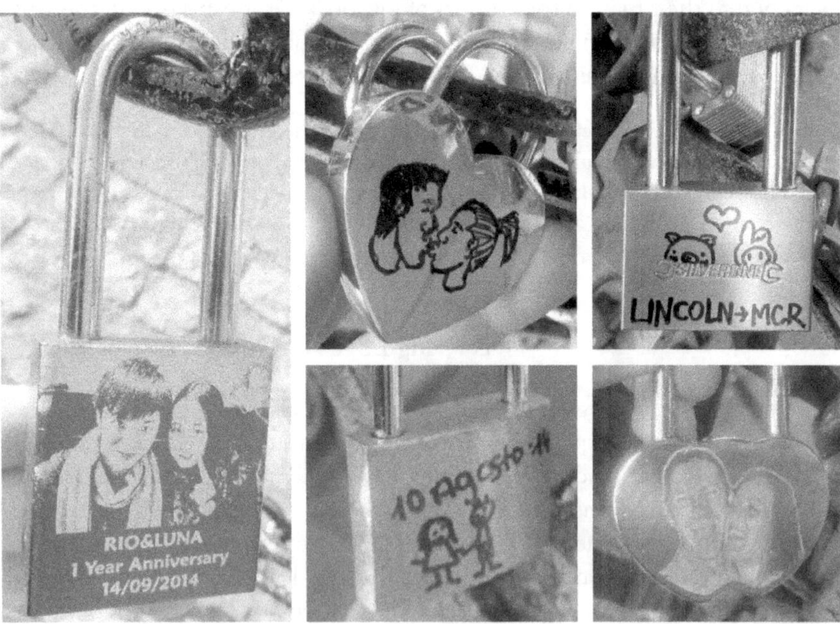

Illustration 4.3. Self-portraits on love-locks in Manchester and Liverpool. Photographs by the author.

identity. Their relationship materialised.[34] So the love-lock symbolises their love –
and by being securely locked, it thus also symbolises the *strength and durability* of
their love.

The public nature of this ritual is also significant. While there may be some
private love-lock assemblages in existence, all of my recorded sites are publicly
accessible, and the vast majority are in areas of high visibility and heavy foot-
fall. So when people are locking their love, they are often enacting the ritual
in public. This is not necessarily the same as having an audience. In most cases,
the people who are sharing the space are focused on their own activities: simply
walking past, examining the assemblage, taking photographs, or even locking
their own love-locks. Depositors can therefore participate in the ritual with some
degree of privacy (the filming and digital sharing of the experience is explored
below). The deposit itself, however, is entirely public.

A five-minute observation starting 12:25PM on a February Tuesday on Manchester's Oxford Road assemblage yielded the following results. Of the 121 people
who crossed the bridge, 34 glanced at or pointed to the love-locks; two people
stopped to examine them; and one person stopped to photograph them. These
statistics may not sound significant, but this was a mere five-minute period on a
cold, midweek afternoon. If we say that Oxford Road experiences at least this
amount of traffic for at least twelve hours a day, then this could amount to 4,896
people glancing/pointing at the love-locks; 288 people stopping to examine
them; and 144 people taking photographs. That could be 1,008 photographers a
week; 52,416 a year. These are very rough estimates, but they clearly show a high
level of engagement with a relatively small love-lock assemblage.

Most of the depositors must know, therefore, that their love-lock will likely
be viewed and may well be photographed by others. Their inscriptions, declaring
love and providing personal information such as names, dates and places, will be
read by strangers. They may even end up in a book entitled *Unlocking the Love-
Lock*. However, the public nature of love-locking is not incidental to the ritual;
it is not a tolerated drawback. It is central. The love-lock custom is about *publicly*
declaring love and commitment. It is about having enough confidence in the
strength and durability of a relationship to share it with the world – or at least
the fraction of the world that encounters that particular assemblage. The apparent importance of sharing this ritual will be explored in greater detail below.

The Love-Lock as Object of Emotion

At the centre of the love-locking custom is the love-lock itself. This is not simply
a ritual accoutrement but is the focus at every stage of activity. Even the act of
relinquishing the key hinges on the love-lock; the key is significant because of
its respective padlock, which it is now rendering immovable. The gravity of the

love-lock lies in its symbolism, which will be explored in the next chapter, but for this chapter I want to consider what the love-lock, as a tangible object, means to its depositors.

It was noted in *Chapter Three: Excavating Love* that padlocks are relatively cheap, mundane, homogenous objects. They are also alienable, in that they can be easily divorced from their owners. Rarely are padlocks personal items, family heirlooms or treasured gifts. They are not inherently special. However, to quote Nicholas Thomas, a thing 'is not immutable'.[35] Through the act of personalising and depositing it, the padlock is ritually recycled as a love-lock and as an inalienable ritual deposit. It becomes metonymically linked or 'entangled' with its depositor.[36] It becomes an object of emotion or, to use a phrase coined by Downes et al., a 'feeling thing'.[37] Some objects, observes Joanne Bergiato, 'have become feeling things . . . simply because a human associates them with events and circumstances that produce particular emotions'.[38]

The fact that (most) love-locks are relatively inexpensive does not belittle their value. Sarah Randles, who considers the thousands of pilgrimage tokens produced and sold cheaply to pilgrims in the Middle Ages as 'feeling things', notes that objects of low monetary value can still 'hold significant emotional value for the people who acquired and used them'.[39] Emotional or sentimental value can be attained through the nature of acquisition. As philosopher Guy Fletcher explains:

> something is sentimentally valuable if and only if the thing is valuable for its own sake in virtue of a subset of its relational properties, where the properties include any or all of having belonged to, having been given to or by, or having been used by, people or animals, within a relationship of family, friendship, or romantic love, or having been used or acquired during a significant experience . . .[40]

In the case of pilgrim tokens, it is the purchase of them at shrines and the pilgrimage they represent that imbues them with emotional value. In the case of love-locks, it is the fact that they have been used (i.e. deposited) by people within a relationship of family, friendship or – more likely – romantic love during a significant experience. They may even have been given as a gift from one of the depositors to the other: Mark gifted Àine their love-lock on a trip to Paris, as Andy gifted one to Kirsty on her birthday. And if adorned with handwritten messages and hand-drawn images, its sentimental value increases even further.[41]

However, the love-lock is more than an object of emotion and sentimental value. It also becomes, to use a term by Taryn Bell and Penny Spikins, an 'attachment object': 'a particular class of objects which provoke positive social feelings. Such objects provoke specific emotions related to the intense closeness we feel with our care-givers as a child and with close loved ones as adults in relationships in which we feel supported and cared for.'[42] The wedding ring is a prime example of an attachment object, which has been compared to a love-lock in terms of the feelings it evokes.[43] And even though the love-lock does not fit Bell and Spikins' further qualification of attachment objects as those that 'tend to be much cared for, typically often handled and portable in nature',[44] the fact that love-locks are owned for only a short amount of time and then relinquished does not lessen their status as attachment objects. They continue to embody the positive social feelings – attachment, closeness, love – experienced between the depositors at the time of deposition.

The Love-Lock as Mnemonic

A locked love-lock not only represents the couple or symbolises the strength of their relationship. It also materialises the moment shared as they enacted the ritual, creating a tangible mnemonic of that time together and of their connection to that particular place. Interviewee Clair told me she deposited a love-lock in Leeds with Drew because 'Drew was visiting for such a short time, and I wasn't sure I'd ever see him again – so wanted to add my own memory'. Andy and Naomi told me of the 'memories' they have with their love-lock, while Kirsty and Andy said of their lock that 'It is a sentimental item that reminds us of a lovely time'. AJ and his fiancé Emily deposit love-locks in the different cities they visit because 'They make good memories'.

Love-locks are mnemonic artefacts, offering a prime example of Michael Rowlands's 'material culture of remembering'.[45] As Bell and Spikins observe, adult attachment objects are often mnemonic devices, 'providing reminders of significant places, people, or events'.[46] Objects transmit memory through 'inscribed practices', as described by archaeologist Richard Bradley,[47] because of their tangibility, their durability and – most appropriately – the inscriptions they bear. These inscriptions summarise in minimal characters the memories they are capturing, celebrating and materialising and the names or initials of the depositors who were together at the time of deposition. Perhaps the love-lock also bears the date of deposition or details of a significant event worthy of celebration, such as the words '1st Wedding Anniversary' on Trisha and Mandy's love-lock; 'Billy Elliot' on AJ and Emily's; 'baby K' on Andy and Kirsty's. Other inscriptions may be more obscure, recognisable as a mnemonic device only to the depositors: Àine and Mark's lock bore nine inscribed 'X's to signify nine months together at the point of deposition.

So, through the act of deposition, the love-lock can evoke the memory of a place and an experience, acting as a snapshot of the depositor's engagement with that site. In this sense, the love-lock fits one of Gell's most basic binary relations between the depositor (the 'artist') and the deposit (the 'index'): the index responding as patient to the artist's agency. 'The index is', Gell writes, 'in these instances, a congealed "trace" of the artist's creative performance'.[48] An object absorbs part of its creator, becoming a snapshot of their creative experience; a 'congealed residue of performance and agency in object-form'.[49] Likewise, the love-lock becomes a physical trace of the couple's experience at the love-lock site.

The emotions associated with the love-lock and the memories it evokes may, of course, change over time. As Bergiato observes, 'Emotional objects are also created in the flow of human relationships, and thus change over personal and historical time, since relationships shift too.'[50] Relationships can end. Break-ups, divorce and bereavement will all transform how a depositor thinks about their love-lock: an object that was intended to signify the durability of their relationship. It may lessen the emotional value of the object or taint the memory it encapsulates.[51] After all, memories are not immutable and neither are objects, even after they have been deposited. However, a changing relationship may also strengthen the memory or increase the object's emotional value, especially in the event of a loss.

The ability of the love-lock to materialise a moment also feeds into its memorialising role, as briefly mentioned in the previous chapter. Many assemblages worldwide feature commemorative love-locks as well as celebratory, inscribed with messages of 'rest in peace' and of missing a person, often identified as a family member. A 2018 feature in the Folklore Society's Newsletter by Rosalind Johnson describes a set of seven padlocks locked to a footbridge over Churchill Way in Salisbury, which she believes may be a 'more permanent memorial' to a young man who fell to his death there a few years before.[52] In Newcastle, a local newspaper reported on a man who had attached a love-lock to High Level Bridge to commemorate his cousin: 'My cousin died there 19 months ago. He was 29, the same age as I am now, and we put a padlock on the bridge in memory of him.'[53] Another set of locks on the same bridge were deposited in memory of a man who had died of cancer. As the *Chronicle* reported in March 2019, several members of the man's family attached love-locks to the bridge in 2015. The man's wife is quoted as saying 'I said to my great grandson to put the key in the water for his great granddad.'[54]

Mary Bradbury observes people's desire for a 'concrete representation' of their loved ones in her work on memorialisation, and, as Petts notes, durable items 'serve to crystallize into physical form the dynamic act of remembrance'.[55] What is more durable (literally and symbolically) than a padlock?

The Love-Lock's Continued Biography

The working definition for 'ritual deposit' is that which is relinquished with no intention of retrieval. According to this then, once a love-lock is locked in place and the key disposed of, it is meant to remain there indefinitely. The depositors have surrendered it as an integral part of the ritual symbolising their confidence in the durability of their relationship. The very purpose of a love-lock is to be immovable; to stay where it was left. So, if we perceive an object as having a biography – as we have been doing since Kopytoff's seminal 'The Cultural Biography of Things'[56] – then are we to assume that the love-lock's biography ends at its moment of deposition? The answer to this is no, on three levels.

The first level recognises the love-lock as a tangible object, independent of its depositors. As Rowlands asserts, 'Objects of a durable kind assert their own memories, their own forms of commentary and therefore come to possess their own personal trajectories.'[57] Those who deposited the love-lock may never engage with it again, but it still exists. The love-lock has a biography in its own right that continues beyond deposition. It will be looked at, possibly photographed, and maybe even ritually recycled by others who come after, as was explored in *Chapter Three: Excavating Love*. It may be obscured behind later deposits, forming part of a dynamically shifting assemblage, with every new contribution supplementing and transforming the whole. It will endure weather, it will rust, its inscription will fade. It may be removed by authorities, its shaft broken, thrown into a bucket, held in storage. As we will discover in *Chapter Seven: Unlocking Love*, it may find itself catalogued by a folklorist, exhibited in a museum, auctioned off for charity, or melted down to form a sculpture. In such ways, the love-lock experiences various life stages. I prefer this term to the more common 'afterlife', which implies that the object dies at the end of its intended use and anything that comes after is postscript. 'Life stages' on the other hand recognises that objects, like people, undergo numerous stages in their lives, none of which hold more value or inherent significance than the others.

The second level of the love-lock's continued biography involves the object in abstract form, via its inalienable link with its depositor. Simply put, the depositor remembers their love-lock. This may be unaided or with the help of photographs or videos, which they can look back on, as mnemonic devices for a mnemonic artefact (see below). So the love-lock's status as an object of emotion creates an alternate life stage where its biography diverges from its tangible existence and continues in a person's mind and memory. As Mills argues, referring to dedicatory offerings secreted away in niches of the buildings at Chaco Canyon, a prehistoric complex in the south west USA, such depositions are central to processes of memory making. 'Although out of sight, sometimes permanently', she writes, 'the location of those objects may be remembered for long periods of time'.[58]

Both of these levels can be applied to most ritual deposits, unless deposit or depositor is entirely destroyed. However, the third level is not as evident in many other depositional contexts: the depositor's continued physical engagement with the deposit. This would not be evident in the material record and so would be missed by a purely material culture approach, but an ethnography of love-locking makes it clear. People like to revisit their love-lock. Not to amend or supplement it in any way but simply to see it again. Mandy and Trisha visited their lock on High Level Bridge on their second wedding anniversary and planned to go again on their fifth. Kirsty and Andy would periodically search for their lock on Leeds Centenary Bridge whenever crossing it, as did Clair – 'with Drew being so far away it was always nice to see it' – who also took a photograph of her lock a month or so after locking it and sent it to Drew. AJ and Emily like to visit their various love-locks: they 'are good to visit and find them again . . . Every time we get a chance to visit we will; we go to Manchester & Liverpool regularly', while Claire and her husband hope to search for their lock on the Flame of Liberty if they return to Paris.

People's desires to return to the site at a later date in order to visit their love-lock is a nostalgic sentiment that affirms the love-lock's status as a mnemonic artefact or a memento: an object that serves as a reminder. In a sense, the love-lock also fits Susan Stewart's term: the 'souvenir'.[59] This is defined by the *Oxford English Dictionary* as 'Something that is given or kept as a reminder of a place, person, event'.[60] Technically, any ritual deposit is the antithesis to the souvenir in that it is, by definition, deliberately *left*. But by revisiting their love-lock, the depositors are in a sense *keeping* their deposit, retaining ownership of it, endowing it with the status of keepsake, metaphorically at least. Their emotional attachment to the object is not severed at the moment of deposition. And nowhere do we witness this more blatantly than in people's reactions to the removal of their lock.

The controversial mass removal of love-locks by local authorities is the focus of *Chapter Seven: Unlocking Love*. The two relevant examples here are the removal of love-locks from Leeds Centenary Bridge in October 2016 and High Level Bridge, Newcastle, in March 2019. Reactions were strong. The depositor who had attached a love-lock in memory of his cousin told a local newspaper, 'This is terrible, absolutely awful. I can't believe that someone has decided to do this. Those locks mean so much to so many people. It breaks my heart what they are doing.'[61] And the woman who attached a lock for her late husband claimed, 'I was heartbroken. I could not believe it . . . These locks mean a lot to people.'[62]

In both cases, authorities gave depositors the opportunity to collect their removed locks – and many did, often going to the trouble of travelling to the council buildings and searching through a mass of locks to find theirs. Andy and Naomi collected theirs and now keep it in a 'box of memories and keepsakes for things we've done together or places we've been'. Clair plans on keeping hers 'somewhere special – or maybe frame it as a gift for Drew', while Kirsty and Andy have put theirs in 'a keepsake box with other important things that we have for our son'. Mandy and Trisha also plan on retrieving theirs: 'Our love-lock is a very sentimental item, and we would like to place it somewhere else. If we cannot do that, we have decided to get it framed in a 3D frame and hang it in our home.'

Granted, these depositors-turned-retrievers are in the minority. The vast majority of love-locks remain unclaimed, but a number of factors could account for this. Firstly, many may not know that the locks have been removed, particularly if they did not live locally to the assemblage. Secondly, those who do know that the locks have been removed may not know that there is the opportunity to retrieve theirs. And thirdly, even if people are aware, they may not have the time or resources for retrieval – especially if they were tourists when making their deposit.

The fact remains, though, that some depositors at least care enough about their love-lock to not only retrieve it but to keep it somewhere special within the home: a box or a frame. In these cases, the love-lock transitions from metaphorical souvenir to literal souvenir; from ritual deposit to keepsake, which is quite a reversal. The love-lock thus enters a new life stage in its continued biography. This provides an important lesson in the theory of ritual deposition: while the general concept behind the act of deposition may be that a person surrenders an object with no intention of retrieval, this may not be the reality. The emotional attachment remains, and the inalienable link between depositor and deposit is more than an abstract notion.

Documenting Love

Another form of retention is documentation, which again can be witnessed in the stories outlined at the beginning of this chapter. After Andy and Naomi had attached their love-lock to the Centenary Bridge, they photographed it. Mandy and Trisha did the same with theirs on High Level Bridge before sharing it on Instagram (Illustration 4.4.). It was through having seen photographs of love-locks on Instagram that Claire and her husband decided to participate in the custom themselves, likewise photographing their love-lock post-deposition, as it hung from the fence around the Flame of Liberty. Finally, Àine and Mark also taking a post-deposition photo, on the Pont des Arts (Illustration 4.5.), had earlier photographed their love-lock before leaving their hotel room.

Photography is clearly an important aspect of the love-lock ritual. It is one of the steps, often slotting between attachment of the lock and disposal of the key, or acting as the final stage before the depositor moves on. This is consistent with my netnography findings: the thousands of photographs shared on Instagram and Twitter showing close-ups of love-locks or 'selfies' of couples standing in front of love-lock assemblages. People not only photograph their deposit and experience though; they also film them. Thousands of 'amateur' videos are posted on YouTube, showing people as they deposit their love-locks.[63] Some are short and shaky videos, briefly (some are mere seconds long) capturing the moment of locking

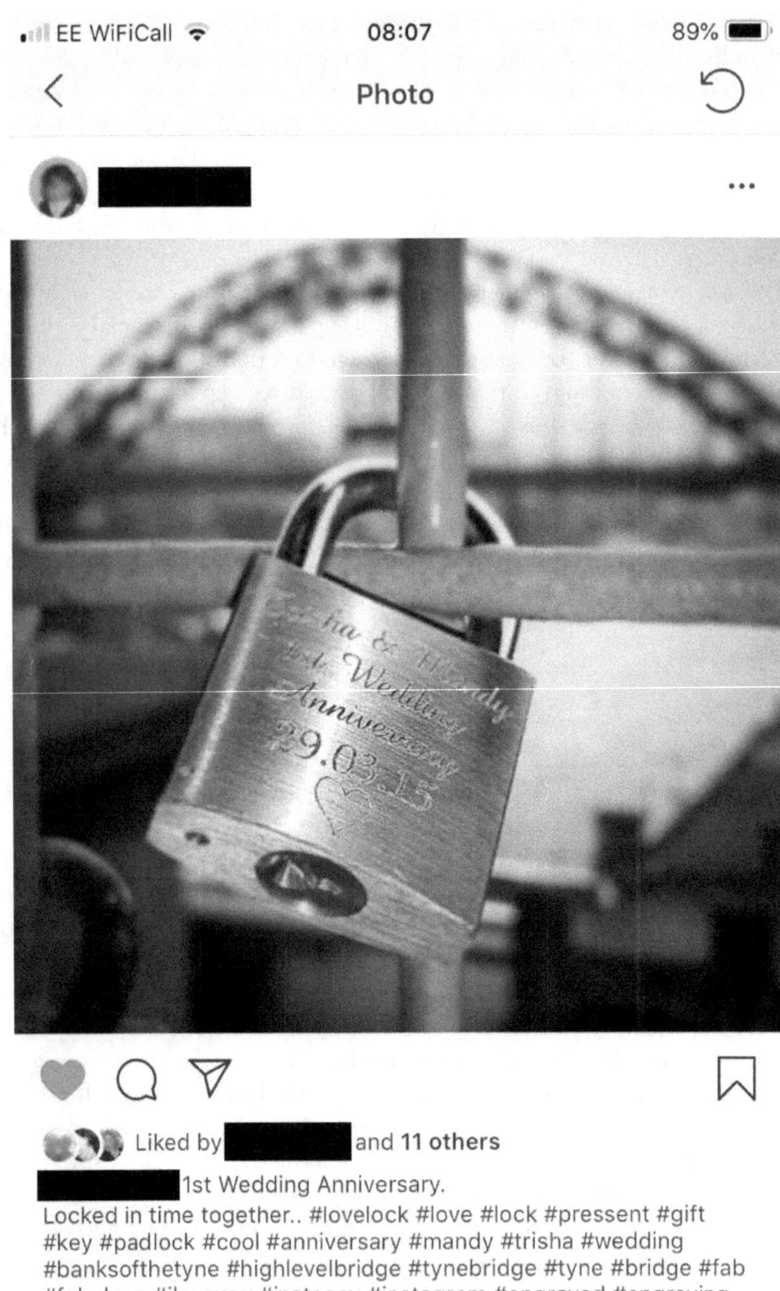

Illustration 4.4. Mandy and Trisha's love-lock, photographed and shared via Instagram by the depositors. Photograph by Trisha Doyle.

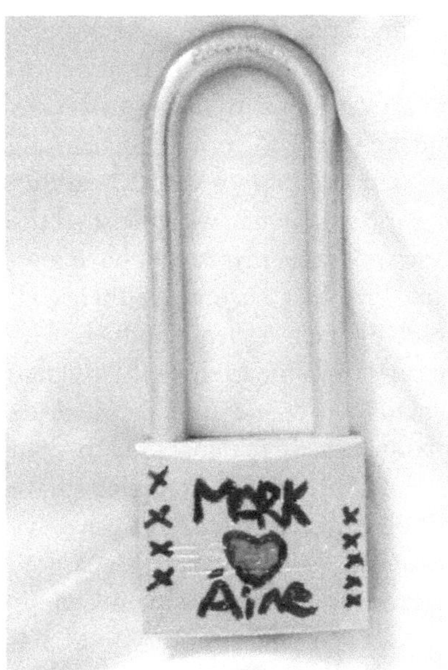

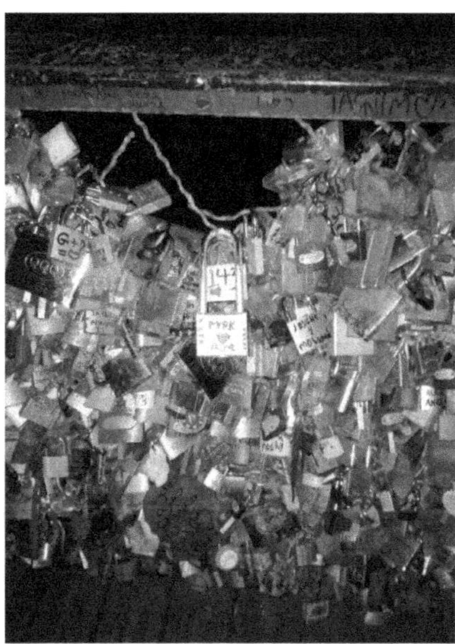

Illustration 4.5. Àine and Mark's love-lock, first in their hotel room and then hanging on the Pont des Arts. Photographs by Àine and Mark.

the love-lock in place or disposing of the key. Other videos are lengthier or more stylised in terms of camera work and editing, occasionally with themed background music and text captions added in. Often one or more of the depositors are narrating, sometimes detailing where they are – 'We're on Brooklyn Bridge, New York'; 'Here we are in Paris, this is the love-lock bridge'; 'We're about to make our mark here in Paris' – and what they are doing – 'This is the lock, our lock, our lock of love. We're putting it on the bridge'; 'Throwing our key, forever together, in the river'; 'I am writing a love-lock to my future husband'; 'Splash!'

These examples of photography and filming are all forms of documentation. They tangibly capture the experience; they provide a way of retaining, to an extent, an object that one is relinquishing. This links back to the concept of the mnemonic. Paul Frosh notes the important role played by photography in the remembrance of romantic intimacy: 'the photograph is designed for the future recollection of past intimacy by the *lovers themselves*' (emphases in original).[64] This is, Frosh notes, most applicable to photographs of special events and holidays, those that we particularly wish to remember (which account for the vast majority of people's photograph albums), in which case we return again to the notion of the souvenir. In his work on tourism, John Taylor observes that 'photography is intimately connected to the processes and products of souveniring practice'.[65] The same is equally true of the production of videos, which Rosalind Morris designates 'personal memory banks' and Lange identifies as media of 'memory preservation'.[66] The photograph or the video can act as a time capsule, preserving the memory of love-locking for future recollection. In the case of the love-lock, the photograph or video becomes a kept souvenir of a deposited souvenir.

However, these photographers and filmmakers are not only documenting their experiences. They are sharing them. As Borraz observed in his ethnographic study of love-locking in Paris, sharing the experience with others is the postliminal stage of the love-lock ritual.[67] Granted, some people will have photographed or filmed their participation in the love-lock custom for their own personal archives, to be viewed only by themselves or close friends and relatives. However, a significant number of participants are choosing to share their videos on YouTube and their photographs on Instagram, Twitter and other social media platforms, where they are publicly accessible and easily searchable with their hashtags of #lovelock and #lovelockbridge. All of the many examples I have recorded have been available for viewing without subscription to the respective online platforms. As was outlined in *Chapter One: Dating Love*, documenting an experience and sharing it with others is a primary tourist activity in keeping with the 'I share therefore I am' culture of the twenty-first century (and also one of the driving forces behind the love-lock's dissemination). This behaviour is therefore consistent with tourist culture; Crouch and Lübbern referred to it as the 'Kodakization' of tourism in 2003, but today 'Instagramization' would be more applicable.[68]

The documentation of a ritual and subsequent sharing of the visual media online is not, however, only a feature of tourism. Gender reveal parties, graduations, birthday parties and weddings all feature heavily on social media and on video-sharing platforms, and as Pauline Greenhill asserts, 'These videos can offer material for analysis in their own right, and their production can also shed light on particular kinds of traditional events.'[69] Such documentation is useful to us as researchers for what it can reveal about the events and practices themselves – in the case of love-locking: the elements of the ritual, the atmosphere of the ritual but also the significance of the documentation. What does it say about love-locking that so many participants have deemed it worthy to be photographed, filmed and shared online with hundreds, even thousands, of people worldwide?

Love-locking is a public declaration of love, in more ways than one. Not only is the lock deposited in a public, often busy place, and left on show with an inscription for anyone to read, but the ritual of deposition is often shared: conducted with an audience (albeit often a disinterested one) or filmed and shared for later viewers – often both. Love-locking is therefore a performance; a performance of love and of the depositors' collective identity. As we explored above, the love-lock is constructed as a metonymy of its depositors, and the ritual itself fulfils a similar function. By documenting and sharing it, the performance is thus ensured an audience. Videos serve as 'experiential communication' and 'identity negotiation', as outlined by Lange,[70] and there is a certain self-consciousness to their productions: sheepish smiles, artistic shots, background music. The same can be said of some of the photographs, framed for best effect, preferably foregrounding a pleasant view or interesting landmark. It is telling, for instance, that of the twenty-three love-locks recorded on Millennium Bridge, London, in March 2017, twenty were on the east side – the side overlooking the Globe, the Shard and Tower Bridge. Only three locks had been deposited on the west side, with views of nothing-very-much as backdrop. Borraz noted a similar pattern with the love-locks in Paris: the west side of the Pont des Arts featuring the Eiffel Tower, for example, is more popular than the east.[71]

Documentation does more than demonstrate the performative nature of the ritual; it can impact the ritual. Ori Schwartz demonstrates how camera phones have reshaped Jewish rituals, such as mass prayers, leading to new practices where filming and the sharing of videos are at the centre of mediated interaction with the sacred.[72] Mattijs van de Port likewise explores how video technology has affected the ritual performances of Candomblé, an Afro-Brazilian spirit-possession cult. Despite this being a highly secretive cult, a relatively recent 'tradition' has emerged of the production of photograph albums and videos of the ceremonies marking the progress of a cultist during their initiation process.[73] In both of the above contexts, photographic and video documentation has resulted in the redefinition of sacred time and space, with rituals having to be adapted to accommodate participants and attendees wielding their cameras and their camera phones, snapping photographs, positioning themselves for optimum angles and sharing the finished media with external audiences who otherwise would not have witnessed the event. Clearly, as McNeill has asserted, 'technologically mediated communication affects cultural expression'.[74]

Documentation also constructs significance. Looking primarily at large-scale urban events, Karin Becker has examined the role of photography and filming in the framing of activity as ritual.[75] The camera demarcates ritual: it denotes the beginning and the end of the activities, and it denotes the performance space, while the people before the camera perform to and for it, conscious of (and often involved in) the process of documentation and aware that in some sense it authenticates the ritual *as ritual*. It 'authenticates an event's significance', to use Becker's words, and it plays a crucial role 'in the ways ritual events accrue and gather new significance over time'.[76] This new significance is not only felt by the participants of the ritual but also the audience – who do not need to be present in order to witness it.

Through documentation, the size of a potential audience vastly multiplies. As was outlined in *Chapter One: Dating Love*, a random selection of 100 YouTube love-lock videos produced from 2014 to 2018 reported a total of almost 500,000 views. This number will probably have increased, and those 100 videos are only a small sample of the myriad 'amateur' love-lock films circulating on YouTube, which is only one of the many online platforms on which the love-lock ritual is being documented and shared. Thinking of the thousands of love-lock photographs that have been posted on Twitter, Instagram and other social media platforms, which are 'liked', 'favourited', 're-tweeted' and continue to be added to, it is impossible to quantify exactly how many people worldwide have witnessed the ritual of love-locking. Whether or not they have participated themselves, even regardless of whether or not they have ever actually physically encountered a love-lock assemblage, they may well have engaged with this custom through witnessing another's performance of it. Via documentation, therefore, countless others are becoming entangled with the love-lock beyond its moment of deposition.

Conclusion

The aim of this chapter was to present an ethnography of love-locking, to demonstrate the ways in which people are engaging with this custom today. It complements the previous chapter's focus on the material culture of the love-lock by centralising the human experience. However, the two are not dichotomised; it is through people that the love-lock is given a life beyond that of a utilitarian padlock, and it is through the love-lock that people participate in the custom, materialising and performing their emotions and identities. Love-lock and love-locker are entangled, and neither can be fully understood without the other. It is through an ethnography of love-locking that we see how the love-lock transitions through various life stages, from padlock to ritual deposit and to keepsake.

This chapter began with what was essentially a set of love stories, and through these it became clear that very few – if any – aspects of the love-lock custom are incidental. From the purchasing and designing of the lock to the choice of when and where to deposit it, thought and personal factors went into the decision making. The stylised, performative, symbolic actions involved in deposition demonstrate the ritualised nature of love-locking, but observations and netnography demonstrated a light-heartedness, a 'ritual levity', that appears integral to the custom. Also integral is the love-lock's role as mnemonic artefact; it materialises the memory of the event of deposition as well as the relationship it symbolises. This role feeds into the depositor's continued engagement with their deposit, in memory but also in reality, with many people returning to visit their lock and many others documenting their experience for future recollection and to share the performance with an immeasurable audience, who in turn become entangled with the love-lock. And so the love-lock's biography continues beyond its locking. Deposition is not the same as relinquishment.

Notes

1. Fieldwork was conducted at love-lock assemblages in St. Petersburg, Russia (2014); Moscow, Russia (2014); Stockholm, Sweden (2014); Manchester, UK (2014–2019); the Cinque Terre, Italy (2014); Liverpool, UK (2014); Prague, Czech Republic (2014); Verona, Italy (2014); Bristol, UK (2014 and 2017); Belfast, Northern Ireland (2014); Berlin, Germany (2015); Hannover, Germany (2015); York, UK (2015); Chester, UK (2015 and 2016); Leeds, UK (2015 and 2016); London, UK (2015, 2016 and 2018); Bakewell, UK (2015 and 2016); Paris, France (2016); Stonehaven, UK (2016); Barcelona, Spain (2016); Reykjavik, Iceland (2016); Athens, Greece (2017); Bologna, Italy (2017); Dublin, Ireland (2017); Edinburgh, UK (2017); Sydney, Australia (2017); Budapest, Hungary (2017); Quimper, Spain (2018); Amsterdam, Holland (2018); Amalfi, Italy (2019); and Graz, Austria (2019).

2. See Robert Kozinets's 2010 work *Netnography: Doing Ethnographic Research Online*, which centralises the knowledge that 'Our social worlds are going digital. As a consequence, social scientists around the world are finding that to understand society they must follow people's social activities and encounters onto the Internet and through other technologically-mediated communications' (Kozinets, *Netnography*, 1). As well as 'netnography', Mariann Domokos lists 'cyberethnography', 'virtual ethnography', 'virtual anthropology' and 'e-folklore' as terms that have been applied to online ethnography (Domokos, 'Towards Methodological Issues in Electronic Folklore', 286).

3. Thomas, *Entangled Objects*, 1991.

4. Based on an interview with Andy and Naomi, 05/11/2016.

5. Based on an interview with Mandy, 27/05/2019.

6. Based on an interview with Clair, 26/11/2016.

7. Based on an interview with Àine, 03/03/2017.

8. Based on an interview with AJ, 22/02/2017.

9. Based on an interview with Claire, 07/03/2017.

10. Based on an interview with Kirsty and Andy, 10/11/2016.

11. Houlbrook, 'Small Change', 123; Houlbrook, *The Roots of a Ritual*, 99; Houlbrook, 'Des pieces de monnaie au cadenas', 241–59.

12. Houlbrook, *The Roots of a Ritual*, 53–55, 109–110.

13. Walhouse, 'Rag-Bushes and Kindred Observances', 104.

14. Hulse, 'A Modern Votive Deposit at a North Welsh Holy Well', 33.

15. *Make Love Locks*: https://www.makelovelocks.com/; *Beloved Padlocks*: http://www.beloved padlocks.com.au/engraving-text-ideas/; *Lock-Itz*: http://lock-itz.com/ [Accessed 19/06/2018].

16. See Houlbrook, 'The Mutability of Meaning', 40–59.

17. Sheenagh Pietrobruno regards YouTube as an informal archive of primary sources of popular cultures and practices (Pietrobruno, 'YouTube and the Social Archiving of Intangible Heritage', 1259–76). Montana Miller also notes that the Internet offers a veritable 'treasure trove' of ethnographic data. However, she also remarks on the 'muddy ethical field' of Internet research (Miller, 'Face-to-Face with the Digital Folk', 228), considering what protections are necessary, whether consent should be obtained and how, and noting the ambiguity between private and public space online. These factors led her to question whether the Internet is a suitable forum for academic research into human subjects. However, as the Association of Internet Researchers stress, 'rather than one-size-fits-all pronouncements, ethical decision-making [in Internet research] is best approached through the application of practical judgment attentive to the specific context' (Markham and Buchanan, 'Ethical Decision-Making and Internet Research Version 2', 4). The contexts of the YouTube videos referred to in this book do not, in my opinion, necessitate a great deal of ethical delicacy. They are all publicly accessible, with none requiring online membership, and the contributors do not appear to view the subject matter as sensitive. However, as advocated by Robert Kozinets in his *Netnography*,

the names of the YouTube users will remain anonymous, unless they are clearly advertising a service or product (Kozinets, *Netnography*, 142).

18. Brück, 'Fragmentation, Personhood and the Social Construction of Technology in Middle and Late Bronze Age Britain', 281; Handelman, *Models and Mirrors*, 11.

19. Moore and Myerhoff, *Secular Ritual*, 21.

20. Quoted in Asad, *Genealogies of Religion*, 56.

21. 'Ritual', *Oxford English Dictionary* (2005).

22. Bender, Hamilton and Tilley, 'Leskernick', 148.

23. Brück, 'Ritual and Rationality', 284.

24. Handelman, *Models and Mirrors*, 5; Shils, 'Ritual and Crisis', 447.

25. Rostas, 'From Ritualization to Performativity', 92; Bocock, *Ritual in Industrial Society*, 36; Rappaport, *Ecology, Meaning, and Religion*, 175.

26. Myerhoff, 'We Don't Wrap Herring in a Printed Page', 199; Fernandez, 'Symbolic Consensus in a Fang Reformative Cult', 912.

27. Becker, 'Media and The Ritual Process', 638.

28. Borraz, 'Love and Locks', 7–21.

29. Richter and Pfeiffer-Kloss, 'Bridges, Locks and Love', 195–96.

30. Houlbrook, *The Roots of a Ritual*.

31. Turner, *From Ritual to Theatre*, 85.

32. Raj and Dempsey, 'Introduction', 3.

33. Ibid, 5.

34. See Tilley, 'Objectification', 60–73; Gell, *Art and Agency*.

35. Thomas, *Entangled Objects*, 28.

36. Weiner, *Inalienable Possessions*; Brück, 'Material Metaphors', 313; Fowler, *The Archaeology of Personhood*, 58; Thomas, *Entangled Objects*.

37. Downes, Holloway and Randles, *Feeling Things*.

38. Bergiato, 'Moving Objects', 231.

39. Randles, 'Signs of Emotion', 49.

40. Fletcher, 'Sentimental Value', 56.

41. See Bergiato, 'Moving Objects', 232.

42. Bell and Spikins, 'The Object of My Affection', 26.

43. Richter and Pfeiffer-Kloss, 'Bridges, Locks and Love', 197.

44. Bell and Spikins, 'The Object of my Affection', 28.

45. Rowlands, 'The Role of Memory in the Transmission of Culture', 144.

46. Bell and Spikins, 'The Object of my Affection', 28.

47. Bradley, *The Significance of Monuments*, 90.

48. Gell, *Art and Agency*, 33.

49. Gell, *Art and Agency*, 68.

50. Bergiato, 'Moving Objects', 231.

51. See Randles, 'Signs of Emotion', 49–50.

52. Johnson, 'Love Locks in Memoriam?', 11.

53. Hutchinson, 'Love-Locks are Being Removed from High Level Bridge and it is Causing Outrage'.

54. Lindsay, 'Woman's Heartache After Love-Lock in Memory of Husband is Cut from High Level Bridge'.

55. Bradbury, 'Forget Me Not', 224; Petts, 'Memories in Stone', 194–95.

56. Kopytoff, 'The Cultural Biography of Things', 64–91.

57. Rowlands, 'The Role of Memory in the Transmission of Culture', 144.

58. Mills, 'Remembering While Forgetting', 82.

59. Stewart, *On Longing*.

60. 'Souvenir', *OED* online.

61. Hutchinson, 'Love-Locks are Being Removed from High Level Bridge'.

62. Lindsay, 'Woman's Heartache after Love-Lock in Memory of Husband is Cut from High Level Bridge'.

63. It should be noted that the distinction between 'amateur' and 'professional' film-makers is recognised as ambiguous. See Salvato, who explores YouTube's democratisation of video creation (Salvato, 'Out of Hand', 67–83) and Patricia Lange, who prefers to refer to 'amateur' and 'professional' as a continuum rather than a binary (Lange, 'Video-Mediated Nostalgia and the Aesthetics of Technical Competencies', 25–44).

64. Frosh, *The Image Factory*, 124.

65. Taylor, 'Pikinini in Paradise', 370.

66. Morris, 'A Room with a Voice', 389; Lange, 'Video-Mediated Nostalgia', 25–44. See also Van de Port, 'Visualizing the Sacred', 444–61.

67. Borraz, 'Love and Locks', 13.

68. Crouch and Lübbern, *Visual Culture and Tourism*, 9.

69. Greenhill, 'Folklore and/on Film', 487. See also Buccitelli, 'Performance 2.0', 60–84.

70. Lange, 'Video-Mediated Nostalgia', 25–44.

71. Borraz, 'Love and Locks', 15.

72. Schwartz, 'Praying with a Camera Phone', 177–94.

73. Van de Port, 'Visualizing the Sacred', 444–61.

74. McNeill, 'Real Virtuality', 85.

75. Becker, 'Media and the Ritual Process', 629–46.

76. Ibid., 635 and 642.

CHAPTER 5

SYMBOLISING LOVE

The Semiotics of Love-Locking

It is not hyperbole to claim, as I have been doing throughout this book, that love-locking is a global phenomenon. Love-locks have hung in the romantic capitals of the world: on the Pont des Arts in Paris; on the Ponte Milvio in Rome; beneath Charles Bridge in Prague; on the 'wall of love' in Gretna Green, Scotland. They have hung at the world's major tourist destinations and landmarks: on Sydney Harbour Bridge, on Brooklyn Bridge, on N Seoul Tower, on the Yellow Mountains, on Cape Town's Signal Hill, on London's Tower Bridge, on remnants of the Berlin Wall. And they have hung in more obscure places: an otherwise nondescript fence in Shoreditch, London; a bridge in the southern Iraqi province of Dhi Qar; in Boston on a footbridge over the Massachusetts Turnpike. As outlined in the *Introduction*, love-locks have been recorded in at least 65 countries worldwide, on every continent bar the Antarctica. While many of these assemblages have been instigated and perpetuated by tourists, local residents have also played a large part in the establishment of this custom in many of these places, as was demonstrated in the previous chapter. It is a custom, therefore, that has near universal appeal. The aim of this chapter is to consider why.

The successful establishment of any custom, as folklorist Frank Cushing observed in the 1970s, depends on 'the similarity of the material to the already existing traditions'.[1] The ease of instigation, perpetuation and dissemination can hinge on the custom's relatability. Generally, the more that people can identify with the purpose and symbolism of a practice, the more likely they are to participate. And so if a folk custom is to be successful, it will likely have fed 'on other matter', to paraphrase an expression given by Peter and Iona Opie.[2] New customs harness and draw on older, more established traditions or symbolisms so that their participants can more easily relate and therefore more readily adopt. However, if the love-lock custom's success has rested upon pre-existing traditions or symbolisms, how can we account for its near universal appeal? How has one custom appealed to, and been adopted by, the myriad and myriadly diverse inhabitants of six different continents?

The previous chapter identified symbolism as an integral element to ritual, with Bocock defining 'ritual' as *bodily action in relation to symbols* (emphases in original) and Myerhoff as 'an act or actions intentionally conducted by a group of people employing one or more symbols in a repetitive, formal, precise, highly stylized fashion'.[3] This chapter therefore addresses the questions surrounding the successful establishment of love-locking by exploring the semiotics – the symbol – of the love-lock. It is not a history of the custom; it does not claim that the practices and symbolisms below are the origins of love-locking. Its aim is to consider the long history of padlock symbolism – the 'other matter', as described by the Opies – in various worldwide contexts. This will enable an understanding of why such vast numbers of people today are so receptive to the seemingly contemporary concept of locking a padlock to a public structure in order to declare romantic commitment.

The Padlock as Symbol

Ancient historian Robin Osborne, in his paper on hoards and votive offerings, stresses the 'importance of the dedicated object' in deducing the beliefs behind a custom.[4] He advocates making the object itself central to the study of a dedicatory practice – which is what love-locking essentially is. Vital to this is the question asked by Osborne: 'Why did anyone think that depositing this or that particular object or group of objects was an appropriate way of marking or establishing communications with transcendent powers?'[5] Some dedicated objects were obviously designed and crafted *as* dedicated objects – classical statuettes or medieval pilgrim badges, for example. For other dedicated objects, however, this is not the case; some were made for secular, everyday use before being 'ritually recycled' as dedicated objects. In most cases, this applies to the love-lock.[6]

So, what makes the padlock an appropriate dedicated or deposited object in this custom? Why are people locking padlocks to structures to declare romantic attachment rather than other relatively cheap, portable objects? This is where semiotics – the study of signs and symbols, of objects that stand for something else[7] – is particularly useful. Although we should of course be wary of any attempt to claim a universal symbol, to many people worldwide the symbolism of the padlock is obvious. They are objects that stand for the concepts of security and steadfast unity because that is what the padlock, at its most basic level, is intended for.

Social scientist Kai-Olaf Maiwald, who adopted an objective-hermeneutic approach in his investigation into 'padlocking' (i.e. love-locking) at the Hohenzollern Bridge in Cologne, writes of how this symbolism is inherent to the pad-lock's very materiality and mundane utility: they lock one thing to another. They symbolically lock the depositors to each other and to the site of deposition. They are, as Maiwald words it, a 'copular' in material form.[8] And as was demonstrated in the *Introduction*, they have been for a very long time, in many world cultures. And for every culture that has used a form of padlock to lock one thing to an-other, there are a people who can recognise the padlock's potency as a symbol of security and steadfastness.

This symbolism is made explicit by many depositors in their inscriptions: 'locked in love', 'key 2 my heart', 'I wanna lock your love', 'LOCKED TO-GETHER FOREVER', 'as long as this is locked, so will our hearts', 'LOCKED + SEALED'. More than any other object, they can signify permanence. Moreover, they can (to an extent) ensure permanence. They are metallic objects locked closed. As Maiwald notes, they not only lock things together but they also lock *out*, preventing access to non-depositors: to those outside of the relationship.[9] Unless they are unlocked by someone with the key – or removed with bolt-cutters, which is detailed in *Chapter Seven: Unlocking Love* – they will remain on that bridge. They will not accidentally fall or disintegrate, as other objects might. Granted, not all customs of ritual deposition aim for permanence; some purposely use objects that are ephemeral or transient. The rags of Celtic clootie wells, for example, are strips of cloth tied to the branches of trees to effect a cure, fabric being chosen in this case because as the deposit degrades, the malady was believed to deteriorate also.[10] However, the love-lock has another purpose, one that favours durability: the locking of love.

The love-lock custom evidently and effortlessly draws on the symbolism of the padlock, which hinges on the object's primary mundane purpose and physical attributes. The question remains, though, whether this symbolism is historic and widespread and whether it engendered other customs in the past: 'other matter' from which the modern love-lock feeds upon. The remainder of this chapter will therefore explore historical examples of the ritual recycling of the padlock in a variety of world cultures and time periods. It will not be an exhaustive list – such an endeavour would require a whole book – but it will still demonstrate the wide-spread and long-standing nature of the padlock as a ritual object.

The Lock and Key in Europe

The love-lock features most prominently in Europe and probably originates here. It is therefore perhaps no coincidence that the padlock features extensively in European customs concerning love and sex, from the Middle Ages through to the twentieth century. The symbolism of lock and key, for example, made it a not uncommon object used in medieval magic. In Thomas of Chobham's thirteenth-century confessional manual *Summa for Confessors*, he describes how a man in Paris had been rendered impotent by the malicious magic of a sorceress. This sorceress had purportedly spoken an incantation over a closed lock, thrown the lock into one well and the key into another. To cure the man's impotence, the lock and key were retrieved and the padlock unlocked.[11] Interestingly here, we have a custom very similar to the contemporary love-lock: although the aims of the respective rituals are disparate (romantic commitment on the one hand and a curse of impotence on the other), both call for the locking of a padlock, the separation of lock and key and the deposition of both in/near water. And both rituals are considered undone by the retrieval of the key and the unlocking of the padlock. Clearly, as Catherine Rider observed when noting that locks and impotence continued to be linked during the early modern period, 'The lock has an obvious symbolism.'[12]

Padlocks have also been employed as charms. The Museum of Witchcraft and Magic, Boscastle, holds a miniature metallic padlock that they classify as a 'protective amulet', stating that 'Padlocks are widely used as protective amulets – they keep the things you value most safe from being lost or stolen: your partner's love, your life, even your spirit.'[13] Two similar padlock charms can be found in the Clarke Charms Collection of Scarborough Museum. One, collected locally in 1935, is described in its original record as having been 'carried as an amulet to bring good luck'. The other is dated to 1914–1918 and is described as a 'Padlock Amulet . . . worn to bring good luck by a soldier during the European war'.[14] Again, the mundane purpose of the padlock – to secure – is being harnessed ritually.

It was, however, more common for the padlock to be associated with the binding of love, and Sophie Page makes an explicit connection between modern-day love-locks and medieval magic in her article 'Love in the Time of Demons'. At the heart of medieval love magic, she writes, 'was the intention to bind another person with words, images and the invocation of a supernatural power, an approach that has some parallels with inscriptions and iconography on lovers' gifts in the Middle Ages and today'.[15] The language of binding fits the symbol of the padlock, which is why it was a popular motif in medieval jewellery design: lockets in the shape of padlocks, given as lovers' tokens to bind their love. Page draws on an example currently held in the British Museum of a fifteenth-century gold locket in the form of a padlock, bearing the French inscription 'sauns repentir' ('without regret'),[16] but there are many others.

The British Museum also holds the Fishpool Padlock Locket, which was found amongst a probable fifteenth-century hoard of medieval gold coins and other jewellery in Fishpool, Nottinghamshire. Many of the pieces of jewellery are interesting in this context because they are associated with love: the brooch is heart-shaped, and one of the rings bears the image of a heart and an inscription that probably translates to 'Lift up your whole heart'. The padlock locket itself, gold, bears floral imagery and the French inscription 'de tout' on one side and 'mon cœur' on the other: 'with all my heart'. It is very small, only 0.6 inches in length, and is attached to a key by a chain. As well as being decorative, it was probably used to link two ends of a chain together.[17] A similar but slightly smaller gold padlock locket, likely of a similar date, was also found in Newark.[18]

John Cherry notes a comparable example in statue form. Around the neck of the alabaster effigy of Jane Cockayne, believed to have died in the 1440s, in a church in Ashbourne, Derbyshire, is a chain joined at the front by a rectangular object, which Cherry believes to have been a padlock.[19] Another comparable padlock is one depicted on a fifteenth-century signet ring's oval bezel held by the Museum of London, bearing the French inscription 'ma soveraigne' ('my queen').[20] Later examples include a nineteenth-century gold, diamond encrusted brooch in the form of a padlock bearing a heart and a key on a suspension chain, made in England; a gold brooch set with pearls and pink topazes, with pendants in the forms of a padlock, a key and a heart, also from nineteenth-century England; and another brooch in the form of a padlock and key set with diamonds and sapphires.[21] Another locket held by the British Museum, believed to have belonged to Marie Antoinette, bears a small gold padlock pendant with a key, while the Horniman Museum contains a twentieth-century English love token pendant that bears a miniature padlock and key on either side of two interlocking hearts.[22]

Another English use of the padlock that draws on the symbolism of binding is that of the foundling token. The London Foundling Hospital was founded by royal charter in 1739 to house the babies whose mothers felt they could not keep them. The mothers were asked to leave an identifying token so that if they wished to reclaim the child, they could be identified, and around 5,000 such tokens survive, dating from 1741 to 1760. These identifying tokens, as historian John Styles words it, 'offer numerous expressions of maternal love, hope, yearning and remorse', especially as most of the women would have been illiterate and so resorted to expressing their emotions through material objects.[23] Most were swatches of fabric, but others were objects with more overt symbolism: a heart-shaped pendant, hearts drawn on paper, embroidered hearts, suit-of-heart playing cards, and so on. Included in this list are three padlocks, which may have been selected for convenience; padlocks from, say, storage chests. But they could equally (and simultaneously) have been chosen as tokens of love for their potent symbolism; for their accessibility to those reliant on 'material literacy', to use another of Styles' terms.[24] This is more likely in light of one other foundling token being a ring in the form of a miniature padlock.[25]

Elsewhere in Europe, padlocks are employed in rituals of love and attachment. In northern Russia, for example, young women would lock a padlock and place the key under their pillow or wear it close to the heart as part of a divination ritual. Their future groom would then appear to them in a dream and ask them for the key.[26] Padlocks also played a role in Slavic weddings. An unlocked padlock and key would be placed on or under the threshold when the newly-weds stepped over it; following this, the padlock would be locked and retained in the home while the key was often discarded into a body of water (a river, a well). Oksana Mykytenko writes that 'The aim was to secure the marriage plans, to strengthen the husband and wife's bond, and to ensure that the marriage would be long and happy.'[27] Mykytenko also details how a padlock would be used on the wedding night, with the bride locking a padlock above the groom's head to increase his love and ensure his fidelity.

Clearly padlocks have a long history of use as love tokens, but they are rarely seen without a corresponding key.[28] And in fact keys appear even more popular as love tokens. For example, they feature quite prominently in the decorative imagery of love-spoons: the carved wooden spoons gifted as love tokens – often as a promise of marriage and not unlike an engagement ring – across Wales from the seventeenth to the nineteenth century. Alongside hearts and diamonds, keys and keyholes were popular motifs.[29] One example from the Pinto Collection of Birmingham Museums and Gallery, dated to 1800–1850, contains a heart, a key and a keyhole. The curator believes the keyhole conveyed the message 'my house is yours', and the heart and key signified 'unlocking love'.[30] In Italy, a similar custom involved the gifting of Saint Valentine's keys as romantic symbols, named for the patron saint of love and marriage, martyred in the third century. The Pitt Rivers Museum holds one such key, purchased in Padua, northern Italy.[31]

The Lock and Key Worldwide

In a 2014 article for *Worldviews*, Ole Bruun described the 'little rituals' performed by visitors to Mt Huanghshan (also known as the Yellow Mountains), China. Along with closing their eyes to sense the 'breath' of the mountains and reading aloud inscriptions on the mountains' rocks, visitors also attach 'love padlocks on steel railings at the Heavenly Capital Peak to "lock the soul" into a marriage of partnership'.[32] This notion of locking the soul, evident at a number of love-lock sites across China, is consistent with far earlier examples of Chinese padlock rituals, the most common of which was the use of the padlock as a protective amulet.

Chinese parents from the Qing Dynasty (founded 1636) onwards, concerned for the natural and supernatural dangers that threatened their children, frequently employed padlock-shaped amulets to protect them. Often made of silver, the scallop-design padlock-shaped pendants would be worn around the child's neck. The purpose of the padlock appears to be twofold. Margaret Duda, who dedicates an entire chapter of her work on personal adornment in the Qing Dynasty to 'Symbolic Locks', believes that the padlock amulet stemmed from a custom involving a baby's first and highly ritualised bath. After being bathed, a functioning padlock, with the shackle open, was passed over the child's body from head to foot. As it reached the ground, the shackle would be closed, 'ritually securing the child to earth'.[33] Another belief was that the padlock amulet was intended to 'bind' the child's body and soul together, countering the efforts of any soul-stealing demons. On a more practical level, Duda remarks that the clanging of the metallic lock may also have aided parents in keeping track of any wandering toddlers.[34]

Some Chinese parents would commission special padlock amulets, but many purchased them ready-made at stalls and silversmith shops. Most contained adornments: natural motifs, symbols of good fortune and scenes from mythology, and extra protections such as small beads, believed to repel evil spirits. Most of the padlocks were purely decorative, and those that were functional were rarely opened, the shackle often being soldered shut.[35] Some of these padlocks were known as *Pih kea so* or *bai jia sau* – 'the hundred family-lock' – so named because the father would raise money for its purchase by obtaining donations from a hundred different families, all of whom would then be contributing to the safety and longevity of the child.[36]

An example of a Chinese padlock worn for protection is held by the Pitt Rivers Museum. This silver padlock from Shanghai bears the image of two figures standing near flowers or trees.[37] Such padlock amulets would primarily be worn by young boys, often first-borns. However, different versions were worn by others. The *King keuen so* – 'neck-ring lock' – was worn by women as well as children, again for protection, and Duda gives examples of one worn by a woman at her wedding and another by a teenage boy during New Year celebrations.[38] These were customs that travelled with many Chinese emigrants to North America, and symbolic padlock amulets are still given to young children for protection and posterity.[39]

There are significantly few love-lock assemblages in the Middle East, a point that is considered in *Chapter Seven: Unlocking Love*. Despite this – or perhaps because of this – a large number of padlock rituals feature in the cultural and religious histories of some Middle Eastern countries. In fact, Tanavoli and Wertime dedicated an entire book to padlocks in Iran, and they outline how the 'inherent symbolism' of the lock was harnessed in a number of popular beliefs and rituals, primarily in the twentieth century.[40]

As with China, many of these beliefs and rituals centred on the notion of protection. Iranian padlock amulets, such as the one held by the Pitt Rivers Museum, were believed to protect the wearer from harm or evil.[41] Most often they were made from steel or silver – metals considered particularly powerful – inscribed with prayers and attached to a garment or worn on a chain. Traditionally, they would be worn by women and sometimes for more specific purposes; for example, a particular ritual involved pregnant women hoping to prevent miscarriage. A religious leader speaks a prayer over a miniature padlock, then a cord is tied and blown upon by one woman as another woman reads from the Koran; finally the cord is tied around the pregnant woman's waist and fastened by the padlock. Only during the ninth month is the padlock unlocked.

Tanavoli and Wertime observe that three elements are important in the talismanic use of the padlock: 'the power of the inscription, which is augmented by that of the metal of the lock, and the lock's inherent symbolism of binding or protecting and releasing'.[42] In the above ritual to prevent miscarriage, we witness the padlock's ability to protect and release. Its ability to bind is more commonly employed in love magic. Girls wishing to attract husbands would wear a lock on a chain around their necks on the evening before Chahar Shanbeh Suri, the last Wednesday in the Iranian year. At sunset, the girls would ask the first sayyid (descendent of Mohammad) they encounter to open the lock, in the hope that they will marry a sayyid.[43]

The padlock also plays a part in Iranian marriage customs, with a member of the bride's wedding party opening and closing a padlock during the ceremony. The lock is closed at the last moment, not to be opened again until the night of the marriage consummation. The aim of this is to bind the groom to the bride and to symbolise marital fidelity. This custom, according to Michelle Marcus, was still popular in the 1990s.[44] And once married, the padlock can be ritually employed again, inscribed with images of happy couples to keep the love of husband and wife securely bound.[45]

In terms of binding, the padlock was also used to secure the fulfilment of wishes and good fortune in Iran.[46] This is explicitly linked to Islam, with pilgrims harnessing the padlock as a form of ex voto when visiting the tombs of saints and religious leaders of the past. Typically, a pilgrim would make some request of the saint, vowing to do something in return if their wish is granted. As the vow is made, they either tear off a strip of their clothing and tie it to the grill surrounding the tomb chamber or chains at the shrine's entrance or they attach a padlock. As Tanavoli and Wertime write, 'this signifies the binding of the supplicant to his intercessor and his vow, and also acts as a reminder to the intercessor of the pilgrim's request and promise.'[47] At the fulfilment of the vow, the supplicant may unlock the padlock or may leave it hanging, in the belief that it will miraculously open without need of a key.

As with the Middle East, there are relatively few established love-lock assemblages on the continent of Africa. This may be due to padlocks featuring little in (documented) popular beliefs and rituals here, and when they do appear in these contexts, they are rarely associated with love. Still, the inherent symbolism of binding is prevalent. There are a few padlocks in the Pitt Rivers Museum hailing from Ghana and Nigeria that are identified as a 'charm' or parts of a 'sorcerer's outfit', often combined with organic materials such as animal bones, feathers and flora.[48] Archaeologists Apoh and Gavua hypothesise that padlocks found amidst an assemblage of ritual objects at a nineteenth-century shrine of the Ga people on the Accra Plains of Ghana were 'probably used to lock victims spiritually'.[49]

Amongst the Oyo Yoruba of West Africa, the padlock is ritually employed to compel another person to do one's will, whether that be forcing them to give you money, to offer you a job, or to seduce somebody. In this case, it is the binding properties of the padlock that are harnessed. In both Yorubaland and Accra, padlocks have been used specifically to close court cases, whereby it is the padlock's ability to open and close that seems particularly significant. Marilyn Houlberg describes padlocks amidst the wares of an Abeokuta travelling medicine man in the 1970s:

> He was selling padlocks wrapped with diagonally criss-crossing threads, with the key in the lock and with two little iron pliers for Ogun, the god of iron and war, attached to the lock. He explained that these padlocks were specifically for winning court cases; by turning the key in the lock, one could insure the legal deadlock to be broken and the case decided in one's favor.[50]

The Symbol of the Bridge

Padlocks have provided a wealth of symbolism and prior customs to draw on, but they are not the only component of the love-lock custom. The structures to which they are attached may also offer ritual matter for this modern custom to feed upon. The types of structures on which love-locks accumulate vary greatly. The earliest confidently documented love-lock assemblage, in Janus Pannonius Utca in Pécs, is on a simple fence. Many other fences are likewise adorned: in Paris, overlooking Montmartre's Sacre Coeur; in Shoreditch, London; at Picnic Point Waterfall at Toowoomba, Australia; at the giraffe enclosure of Chester Zoo, UK. Love-locks also adorn many other types of structures: a chain around a tree in the Black Forest, Germany; a sculptural fence around another tree in Erzsébet Square, Budapest; the flag rings of surviving sections of the Berlin Wall; the mesh over a well in Tuscany; lamp posts in St Petersburg. There are also a large number of sculptures being harnessed for this custom, some specifically built to accommodate love-locks, and these are detailed further in the next two chapters.

However, the majority of love-lock accumulations do occur on bridges; as Stéphane Borraz observed in his study of love-locks in Paris, 'There are many places where padlocks may be attached but all places are not equal.'[51] From the records compiled for this research, 118 fences or gates accommodate love-locks, in contrast to 226 bridges, from Paris' Pont des Arts, the Brooklyn Bridge, and Ha'penny Bridge, Dublin, to the lesser-known structures spanning the River Wye in Bakewell, Derbyshire, and the River Wharfe in Otley, Yorkshire. There is something symbolically significant about the bridge as a structure. Please note however that this chapter is not arguing that those earlier depositors made a conscious decision to attach their love-locks to a bridge because of this symbolism, just as it is not claiming that depositors today make the same deliberate selection. It is, however, arguing that the love-lock custom was more readily accepted because of familiarity (conscious or subconscious) with the cultural and ritual significance of the bridge.

The mythologies of many cultures worldwide feature an Otherworld – whether a supernatural realm or the afterlife – separated from us by a barrier, such as a chasm, an ocean, or a river, which is reached via a bridge. The bridge features in Norse mythology in the form of the Bifröst, which spans the gap between earth and heaven, and in the Gjallarbru – the 'Echoing Bridge' – which crosses the river Gjall on the journey into the land of Hel.[52] Travelling a little further west and we find that the theme of the bridge appears in abundance in Celtic legends and medieval romances. Cuchulain must cross a perilous bridge to reach the house of Scathan, and Maol a Chliobain, the heroine of a West Highland oral story, must create a bridge out of a strand of her hair in order to escape a giant.[53] And in the fourteenth-century romance *Rigomer*, Lancelot and Gawain must traverse a myriad of bridges: one of copper, guarded by a serpent; one that can only be lowered by enchantment; and another that is guarded by copper giants.[54]

The bridge's presence in Christian otherworldly visions is no less salient. It appears in the *Vision of Saint Paul*, albeit not in the fourth-century Greek text but in later versions, as a bridge as narrow as a hair connecting the terrestrial realm to paradise.[55] This bridge has been depicted as a high arch, crossed by crawling souls, in an illumination from the fourteenth century, and it makes an appearance in numerous pieces of later European literature and artwork; even the artist of the eighteenth-century work *Pantheon* could not resist sneaking a bridge into the distant background of the scene of Charon and the River Styx.[56] In Islam, we hear of the Sirat Bridge, or Straight Path, which passes over hell and is believed to be 'thinner than a hair, and sharper than the edge of a sword'.[57] This seems to have been adopted, and adapted, from the Persian tradition of the Cinvat Bridge, described as being as 'narrow as the blade of a razor'.[58]

The theme of the otherworldly bridge is also familiar to many native peoples of both the Americas and the Oceanic cultures, to whom the realm of the dead is reached by a bridge, usually in the form of a plank or a log,[59] and this theme is equally prevalent in eastern beliefs. The Chinese in Taiwan, for example, believe that a narrow bamboo bridge aids the crossing into Paradise;[60] in Japan, we hear of how Deguchi Onisaburo (1871–1948), one of the founders of the religious movement Ōmoto, claimed to have crossed two bridges – one of ice and one of gold – on his mantic journey to heaven and hell;[61] and in Tibetan thought, it is a bridge that the dead traverse as they cross into the land of the gods.[62] These examples are only few amongst many and highlight the extensive use of the bridge in cross-cultural eschatological mythology.

On its simplest level, the popularity of the bridge in eschatological mythology can easily be explained. It is, after all, the most literal symbol of 'crossing-over' one can envisage. There are, however, more complex theories behind its prevalence. In the terrestrial realm, the bridge has always been a method of crossing from one land to another, and it has become a symbol of transition. Both Mircea Eliade and Arnold van Gennep, who have studied the prominence of bridge symbolism in cross-cultural initiation rites, note the bridge's intermediary, marginal elements.[63] The bridge is, by its very nature, a liminal object. It is neither part of one realm nor the other; neither on land nor in water. It is a 'bridge of transition', which may account for why it is deemed a suitable place for couples wishing to declare romantic commitment at significant milestones in their relationships: anniversaries, marriages and the birth of children (see *Chapter Three: Excavating Love* and *Chapter Four: Locking Love*).

The bridge also connects. Semiotician Omar Calabrese explores the bridge as pictorial motif, noting the wealth of bridges in folklore, art and popular culture that fulfil the function of connecting one thing – a land, people, territories – to another. A bridge, Calabrese observes, 'always leads something or someone towards something or someone'.[64] This is why 'building bridges' is a linguistic metaphor for reconciliation and making social connections.[65] In this sense, the bridge is much like the padlock: they are both 'copulars' in material form, to return to Maiwald's phrase.[66] They are thus ideal places for the coming together of two people who wish to ritually declare their romantic commitment. As one love-lock depositor in Cologne explained in a 2014 newspaper interview: 'The river represents life, the bridge stands for overcoming barriers and connecting'.[67] Bridges, notes Lucy Blakstad, are popular places for first kisses, marriage proposals and for seeing in the new year. Why? Because they are 'an explicit manifestation of the eternal – and eternally unsatisfied – human desire to link'.[68]

Calabrese identifies the centre of the bridge as symbolically the most 'intense' section of the structure, being the most and equally separate point from both sides.[69] This may explain why on most bridges there is a concentration of love-locks in the centre, a phenomenon recognised by Borraz in his study of love-lock bridges in Paris and by Maiwald in his analysis of the Hohenzollern Bridge, Cologne: 'the padlockers' preference for the middle of the bridge can . . . be explained since it is the ideal endpoint of mutually approaching one another from two equidistant points.'[70] This was evident at Leeds Centenary Bridge, UK, which consists of 38 metal panels from end to end containing 1,436 love-locks in total. The middle 14 panels contained 93 per cent of those love-locks.[71] There could, of course, be a more mundane reason for this distribution: the centre of a bridge tends to provide the best views, linking back to the concept of framing the love-lock as explored in *Chapter Four: Locking Love*. However, it could also be the case that people, consciously or subconsciously, recognise a symbolic and metaphorical significance to the centre point of a bridge.

There is of course the risk of over-interpretation. The popularity of the bridge as a place of deposition may stem from a far simpler reason: its proximity to water. We know that the act of relinquishing the key into a body of water is a significant stage – indeed, one of the two peak moments – of the ritual, and a bridge allows the depositors to enact this stage: they can stand on the bridge and watch as the key disappears from view in the river or canal below. The choice of the bridge as the most popular accommodator of love-locks, therefore, may be more a matter of convenience, but that does not negate the bridge's metaphoric potency.

The Symbolism of Water

Water has a long history of admitting ritual deposits. Countless prehistoric and historic hoards, assemblages and deposits have been discovered in rivers, lakes, marshlands and other watery places; far too many worldwide to detail here.[72] In the interest of concision, the focus will be on Britain – from the range of bent and broken metal objects deposited during the Iron Age in the lake at Llyn Cerrig Bach, Anglesey, to the vast array of coins, jewellery, clay pipes and other objects excavated from the Thames.[73] Coins are objects very frequently deposited in watery places, as offerings to deities, as propitiatory 'sacrifices' to malignant water spirits, or dropped into holy wells as 'payments' to presiding saints, in exchange for health or the fulfilment of wishes. This is a practice that has entered the twenty-first century in the form of the wishing-fountains encountered in parks, tourist destinations and shopping centres.[74]

Some water deposits are more relevant to love-locks than others. Returning to the Thames, a large body of love tokens have been recovered from its riverbed and muddy banks, predominantly eighteenth-, nineteenth- and twentieth-century coins that have been smoothed down and then engraved with initials, names, dates and messages. These engravings are very much akin to what we find inscribed on love-locks: 'FROM VIC TO MAY'; 'M W', 'Jan 11 1921'. The anonymous author of an online post about these finds hypothesises: 'With a great river like the Thames racing down towards the ocean, there is a sense of a connection to the infinite. And there is a sweet romance to the notion of a lover secretly throwing a token into the water, feeling that the strength of their emotions connects them to a force larger than themselves.'[75] No doubt being added to these tokens are the love-lock keys thrown off the bridges of London today; the riverbed of the Thames is a palimpsest of romantic deposits.

Edwin Sidney Hartland described another example of romance-related water deposition: in Wales in the late nineteenth century it was custom for 'a bride and bridegroom to go and lie down beside a well or fountain and throw in pins as a pledge of the new relation into which they have entered'.[76] And another love-related water deposit is the wedding ring. A 2019 contribution to the Folklore

Society Newsletter tells of an underwater archaeologist who has recovered a number of modern wedding rings beneath one of Durham's bridges, on which newly married couples from the nearby church often pose for photographs. Unlike other love-related deposits, Fionnuala Williams believes that the rings were probably deposited at the break-up of a marriage.[77]

Why have pins, coin love tokens and wedding rings been deposited in watery places in rituals of love, found and lost? Focusing on more general water deposition during the Bronze Age, David Fontijn proposes a number of possible reasons for this: 'purity, pollution, regeneration, fertility', as well as the status of the river as a boundary between peoples and worlds, and as a 'central element in people's perception of landscape'.[78] While modern-day love-lockers are unlikely to cite 'purity, pollution, regeneration, fertility' as the factors motivating their decision to attach their love-lock to a bridge and drop their key into a river (indeed, none have referenced or alluded to this when speaking to me or in any of the interviews conducted by Borraz in Paris),[79] might some of these notions have fed discretely, subconsciously, into the contemporary custom?

It may also be appropriate to consider what water *does* rather than what it symbolises. Fontijn, for example, explores the physical qualities of bodies of water:

> They 'seal off' the invisible parts of the world: the muddy bottoms of streams and rivers ... Throwing a gold-glimmering bronze axe into such a place must have been an act whereby the onlookers really got the impression that the object disappeared completely. Sunk to the bottom of the marsh, it could no longer be seen or retrieved anymore.[80]

The dropping of a padlock's key into a river could have the same effect; the depositors can watch as it sinks from view. Richard Bradley, writing of prehistoric hoards, describes how many offerings were deposited in such a fashion so as to be irredeemable, either physically damaged, negating their economic value, or deposited in a location from which they could not be recovered – that is, watery places.[81] The depositors of love-locks employ both methods. The key deposited in the water becomes irredeemable, while the padlock, locked and now lacking a key, can no longer serve a utilitarian function. Nor can it easily be unlocked, indicating the faith the depositors have in the durability of their feelings for each other.

This separation of lock and key is an example of 'fragmentation', to use an archaeological term.[82] This is a word applied to objects that have been broken into parts and deposited incomplete; not subtly or obscurely but in a way that makes their missing parts starkly evident. The fragmented deposits thus denote synecdoche, with archaeologist John Chapman observing that 'the (present) parts clearly signify the (absent) whole'.[83] The padlock without a key is a synecdoche, clearly signifying a padlock that once had a key. Therefore, a love-lock on a bridge signifies a key, irredeemable, in the water below.

Conclusion

The aim of this chapter was to consider why the love-lock custom has been so readily adopted by people the world over. Even just within Europe, if we consider the diversity of the continent's inhabitants it is striking how widespread and how established the custom has become here. The chapter's premise was that the successful establishment of a custom hinges on, as Cushing worded it, 'the similarity of the material to the already existing traditions'.[84] The ease of instigation, perpetuation and dissemination of a custom can depend on its relatability; on how familiar the potential participants are with the symbolism employed within it. We took the three central components of the love-lock custom – the padlock, the bridge and the act of deposition in water – and explored their ritual and semiotic histories within largely global contexts. All three have proven rich.

The padlock has a long and widespread history in customs associated with love, sex, marriage, protection and binding; associations that have no doubt derived from the object's inherent mundane purpose and physical properties. The bridge proves an appropriate accommodator of the love-locking ritual because of its broad identification as a structure of transition and connection that stretches back to many of the world's eschatology myths. The bridge's close proximity to water is also significant: ritual deposits, including love tokens, have long been surrendered to watery places. It is, I argue, water's ability to make something disappear and render it irretrievable that is of importance to most acts of deposition, including that of the love-lock's key.

This chapter was not a history of love-locking. It does not claim that these rituals and symbolisms are the origins of the contemporary practice, nor that modern-day love-locking is an adaptation or reinvention of these older customs. Love-locking is a relatively new custom that has fed on older, more established symbolisms, cultural associations and practices. It has been so rapidly and widely adopted because people cross-culturally can easily recognise the padlock as an object of symbolic security; the bridge as a structure of connection; and water as a ritual place of no return. Most people are literate in the metaphorical language that birthed the love-lock.

Notes

1. Cushing, 'The Cock and the Mouse', 269.

2. Opie and Opie, 'Certain Laws of Folklore', 68.

3. Bocock, *Ritual in Industrial Society*, 36; Myerhoff, 'We Don't Wrap Herring in a Printed Page', 199.

4. Osborne, 'Hoards, Votives, Offerings', 5.

5. Osborne, 'Hoards, Votives, Offerings', 7.

6. This excludes the commissioned, professionally engraved love-locks, some of which do not even come with a key. For 'ritual recycling', see also my work on concealed shoes (Houlbrook, 'Ritual, Recycling, and Recontextualisation', 99–112).

7. Chandler, *Semiotics*.

8. Maiwald, 'An Ever-Fixed Mark?'.

9. Maiwald, 'An Ever-Fixed Mark?'.

10. Bord and Bord, *Sacred Wells*, 59; Foley, 'Performing Health in Place', 473.

11. Cited in Rider, *Magic and Impotence in the Middle Ages*, 97–98.

12. Rider, *Magic and Impotence in the Middle Ages*, 98.

13. Museum of Witchcraft and Magic, '1702 Amulet: Padlock': https://museumofwitchcraftand magic.co.uk/object/amulet-padlock/ [Accessed 17/06/2019].

14. Scarborough Museums & Gallery, Clarke Charms Collection 1946.48; Scarborough Museums & Gallery, Clarke Charms Collection 1946.289.

15. Page, 'Love in the Time of Demons', 60.

16. British Museum, Gold Locket 2010,8023.1. Cited in Page, 'Love in the Time of Demons', 61.

17. Cherry, 'The Medieval Jewellery from the Fishpool, Nottinghamshire, Hoard', 307–21.

18. British Museum, 'Locket', 2010,8023.1: http://www.britishmuseum.org/research/collection_ online/collection_object_details.aspx?objectId=3335914&partId=1&searchText=2010,8023.1&pag e=1 [Accessed 19/01/2018].

19. Cherry, 'The Medieval Jewellery from the Fishpool', 312.

20. Ibid., 313.

21. British Museum, 'Brooch', 1978,1002.612: http://www.britishmuseum.org/research/collecti on_online/collection_object_details.aspx?objectId=78153&partId=1&searchText=1978,1002.612& page=1 [Accessed 19/01/2018].

22. Horniman Museum, 'Love Token', 16.111: https://www.horniman.ac.uk/collections/browse-our-collections/object/62761 [Accessed 19/01/2018].

23. Styles, *Threads of Feeling*, 64. See also Holloway, 'Materializing Maternal Emotions', 154–71.

24. Styles, *Threads of Feeling*, 70.

25. Pers. comm. Alison Duke, Foundling Museum, 20/10/2016.

26. Vlaskina, 'The Types of Divination Used by the Don Cossacks', 306.

27. Mykytenko, 'Padlock and Key as Attributes of the Wedding Ceremony', 489.

28. For the religious symbolism of keys, see Richter and Pfeiffer-Kloss, 'Bridges, Locks and Love', 192–93.

29. Wight, 'Peasant Art in Britain', 18.

30. National Museum Wales, 'Lovespoon', 53.101.15: https://museum.wales/collections/online/ object/fe8fc6e8-f701-3a40-a64b-181bc3e2ad1e/Lovespoon/?field0=string&value0=lovespoon&field 1=with_images&value1=on&page=2&index=14 [Accessed 23/03/2019]; National Museum Wales, 'Lovespoon', 01.374.3: https://museum.wales/collections/online/object/0d5d5437-1a0d-399b-bcf9-e8 7224c60e85/Lovespoon/?field0=string&value0=lovespoon&field1=with_images&value1=on&page =2&index=15 [Accessed 23/03/2019].

31. Pitt Rivers Museum, 'St Valentine Key, Italy', 1985.52.459: http://web.prm.ox.ac.uk/amulets/ index.php/keys-amulet2/index.html [Accessed 23/03/2019].

32. Bruun, '"When You Have Seen the Yellow Mountains"', 20.

33. Duda, *Four Centuries of Silver*, 32.

34. Ibid., 41.

35. Ibid., 35–41.

36. Morrison, 'Some Account of Charms, Talismans, and the Felicitous Appendages Worn about the Person, or Hung Up in the House, &c. used by the Chinese', 285; Doolittle, *Social Life of the Chinese*, 314–15; Werner, 'Chinese Superstitions', 958.

37. Pitt Rivers Museum, 'Silver Padlock & Chain for a Child to Wear as Protection against Spirits', 1909.32.45: http://objects.prm.ox.ac.uk/pages/PRMUID45335.html [Accessed 17/06/2019].

38. Morrison, 'Some Account of Charms', 286; Duda, *Four Centuries of Silver*, 41.

39. Rouse, 'Charmed Lives', 28–29.

40. Tanavoli and Wertime, *Locks from Iran*, 16.

41. Pitt Rivers Museum, 'Amulet in the Form of a Padlock, Iran', 1985.51.738; Tanavoli and Wertime, *Locks from Iran*, 20; Saraçoğlu Çelik, 'Lost Treasures: Locks', 98.

42. Tanavoli and Wertime, *Locks from Iran*, 20.

43. Ibid., 22.

44. Marcus, 'Dressed to Kill', 9.

45. Tanavoli and Wertime, *Locks from Iran*, 22.

46. Saraçoğlu Çelik, 'Lost Treasures', 98.

47. Tanavoli and Wertime, *Locks from Iran*, 24; Wertime, 'Metalwork', 160.

48. Pitt Rivers Museum, 'Charm Made from a Tin Dish Containing a Padlock Set in an Earthen Pack with Feathers, Hair and Plant Stems at One Edge', 1891.40.1: http://objects.prm.ox.ac.uk/pages/PRMUID27373.html; Pitt Rivers Museum, 'Part of a Native Sorcerer's Outfit: Bird Skull with Metal Padlock through the Top, Bound to a Pointed Stick', 1933.93.44: http://objects.prm.ox.ac.uk/pages/PRMUID190633.html; Pitt Rivers Museum, '"Charm" Necklet of Twisted Cotton with Strung Magical Items (Padlock, Tree Seed, 2 Small Horns etc.)', 1925.12.1: http://objects.prm.ox.ac.uk/pages/PRMUID27434.html [Accessed 16/08/2019].

49. Apoh and Gavua, 'Material Culture and Indigenous Spiritism', 225.

50. Houlberg, 'Notes of Egungun Masquerades among the Oyo Yoruba', 61. See also James, 'Ciki and Jiki', 160.

51. Borraz, 'Love and Locks', 15.

52. Turner, *The History of Hell*, 106.

53. Lady Gregory, *Cuchulain of Muirthemne*, 35; Campbell, *Popular Tales of the West Highlands*, 261.

54. Patch, *The Other World*, 299–301.

55. Loomis, *Adventures in the Middle Ages*, 27.

56. Hastings, *Encyclopaedia of Religion and Ethics*, 853.

57. Ivanow, *Kalāmi Pīr*, VII, 107–8.

58. Hughes, *Heaven and Hell in Western Art*, 164–65.

59. Poignant, *Oceanic Mythology*, 135.

60. Forlong, *Faiths of Man*, Volume I, 341.

61. Blacker, 'Other World Journeys in Japan', 66–68.

62. Rock, 'Studies in Na-Khi Literature', 50.

63. Eliade, *Shamanism*, 484; Van Gennep, *The Rites of Passage*, 22.

64. Calabrese, 'The Bridge', 11.

65. See Cameron, 'Patterns of Metaphor Use in Reconciliation Talk', 212–14.

66. Maiwald, 'An Ever-Fixed Mark?'.

67. D. Scherf, 'Herzilein, Der Schlüssel liegt im Rhein', *Der Standard* (15 June 2014), cited in Richter and Pfeiffer-Kloss, 'Bridges, Locks and Love', 190.

68. Blakstad, 'Introduction', 6

69. Calabrese, 'The Bridge', 3.

70. Borraz, 'Love and Locks', 15; Maiwald, 'An Ever-Fixed Mark?'.

71. Based on fieldwork at the site in October 2016.

72. See Laing, *Coins and Archaeology*; Bord and Bord, *Sacred Wells*; Merrifield, *The Archaeology of Ritual and Magic*; Aitchison, 'Roman Wealth, Native Ritual', 270–84; Bradley, *The Significance of Monuments*; Fulford, 'Links with the Past', 199–218; Cool and Richardson, 'Exploring Ritual Deposits in a Well at Rothwell Haigh, Leeds', 1–27.

73. Fox, *A Find of the Early Iron Age from Llyn Cerrig Bach, Anglesey*, 69; 'River Finds', *Thames and Field*.

74. Dowden, *European Paganism*, 51; Tuleja, 'The Tooth Fairy', 409; Houlbrook, 'The Penny's Dropped', 173–89.

75. The Gentle Author, 'Love Tokens from the Thames'.

76. Hartland, 'Pin-Wells and Rag-Bushes', 468.

77. Williams, 'Revoking Vows', 9.

78. Fontijn, *Sacrificial Landscapes*, 263–64.

79. Borraz, 'Love and Locks', 18.

80. Fontijn, *Sacrificial Landscapes*, 266.

81. Bradley, *The Significance of Monuments*.

82. Chapman, *Fragmentation in Archaeology*; Brück, 'Fragmentation, Personhood and The Social Construction of Technology in Middle and Late Bronze Age Britain', 297–315.

83. Chapman, *Fragmentation in Archaeology*, 104.

84. Cushing, 'The Cock and the Mouse', 269.

CHAPTER 6

SELLING LOVE

The Commercialisation of Love-Locking

It's Valentine's Day and couples are standing on the bridge amidst love-heart-shaped balloons, wrapping their arms around each other and kissing as colourful confetti falls like snow from the sky. It would be romantic if not for the cheering and jeering crowds that surround them, the photographers snapping their pictures and the adjudicator timing the minutes of lip-locking. Thirty-two minutes. Thirty-three minutes. Thirty-four minutes, and we have our winners! This is Vrnjačka Banja's annual 'Kiss Me' competition, which has been running since 2009.[1]

Couples from across Serbia visit this spa town to celebrate Valentine's Day (and St. Trifun) not only for the competition but for the town-wide festival that celebrates all things romantic with food, drink, music, prizes for the oldest and most attractive couples and the chance to splurge on love-themed souvenirs. There is even the opportunity to race a candle, floating on a love-heart-shaped 'licidar' cookie, down the Vrnjačka River. The winning cookie earns its couple a romantic evening of massages in a nearby resort. Forget Paris and Venice – this is the new capital of love. Although, as the tourist literature assures us, it is not that 'new' after all, because this is the town that accommodates the Most Ljubavi: the 'Bridge of Love', which claims to be the oldest love-lock bridge in the world, dating back to the First World War.

As was outlined in *Chapter One: Dating Love*, it has proven difficult to separate fact from fiction over the origins of love-locking. This is particularly the case with Vrnjačka Banja. I deliberated long and hard over whether to include this town's love-lock assemblage in the history of love-locking or in this chapter. This section could certainly have belonged in the first chapter, preceding Pécs and the 1980s, because the Vrnjačka Banja Bridge of Love is so often cited as the origins of the custom. Every written source read on the subject attributes the custom to the local legend of Nada, a local schoolteacher, and her lover Relja, who liaised on the bridge while courting. This was at the dawn of the First World War, and Relja was soon sent away to Greece to fight. There, he fell in love with another woman and never returned. The story is not a happy one; Nada soon died of a broken heart. Local girls, determined not to meet the same fate as Nada's, began 'locking their love' onto the bridge, and thus the love-lock custom was born.

This is the story told as historical fact in Vrnjačka Banja's *Tourist Organization Guide* and in the official information board on the bridge. It is repeated in newspaper articles, both Serbian and international; on tourism websites; and on *Wikipedia*, which has a page devoted to the bridge.[2] However, no solid evidence has been identified testifying to the accuracy of this origin story, and this is not through lack of searching. None of the secondary sources cite any primary sources. The earliest online reference I have found to love-locks on the Most Ljubavi is a Serbian article written in 2006, claiming vaguely that 'Vrnjacka girls have been practicing this "magic" for hundreds of years'.[3] And despite having made contact with local archives, museums and libraries in Vrnjačka Banja, no evidence has been forthcoming, other than the opinion that the assemblage is a modern feature and the story created for tourism.[4]

The likeliest explanation is that there was a pre-existing folktale associated with the Most Ljubavi, Nada, and Relja, who may well have been historical figures local to the town. One 2014 article in Serbian tabloid newspaper *Alo!* attempted to historicise Nada through undetailed oral history testimonies, suggesting that she did not die of heartbreak but spent the remainder of her life in a monastery.[5] The story of the two local lovers was probably adapted – perhaps with the addition of the local girls attaching padlocks to avoid Nada's fate – as an aetiological tale, perhaps with tourism in mind, explaining the custom that probably spread to Vrnjačka Banja in the late twentieth or early twenty-first century from Pécs, not far from the Hungarian-Serbian border.[6]

Apocryphal or not, the origin story of Nada and Relja has become so ingrained in the cultural identity of Vrnjačka Banja that the town hosts its annual festival of love in honour of it, and it features prominently in the tourist literature.[7] On the popular travel review website *TripAdvisor*, the bridge is listed as '#2' of 'things to do in Vrnjačka Banja', with a nearby stall selling padlocks to perpetuate (and profit from) the custom.[8] Alongside the spa resorts, the love-lock custom has therefore become central to the town's tourist industry.

This chapter considers the myriad other examples of love-locks being harnessed for tourism and commercial gain, exploring the various facets of the marketing of custom worldwide. In some instances, love-locking is encouraged; in others, it is deliberately implemented, whether for the revenue it creates or to foster a sense of communal identity. Other examples see the love-locking custom utilised for advertisements or commodified and sold in other forms. Across the majority of these cases is a sense that, through commercialisation, the custom has become inherent to the sites, through the processes of place-marketing and place-making.

'An Ancient Chinese Tradition'?

Most descriptions of love-locks in the press attribute the custom to Nada and Relja's ill-fated love in Vrnjačka Banja – it has been repeated enough times so as to become canon. There are some, however, which give the practice even greater antiquity. Love-locking is 'an ancient custom, which is believed to have originated in China', writes the author of one online news article, while *The Guardian* observes 'According to some, it stems from an ancient Chinese tradition.'[9] The companies dedicated to selling commissioned love-locks, professionally engraved (which are considered below), repeat this theory: 'Inspired by an an [sic] ancient custom' and 'Here at LoveLocks, Inc. we have been inspired by an ancient custom, which is believed to have originated in China.'[10]

Is there any truth to this claim? There is a site on Mt. Huangshan (also known as the Yellow Mountains) in eastern China where thousands of love-locks encrust a fence overlooking Jade Peak. A Chinese tour operator associates the deposits with a local 'legend':

> There is a legend about the lover locks on Mt. Huangshan. A long time ago, a beautiful girl fell in love with a poor young man, but her father didn't want her daughter to live a poor life. The father let his daughter marry a rich man. On the day of the wedding, the poor young man stole the girl and they ran away to the Huangshan Mountain. In that situation, they held hands and jumped into the deep cliff. Their wonderful dialogue kills people's minds – 'I have the same mind with you, faithful to you, I have my infatuation for you, and never change my mind.'[11]

This legend provides an origin story for the love-locks, vaguely dated to a 'long time ago'. However, evidence points to a date closer to the twenty-first century. Dr Trevor Sofield, who was employed as the international expert with a team of Chinese planners to formulate a Tourism Master Plan for Huangshan, and who co-authored the 2006 paper 'World Heritage Listing: The Case of Huangshan (Yellow Mountains), China',[12] believes the custom began on Mt. Huangshan in 1999 or 2000. This estimation is based on his frequent visits to the site, including one in 1998, when he saw no evidence of the practice. He first noticed love-locks on the mountain at the Host Welcoming Guests Pine Tree in 2000, and by 2004 'there were thousands adorning every chain link fence around the mountains'.[13]

This 'ancient Chinese tradition' proves to be not so very ancient. This is certainly not the first custom or 'tradition' to be perceived or presented as far older than it is. Eric Hobsbawm and Terence Ranger note the myriad 'traditions' –

from ceremonies of the British monarchy to Scottish tartans – which 'appear or claim to be old [but] are often quite recent in origin'.[14] Why? Value is attributed to age. A custom will feel more firmly established if it is bestowed with a sense of antiquity. In this way, age authenticates; it 'lends it status'.[15] As Sefryn Penrose observes, 'the older something becomes the more important it tends to be thought.'[16] The same applies to customs, which are viewed by many as only interesting insofar as they are seasoned 'survivals' from an earlier time.[17]

This not-so-ancient 'Chinese custom' is also unlikely to have originated in China, given the late date of its appearance in comparison with assemblages in Serbia, Hungary and Italy. Why, then, is it so frequently attributed to China? Historian of modern Italy Catherine Kovesi, who wrote a critical piece on the love-lock custom in 2014 (see *Chapter Seven: Unlocking Love*), observes that China is 'always a safely nebulous location for the origins of a myth'.[18] China also has a long history of being viewed by the Western world as 'a place of romance', to use Edward Said's words, and as having 'an aura of mystery', to use Zhang Longxi's.[19] Where better then, the argument presumably goes, to locate the mysterious origins of a curious custom.

However, the attribution of love-locks to a local Chinese legend from a 'long time ago' is not only externally fostered by Western journalists and travel bloggers. It appears to have been strongly cultivated by the Huangshan Parks Authority itself. Sofield informs me that the introduction of the custom was deliberately implemented by the park's authority, who entered into a commercial arrangement with a padlock company, the Double Heart Lock Development Co Ltd., to provide locks for tourists. They also replaced and installed new chain link fences (more accommodating for love-locks than the original concrete 'timber' design) in key scenic spots; set up around twenty stalls amidst the mountain trails selling locks; and provided 'photo opportunities', charging visitors for instant photographs of them making their romantic deposits. As more and more locks filled the fences, the vendors adapted to demand. To ensure more could fit, they began selling larger locks with longer shafts, and accordingly increased the price from Yen 6 (70 pence) to Yen 60 (£7).[20]

As to the story of the ill-fated lovers, the term 'legend' is used because of the implied antiquity that comes with it and for its historical ambiguity. This is not the only 'legend' we have associated with love-locking. Vrnjačka Banja has its own, as do other locations. In Montevideo, Uruguay, for example, the love-lock assemblage on the railings surrounding a fountain is accompanied by a plaque naming the structure *Fuente de los Candados* ('Locks Fountain') and explaining: 'The legend of this young fountain tells us that if a lock with the initials of two people in love is placed in it, they will return together to the fountain and their love will be forever locked.'[21] This does not present an origin story for love-locking, but it does imply a connection between the custom and the place – and again, that term 'legend' lends a sense of antiquity that probably does not exist.

In his chapter on tourism and the 'politics of authenticity', Craig Fees details how a 'Myth' can be implemented by residents that becomes so firmly entrenched in a place's identity that it comes to be perceived as factual history. Tracing the 'Myth' of a Londoner who moved to Campden, a town in the Cotswolds, England, at the start of the twentieth century, purportedly toppling a feudal social structure, revitalising the town and reviving forgotten customs, Fees observes that 'what was presented almost universally in books and magazines, television and radio programmes, tourist guides and journals as the history of modern Campden was in fact a Myth . . . What was treated as history was in fact tradition.'[22] This is the process that has occurred on Mt. Huangshan and in Vrnjačka Banja: the 'tradition' of the custom's origins has become so firmly established that it is repeated, by both insiders and outsiders, as historical fact.

Returning to the Mt. Huangshan legend, Sofield notes that the 'Chinese tourist authorities are very good at inventing "ancient" folk tales to verify or authenticate all sorts of things that are in fact often very new'.[23] This is evident with the official 2002 renaming of Zhongdian County in the Yunnan Province as 'Shangri-La'; a (successful) marketing strategy to 'package' the area as the real location on which the mythical paradise of James Hilton's 1933 *Lost Horizon* was based.[24] It was, to use Ben Hillman's words, 'the icing on the cake for tourism promotion and a certainty to put the area on the map.'[25] This process of 'inventing tradition' for the purposes of tourism, however, is certainly not exclusive to China. After all, to quote Tom Selwyn, 'Tourism is about the invention and re-invention of tradition. It is about the production and consumption of myths and staged inauthenticities.'[26]

As folklorist Venetia Newall observes, often what we perceive as the continuation of a custom or tradition actually proves to be a 'deliberately inserted renaissance'. Practices that appear old, from national anthems to Christmas carols, are actually the result of recent and conscious invention, and folk customs are subject to a similar ambiguity of 'authenticity'.[27] Their malleability, so vital to their survival, makes them all the more susceptible to appropriation, modification and recontextualisation. Commercialisation, such as tourism, is often the motivation behind such inventions or reinventions.

Many scholars have examined the creation of what Selwyn describes as 'tourist myths', considering how tourism has impacted and modified folk traditions worldwide.[28] Gabriela Muri, for example, explores the centrality of tourism to the process of imparting and interpreting folk traditions in the Montafon Valley, Austria. John Creighton considers the impact 'nostalgia tourism' has on the folk traditions of Japan, whilst Helaine Silverman studies how archaeological tourism has influenced contemporary constructions of Peruvian traditions.[29] Often, these traditions and customs are not invented from scratch, so to speak; most tend to be drawn on from pre-existing legends or practices, revitalised or commercialised for tourism. In the process, said legends or practices become so firmly entrenched in the identity and history of the place that it becomes difficult to separate fact from fiction.

Marketing Customs

In a forest in Nottinghamshire, one tree stands apart from the rest, protected behind fencing, its aged limbs supported by numerous metal props. It is monitored daily by the Forest Rangers, and an external arboricultural specialist survey is conducted on the tree every eighteen months.[30] It is a very old oak, yes, but this does not account for the level of care and attention it receives. Why then is it so heavily protected? Because it stands in Sherwood Forest, and this is the particular tree that antiquarian Major Hayman Rooke identified in the eighteenth century as being so large and so old that it could have been there at the time of Robin Hood. Since then the tree, known as the Major Oak, has been, both romantically and commercially, associated with the legendary figure of Robin Hood, identified as the historic hideout of the outlaw – despite both its size and age discrediting the theory. From the nineteenth century onwards, the tree was established as a national attraction, featuring on postcards and adopted as a corporate symbol of Nottinghamshire County Council.

It is not only the tree that has been drawn into the county's identity. Connected with the quasi-historical character of Robin Hood since the late medieval ballads, Sherwood Forest and the town contained within it, Edwinstowe, contain many gift shops and restaurants that commercialise this connection ('Robin Hood's Plaice' fish and chip shop, for example). Nottinghamshire, which brands itself as 'Robin Hood County', has hosted an exhibition on *The World of Robin Hood*, created *The Tales of Robin Hood* theme park, and the County Library has contained a Robin Hood archive since the nineteenth century.[31] Roy Jones observes that the legends surrounding Robin Hood have been 'co-opted, not merely into becoming the bases of local heritage tourism attractions, but also into being catalysts for place marketing'.[32]

Legends and traditions have similarly been utilised as tourist hooks elsewhere. In the centre of Point Pleasant, West Virginia, a large metal statue with mottled moth's wings very tangibly entrenches the history of 'Mothman' sightings into the identity of the town. The supernatural creature, reportedly seen by many of Point Pleasant's inhabitants during 1966–67 – and believed to have forecasted a major bridge disaster, which killed forty-six people – has become, to use Joe Laycock's phrase, the town's 'monstrous patron'; a symbol of their identity.[33] As well as the statue, the town's Gunn Park has been renamed Mothman Park; an annual festival is held in the creature's honour; the Mothman Museum and Research Center opened in 2006; and various local businesses capitalise on the legend (a pizzeria's 'Mothman Special', for example).[34]

The same process explains the McDonald's shaped like a flying saucer, the alien-head lamp posts and the 'alien specials' on offer in the local diners of Roswell, New Mexico. 'Whether one believes that . . . visitors from another world crashed in New Mexico is beside the point,' writes Jeremy Ricketts, because this supposed event of 1947 is 'now enshrined in the national collective consciousness'.[35] These are all examples of places becoming inseparable from the legends and traditions that are narrated, presented and commercialised. The name Roswell is synonymous with aliens; Point Pleasant with Mothman; and Sherwood Forest with Robin Hood. In much the same vein, love-locking has become such a prominent aspect of place-marketing and place-making on Mt. Huangshan that the custom is now inalienable from the place.

Global sociologist Ole Bruun writes the following on how visitors today engage with the landscape of Mt. Huangshan:

> Visitors perform little rituals in distinct places, such as closing their eyes to sense the 'breath' of the mountains like the famous poets and painters were believed to do, reading aloud inscriptions on rocks, marvelling at a sunrise over a sea of clouds, or putting love padlocks on steel railings at the Heavenly Capital Peak to 'lock the soul' into a marriage of partnership.[36]

To install a love-lock and snap a photograph in the process has become one of the key, almost obligatory rituals enacted on the mountain. This is despite the fact that the custom here is not more than two decades old. The same is very much true of other love-lock sites, in particular Vrnjačka Banja, as outlined above, and Paris. For example, prior to their removal, the love-lock assemblages of Paris were frequently included in lists of the most romantic places to visit in the French capital in articles and on travel websites.[37] At the height of the custom, locking a love-lock was viewed as one of *the* things to do as a tourist, especially anyone travelling as a couple; an essential component of a romantic trip to Paris.

Implementing the Custom

The primary difference between Paris and the other sites considered in this chapter is that love-locking was not implemented or encouraged by local authorities, who have been adamantly opposed to the custom since 2010 (see *Chapter Seven: Unlocking Love*).[38] The persistence of the practice in Paris was in part enabled by the many hawkers who illegally sold padlocks on the Pont des Arts and Pont Neuf but overall appears to have been self-perpetuating – no doubt due to widespread awareness of the custom through news and social media. It became an established part of Paris's identity in direct defiance of Paris City Hall's wishes. This is in contrast to the example of Mt. Huangshan, where the park authorities not only encouraged the practice of love-locking but appear to have implemented it.

Worldwide, there are many other examples of landowners, managers or local authorities facilitating the custom. A small town in Nevada is capitalising on its name – Lovelock, after English settler George Lovelock – to market itself as 'the nation's official love-locking destination', boasted by the town's tourism website and promotional video.[39] As Kirsten Hertz of the Lovelock Chamber of Commerce explains in the video, they 'were in the process of looking for an idea to really put Lovelock on the map'. Hearing about the 'ancient Chinese custom' of love-locking, they 'built on it here and created [their] own Nevada version'.[40] And so on Valentine's Day 2006, a circle of chain-link fences behind the County Courthouse was officially dedicated to the custom and dubbed 'Lovers Lock Plaza'. The website advises visitors that they can purchase padlocks at 'participating businesses throughout Lovelock. Look for the Lovers Lock posters in storefront windows,' with the shops also offering an instant photography service, taking shots of those locking their love.

Unsurprisingly, wedding venues have also adopted the custom. Famed resort of elopers, Gretna Green, Scotland, commissioned what they have dubbed a 'wall of love' in 2015. This 6x20-foot sculpture spells out the word 'LOVE' in metal crisscross netting, allowing for the installation of love-locks.[41] The tourist website (which attributes the practice to both 'an ancient Chinese custom' and Vrnjačka Banja) recommends that visitors wishing to own or install a love-lock should either purchase one from the Gretna Green gift shop (for £19.99) or order one online; in partnership with the Love Locks UK company, they sell padlocks in the shape of two interlocking hearts engraved with 'GRETNA GREEN SINCE 1754' (referring to the 1754 Marriage Act preventing clandestine weddings, which did not apply to Scotland) (Illustrations 6.1.–6.2.).[42] In February 2019, they also offered a 'Valentines Handfasting Package' for £79 per couple, which included a handfasting ceremony, photographs and a love-lock. Already capitalising on their reputation as a romantic destination, with a swathe of wedding venues and a 'Courtship Maze', it is not surprising that they have also embraced the love-lock custom.

Other wedding venues facilitating the custom include Baker's Ranch in Tampa Bay, Florida, which hosts a 'love lock bridge'. This small decorative bridge, containing love-locks deposited by previous brides and grooms, can be used either as a ceremony venue or a 'dreamy backdrop' to the wedding photographs.[43] Likewise, Statham Lodge in Cheshire and Harvey's Point, Donegal, Ireland offer love-lock commission services and a 'love-gate' and 'Lovers Bridge' respectively for couples to attach their love-locks to on their special day.[44]

Less obviously romantic locations are also adopting the custom. In 2018, the Frenchgate Shopping Centre in Doncaster, UK, incorporated love-locking into their celebrations of the fiftieth anniversary of the *Frenchgate Lovers* statue, on display at the centre. A love-heart-shaped structure with criss-cross panelling was

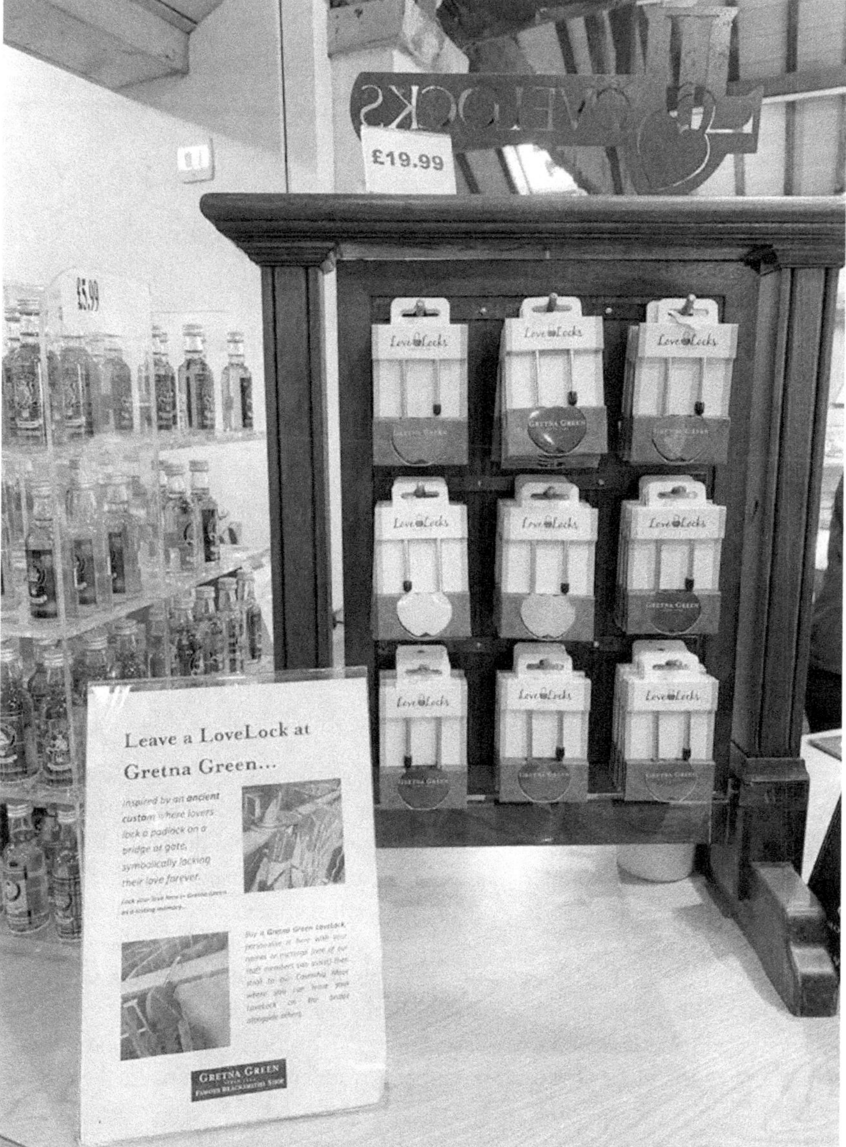

Illustration 6.1. Love-locks on sale at Gretna Green. Photograph by the author.

installed for Valentine's Day alongside a pop-up banner reading: 'We're bringing the romance back to Frenchgate by giving you the opportunity to declare your affections in the form of a message attached to a padlock, just like they do in the city of love, Paris … Let's celebrate 50 years of love at Frenchgate.' Padlocks were available for purchase at Guest Services for £2, with the proceeds going to Doncaster Cancer Detection Trust (see below for charitable causes).

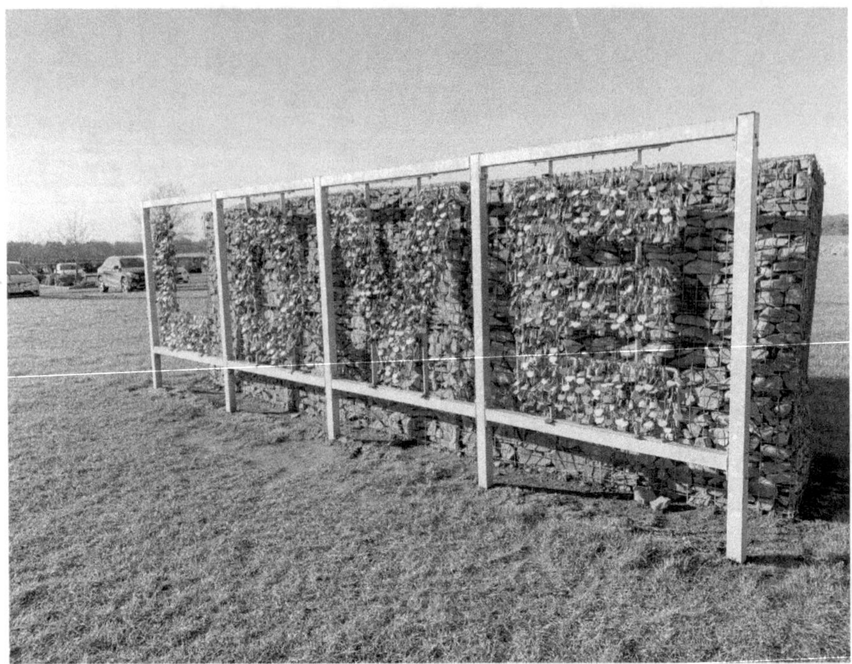

Illustration 6.2. Gretna Green's 'wall of love'. Photograph by the author.

Fence Stile Vineyards and Winery in Missouri, the US, have likewise installed red criss-cross panelling to a wall – dubbed the 'Love Lock Wall' – in their vineyard specifically to accommodate love-locks, which are sold on site.[45] While the Franklin Victorian Bed and Breakfast in Sparta, Wisconsin, advertise a 'Love Locks Arbor' on their property and likewise sell padlocks for the privilege.[46] In fact, love-lock gates and fences, described as 'Lovescapes', have been implemented in many locations across the US, such as in St George, Salem Pond and Zion National Park, Utah, and in the Dothan Area Botanical Gardens in Kinsey, Alabama, to name only some.[47] In Australia, Perth's Bell Tower sells professionally engraved love-locks for their assemblage – advertised as being 'locked in the heart of Perth' – for AU$30.

In South Africa, love-locks have been harnessed in celebration of national 'SA [South African] Marriage Week', the mission of which is: 'To inspire and motivate couples to focus on the wellbeing of their marriage and thus establish a whole family and consequently a healthy society.'[48] In September 2014, the 'Love Bridge' was set up in Magnolia Dell, Pretoria, and launched during Marriage Week. In an interview with SABC (South African Broadcasting Corporation), founder of SA Marriage Week Liezel van der Merwe contrasted this bridge with others worldwide where authorities discourage the practice and spoke of the importance of planning when designing this site, taking safety, weight management and accessibility into consideration. The establishment of this love-lock bridge was not (directly) about economic gain; although you can purchase a lock on site, Van der Merwe also mentions you can buy a lock cheaply from elsewhere and bring it with you. It was more about raising awareness of SA Marriage Week and about place-making, with Van der Merwe explaining in her interview that:

> it's there forever and ever. It's a new landmark for Pretoria, and I believe that many people will come there, tourists but obviously from South Africa, people from our country will visit Magnolia Dell and put their love-lock on our bridge . . . It's very nice to take a moment and just to reaffirm your vows, reaffirm your love for one another.[49]

Capitalising on the Custom

The custom of love-locking is evidently, in some places, actively implemented by landowners and managers, and local authorities. The reasons appear twofold: firstly, for the immediate monetary profits of selling padlocks on site or through online services, and secondly, for the longer-term (but still commercial) value of imbuing a location with romantic character and consequently promoting it as a destination worthy of visiting. 'So make the trip out here to Lovelock,' concludes Lovelock Nevada's promotional video, 'and see how locking your love will make it last forever.' These are not just cases of place-marketing but of place-making. Prior to the love-lock phenomenon, Lovelock Nevada was associated with English settler George Lovelock. Now, following the appropriation of Lovelock's name, the town is identified as the '"Heart" of Nevada', with an image of a love-lock incorporated into its Chamber of Commerce logo.[50] The adoption of the love-lock custom has impacted the physicality and the identity of this town – as it has, to both greater and lesser extents, at the other locations detailed above.

However, in most cases these processes of place-marketing and place-making are not the result of any official active implementation of the love-lock custom. More commonly, the custom embeds itself into a location more organically, through the actions of the depositors with a pre-existing structure, rather than through any formal decision to facilitate the practice. But landowners and managers, and local authorities, do still react to the introduction of this custom, and while some disapprove of it (see the next chapter), many others decide to capitalise on it.

Often this is simply a case of selling padlocks on site to allow the continuation of the custom. While in Paris the hawkers who once touted their padlocks on the Pont des Arts and Pont Neuf did so illegally and therefore covertly, in many other locations the sale of padlocks are officially sanctioned and often officially implemented in gift shops or at stalls nearby.[51] The purchase of padlocks has reached new heights of convenience in Asia, where love-lock assemblages at Singapore's Clarke Quay Central Mall and Seoul's Namsan Tower are accompanied by padlock vending machines offering a variety of colours to choose from.[52]

By accepting or fostering the custom, local authorities allow or encourage love-locking to shape the site's identity. For example, in Casa di Giulietta, Verona – the purported 'House of Juliet Capulet' of Shakespeare fame – love-locks were being deposited on the chains within the courtyard beneath 'Juliet's balcony'. Rather than ban the custom, management decided to embrace it. You can now purchase love-heart shaped padlocks packaged with marker pens from the gift shop, as well as t-shirts bearing love-lock imagery (Illustration 6.3.). As with

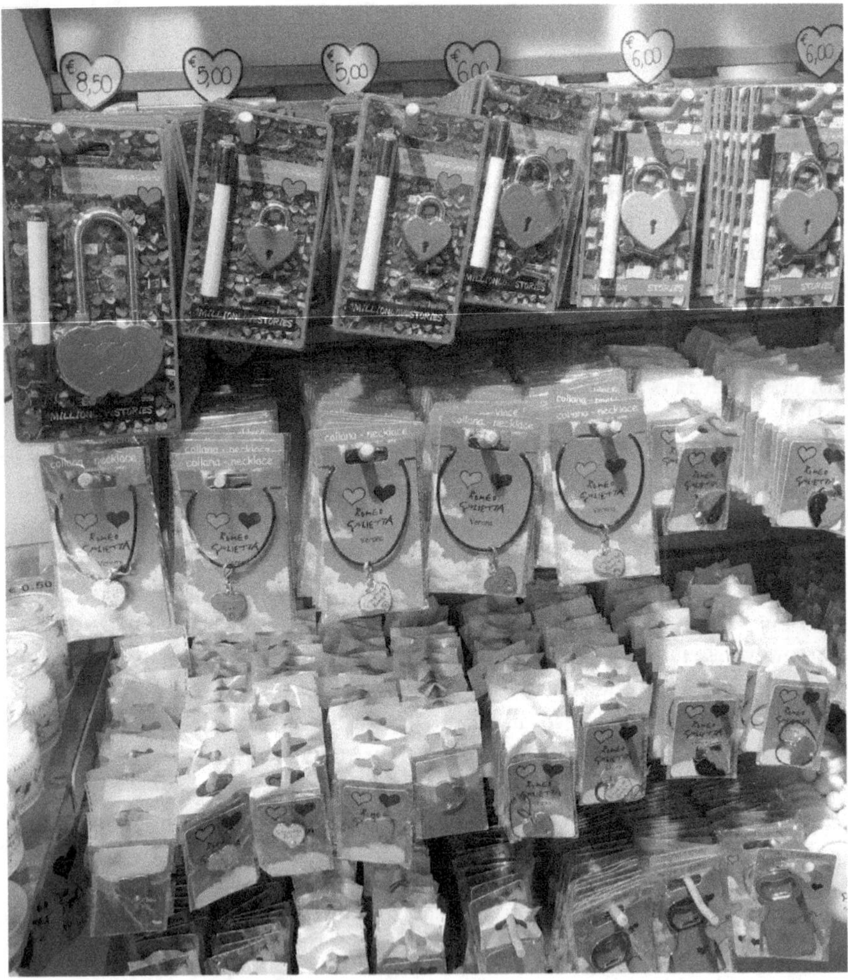

Illustration 6.3. Love-locks for sale at the gift shop of Casa di Giulietta, Verona. Photograph by Malcolm Gaskill.

Gretna Green, it is unsurprising that this inherently romantic site should market the custom, encouraging it to become one of the many tourist rituals enacted on site, alongside standing on the balcony in imitation of Juliet, rubbing the breast of Juliet's statue for luck, writing letters to 'Juliet' and sticking chewing gum to the walls of the building.[53] A similar story is seen on the Via dell'Amore ('Pathway of Love'), a coastal trail connecting two Cinque Terre towns in Italy. Named for its reputation as a meeting place for lovers from the different towns, it is not surprising that love-locks began appearing on the handrails – and also not surprising that padlocks began to be sold in various shops and restaurants in the area.[54]

However, not all cases of capitalisation of the custom centre on the selling of padlocks. Some are more focused on how the custom is presented by local authorities, and this can change over time. We have already encountered the love-lock assemblage of Pécs, Hungary in *Chapter One: Dating Love*, which was illegally and covertly instigated in the 1980s, possibly as part of the Punk music subculture. Initially, the custom was viewed negatively by local authorities, with efforts to contain it being made into the 2000s. However, as Cynthia Hammond observes, by 2007 there had been a perceptible shift in attitude. Photographs of the assemblage began appearing on the city's official website and tourism literature, marking it out as a site worthy of visiting and demonstrating that it had been incorporated into the sanctioned image – and therefore identity – of the city. The love-locks had thus transformed, to use Hammond's words, 'from a "plague of padlocks" to a respectable and desirable addition to the urban landscape of the city'.[55] Again, love-locks are being used in place-marketing and place-making.

Assemblages of Altruism

In 2015, the Forth Road Bridge, Scotland, celebrated its 50th birthday. The Forth Bridges Festival took place in September, and as part of the celebrations an initiative was set up by the Forth Estuary Transport Authority. Two panels were hung on the bridge in South Queensferry and, in collaboration with online company *Love Locks UK*, visitors were encouraged to purchase a specially engraved 'Forth Road Bridge' padlock – akin to the Gretna Green example above. Each lock cost £15 with £3.46 going towards RNLI Queensferry Lifeboat Station. Over 5,000 locks were purchased, many – if not all – of them installed on the bridge's panels, and the total raised was £10,300.[56]

Two years earlier, in 2013, the British Heart Foundation had commissioned creative agency GOOD Agency to design a campaign around Valentine's Day to raise money for National Heart Month. Their brief, explains GOOD Creative Partner Reuben Turner, was to help 'people mark their love for others. We looked at the cultural trend of "love locks"', he continues, 'and realised we could provide a temporary version that would enable the same gesture while allowing people to support heart research, and provide a powerful visual display to raise awareness'.[57] So they set up a large metallic frame spelling out the word 'LOVE', accompanied by a heart, designed to accommodate love-locks, in Covent Garden, London. The installation was planned for a fortnight but proved so popular it was extended to a month. It featured in *Time Out*'s 'best things to do in London' over the period and sold c.10,000 padlocks at £3 each.[58]

Ultimately all love-lock assemblages have some commercial implications (whether to padlock pedlars or to a site's tourist industry). In the cases of the Forth Road Bridge and Covent Garden, however, these have been put to philanthropic use. Similar initiatives have been seen elsewhere, with assemblages instigated by organisations and the proceeds from padlock sales going to charities. In Liverpool, love-locks were used to raise money by Liverpool Women's Charity for a maternity hospital; in Locks Heath Shopping Village, Southampton, for Breast Cancer Haven; at Ladysmith Shopping Centre, Ashton-under-Lyne, for the Believe & Achieve Trust.[59] This trend goes beyond Britain: in Dayton Mall, Ohio, for example, a large heart-shaped sculpture has been set up for love-locks, with proceeds going to a range of local charities; in Calgary, the money from love-locks goes to the Alzheimer's Society; while in Hong Kong, the money raised is donated to Care for Children, to name only a few examples.[60] We will see love-locks being employed for charity also in the next chapter.

This is certainly not the first time ritual deposits have been employed for altruistic purposes. Coins, for instance, have a long history of being ritually deposited and then put to good use. Many Christian holy wells in Britain contained receptacles for coins, deposited to the presiding saint in exchange for a cure, which would be collected by the guardians of the well and put towards its maintenance.[61] The wishing fountain is the modern equivalent, sometimes installed with the express purpose of encouraging charitable donations in the form of coin deposits.[62]

In 1961, Edward Block filed the patent for a 'Wishing-Well Type Coin Collector', which describes the device as:

> ... representing a 'wishing-well', the 'wishing-well' bearing a religious, or other inscription thereon which creates interest in the aspect of the simulated well and the inscription thereon whereby the observer will have a distinct mental inclination toward the doing, obtaining, attaining of something, or an expression of a wish, often one of a kindly or courteous nature, and to obtain the same the observer will drop a coin, or the like, into the simulated well, the observer knowing the coin will be used for charity, or other almsgiving or public relief or unfortunate or needy persons, the observer leaving the well with a feeling of benevolence.[63]

This device was intended to be installed in public places, and folklorist Alan Dundes, writing a year later, attests to its success: 'Despite the supposed present-day scientific mindedness, the fact that some charity fund raisers have constructed wishing wells in order to collect contributions attests to the extraordinary appeal of the custom'.[64] Today, many of these installations can be found in shopping centres (malls). The Trafford Centre, Greater Manchester, for example, established a 'Fountain Fund' in 1999, donating all money deposited by shoppers in the centre's fountains to charities in the North West of England.[65] Likewise, The Mall at Cribbs Causeway, Bristol, established the Mall Fountain Fund Grant in 2003. Using the coins deposited in The Mall's fountain, which they estimate can total around £10,000 a year, the Fountain Fund provides grants to local charitable organisations.[66]

It is not only coins that have been employed for such purposes. In Germany during the First World War, assemblages of nails were set up to raise money for the war efforts in the form of *Nagelfiguren*. These were wooden sculptures of various forms – knights, shields, blacksmiths, crosses, eagles, ranging in size up to twelve metres high – which were set up in streets and schools by local communities and associations. Civilians and soldiers would purchase nails for ritual deposition, hammering them into the sculpture with the aim of creating an encompassing metal surface, literally but also symbolically 'steeling' the *Nagelfiguren*. The money raised in the sale of the nails was donated to the Red Cross and the army, for supporting injured soldiers and war widows and orphans.[67]

Susan Brandt believes that the ritual assemblages of the *Nagelfiguren* 'may reflect the desire [of the depositors] to feel a part of a strong community which stands together in times of danger'.[68] While the love-lock assemblages may not be employed to raise money for war or the defence of a country, a similar mentality no doubt applies. Given the social influences on charity giving, it is unsurprising that folk assemblages – popular for the satisfaction of contributing to collective pieces and the sense of community they evoke[69] – also prove successful in fundraising initiatives. People see that others have given their money to a particular cause and are more inclined to contribute themselves. This is especially the case with the above love-lock structures, where the kindness of donors is manifested physically in the growing love-lock assemblage. A person's charitable donation is not just signified by numbers in an organisation's bank account but tangibly by a growing collective piece in a particularly public and visible space.

Love-lock assemblages are also suitable for fundraising because of their symbolism, with charities often appealing to love or the heart in their campaigns. The slogan for Dayton's love-lock heart sculpture, referred to above, reads: 'Dayton has a big heart, open yours,' while in Hong Kong, potential donors are asked: 'Trying to think of how to show your love to friends or family this year? How about shouting it aloud at Care for Children's Love Locks installation in Hong Kong?'[70] The connection between love-locks and the British *Heart* Foundation is even more obvious, the harnessing of which has been commended by Third Sector, the UK's leading publication on the not-for-profit sector. Rachel Beer, fundraising and marketing consultant, gave her expert view on the Covent Garden love-lock campaign: 'I love the clever interpretation of the Paris tradition. Adapting an existing trend is often a better recipe for success than inventing something.'[71] The love-lock custom thus proves itself malleable again.

Commodifying Love-Locks

Some forms of love-lock commercialisation are not location specific and are therefore not bound up in place-marketing and place-making. They do, however, play a role in the perpetuation of the custom. Particularly significant are the online companies marketing professionally inscribed love-locks. As observed in previous chapters, such love-locks are physically different to the utilitarian padlocks repurposed for the custom. Some are in the shape, or bear engravings, of love-hearts. They come in a variety of colours. Inscriptions are neater than those handwritten. Some even have photographs of the couple imposed on.

Myriad e-commerce shopping websites, such as Amazon and Etsy, sell these love-locks, offering personalised inscription services. A company called 'Engravables', which sells love-locks for £4.49 (excluding post and packaging), presents the following information to its customers:

> A brand new solid brass 40mm padlock engraved with any message of your choice to the style laid out in the photo. We will engrave your personal message with bold, permanent, contrasting text[,] which can be seen under most light conditions. Your Padlock will be beautifully presented in an Engravables black gift box. This is a perfect gift for Valentine's day, Weddings, Anniversaries, Engagements, Birthdays or to celebrate any special occasion. When you place your order, please add your engraving information to the 'note to seller box' to confirm what you want engraved on the Love Lock. Please separate each line with an asterisk (*). For Example: Line 1 *Line 2 *Line 3. A typical message might look like: Lily * & * Danny xx * 14th February 2016 . . .[72]

Some companies are solely dedicated to selling love-locks, having emerged in the 2010s to meet demand. *Love Locks UK* is one such company, who state on their website that their locks, shaped as two interlocking hearts, are designed with the pragmatics of the love-locking custom specifically in mind. They are made to be lightweight ('Thus posing less of a weight burden on structures'), and they come without a key ('meaning that once the lock is sealed it is kept sealed forever – plus, there is no key-litter').[73] Other companies include US-based *LoveLocks, Inc.*, *MakeLoveLocks* and *Lock-itz*.[74]

Other examples of commoditisation testify less to the demand for love-locks and more to how established the love-lock has become as a familiar symbol of love. International jewellery manufacturer and retailer Pandora, well-known for its customisable charm bracelets, sell several variations of explicitly described 'love lock' charms. One that is sold in the US for $80 is described as: 'Featuring two connected padlock hearts in sterling silver and 14K gold, this sweet charm is inspired by the tradition of sweethearts leaving padlocks in cities around the world to symbolize their everlasting love.'[75] In the UK, £40 gets you a love-lock ring ('Lock away feelings of love with this beautifully crafted sterling silver band ring') and a matching pair of earrings for a further £35 ('Turn your promise of love into a commitment with this pair of sterling silver padlock-inspired earrings'). Similar charms and pendants are sold across the spectrum of jewellers: for £690 you can purchase a 'Love Lock Necklace' from Tiffany & Co., while River Island sells a padlock pendant for £4.[76]

Love-locks are not only being commodified in jewellery. Louis Vuitton has a range of 'Love Lock Charm' handbags and keychains. One such handbag, the price tellingly absent from the website, is described: 'Crafted from black Epi leather, the Twist MM LV Love Lock Charms handbag is embellished with a removable ornemental [sic] chain hung with locks, keys and other charms in silver and gold-tone metal.' Far more affordable, for €4.99, you can purchase an 80g milk chocolate model of a love-lock, complete with key, from German chocolatiers Hussel. For the person who 'wants to show that love will last forever', the website advertises, 'What could express this better than the delicious love lock made of milk chocolate . . . ?'

In some cases, the symbolism of love-locks is harnessed in the marketing of other products. For example, a café close to Butcher's Bridge in Ljubljana, Slovenia, is named Lockal in honour of the nearby love-lock assemblage. The café's logos feature a glass of beer and a cup, both in the shapes of padlocks; the banner image on their Facebook page is of love-locks on Butcher's Bridge; and their menus are held together by two padlocks.[77] In this case, the love-lock is a referent to location, making the most of a nearby tourist attraction – just as establishments close to the Eiffel Tower, the Leaning Tower of Pisa or the Sagrada Familia draw on the iconography of these in their marketing material. In other cases, the love-lock itself symbolises something appropriate to the service offered. For instance, on the front cover of a 2018 Lloyds Bank brochure for home insurance is a red heart-shaped love-lock placed on two overlapping hands, intended no doubt to connote a sense of security and stability.[78] And on a poster advertising a dating event in a pub in Rochester, UK, in 2019, a padlock and key – apparently stock symbols for romance now, as we saw in the *Introduction* – are the prominent images.

Other examples of commoditisation see actual love-locks being physically harnessed for promotional purposes. In these cases, the love-locks are not 'authentic', in the sense that they are not deposited in declaration of love but for commercial reasons. In Manchester, one love-lock bears a sticker advertising a dating website. Another in Budapest promotes the German website *SmartLoveLock*, which offers professionally engraved love-locks also bearing an NFC chip and a QR code, linked to a personal website or social media page. The idea behind this is that anyone with a smartphone coming across one of these love-locks could scan the code and then access the depositors' love story online.[79] Having not encountered any such 'smart' love-locks in the wild, so to speak, I do not believe that the concept has been widely adopted.

Another example is both an 'authentic' love-lock and a promotional device. In April 2018, successful Canadian video blogger ('vlogger') Sham Idrees and his fiancé travelled to Paris. In a video entitled 'WE PLACED A LOCK on THE LOVE BRIDGE' they attach a love-lock to the Pont Neuf bearing their names. They toss two of the keys into the Seine but give the third to a friend living in Paris, with the instructions to their 1.7 million followers that anyone who retrieves the key and films themselves unlocking their love-lock would win an invitation to their (then upcoming) wedding.[80]

This use of a love-lock in what is essentially a game is similar to the custom's adoption in *Geocaching*, a real-world outdoor treasure hunt. First played in 2000 in the US, this game consists of people using GPS-enabled devices to locate over 3 million caches worldwide.[81] A number of these caches (discrete containers hidden in public spaces) have taken the form of love-locks. One example of this is in Manchester, which, instead of the usual declarations of love, bears a large black cross above the word 'GEOCACHE' and on the reverse a plea: 'Please do not disturb! This is part of an official game.' In place of a keyhole at the bottom is a plastic cap, which is extractable with tweezers. Inside is a rolled-up piece of paper bearing the names of the players ('Geocachers') who have successfully found it, logged with dates. This, like the two examples above, is not an 'authentic' love-lock but has been deposited as part of (and to advertise) a game. Working with Adam Parker, an archaeologist and Geocacher himself, I have catalogued 100 examples of Geocaches that feature love-locks in some way, the details and conceptual implications of which are detailed elsewhere.[82]

Conclusion: The Love-Lock as 'Fakelore'?

Tourism and commercialisation have, in the past, been viewed as banes of the traditional custom. Davydd Greenwood, writing in 1989, asserted that 'the commoditization of local culture in the tourism industry is . . . fundamentally destructive.'[83] Citing various worldwide examples, from Balinese dances to voodoo ceremonies, he laments how traditional customs packaged as tourist attractions have become altered in the process, have lost their meaning and have in some instances 'died' because of culture commoditisation.[84] However, the tactical adaptation of folklore is not always regarded in scholarship as a negative process. Jeremy Boissevain, responding to Greenwood, disagrees that such commoditisation necessarily has detrimental effects on customs and rituals. Focusing on a Maltese case study, he argues that 'While Malta is indeed now selling its colourful rituals to tourists, this commoditization is not destroying them. On the contrary, it has imbued them with new meaning.'[85]

Other folklorists have acknowledged that folk 'traditions' are fluid and malleable, and their employment and adaptation for commercial reasons can have positive effects. Muri, in her study of tourism's impact on Austrian folk traditions, advocates that mass media has 'been instrumental in preserving traditions', while Creighton, in her consideration of the commoditisation of tradition in the Japanese travel industry, asserts that in some cases tourism has provided rural Japanese communities with the economic means to sustain themselves and retain their traditions. 'One may bemoan the loss of tradition to commercialization . . .' she observes, 'but in some cases these forces have also brought about the means to keep traditions bemoaned as lost from disappearing altogether'.[86]

Love-locking, often deliberately implemented or facilitated for commercial purposes, has a place within this debate. However, it differs from the above examples because of the custom's seemingly recent genesis. This is not a case of an old, well-established tradition being employed and adapted for tourism. Instead, it is – to most of the locations – a new custom, introduced, encouraged or repurposed from elsewhere for commercial gain and to foster a sense of place. Love-locks thus fall under the category of 'invented tradition',[87] and American folklorist Richard Dorson would probably have viewed them with a suspicious eye. Had he been writing in a time of love-locks, he may well have labelled them 'fakelore', as that which is spurious and synthetic, rather than as 'authentic' folklore.[88] In the sense that the custom is often repurposed from other locations, it equally could be labelled 'folklorismus', a term coined by Hans Moser in 1962 to describe a 'mixture of genuine and falsified materials from folk culture'.[89]

There is no denying that folklore is, as Dorson terms it, 'big business', particularly within the tourist industry.[90] There is also no denying that tourist literature draws on, or creates, folklore as romantic aetiological tales for the love-lock custom, such as the tragic love affairs of Vrnjačka Banja and Mt. Huangshan. However, is this a necessarily negative process? Is such 'fakelore' unworthy of folkloric study? Dorson himself quotes folklorist Edwin Sidney Hartland, who in 1885 contended that 'Tradition is always being created anew, and that traditions of modern origin wherever found are as much within our province as ancient ones.'[91]

Dorson's successors have not all viewed fakelore with the same disdain that Dorson exhibited. As Anthony Bak Buccitelli observes, it was Alan Dundes who paved the way for a more nuanced understanding of the commercial forces of and in folklore, challenging the traditional view of the opposition between 'authentic folklore' and 'commercialized fakelore'.[92] Dundes advocated the study of fakelore and folklorismus for a number of reasons. For one, 'folklorismus and fakelore are not really new at all.'[93] Tracing the commercialisation of folklore back to eighteenth-century Scotland, he demonstrates the antiquity, as well as the pervasiveness, of this process. Secondly, the folklorist 'cannot prevent people from believing that fakelore is folklore'.[94] Regardless of the contemporaneity of the love-locks' origin tale on Mt. Huangshan, for example, visitors presumably believe it to be 'authentic' folklore, and journalists and business-owners world-wide believe it enough to describe love-locking as an 'ancient Chinese custom'. This leads to Dundes's third point: 'fakelore can in theory become folklore.'[95] Jane Yolen, in her vociferous critique of the term 'fakelore', observes how it can become canon, given enough time and enough tellers.[96]

Fortunately, many folklorists are following Dundes's advice that we 'accept the fact that fakelore may be an integral element of culture just as folklore is'[97] and have taken this a good leap further by largely dispensing with the term 'fakelore' – and, indeed, the term 'authentic'. Folklore, created or adapted for commercial reasons, is no longer viewed as the inauthentic result of a necessarily negative process. Folklorists should therefore not view the love-lock custom and the myriad tales surrounding it, regardless of their origins and ages, with antipathy, nor with indifference, as something unworthy of study. They are, to use Dundes's words again, an 'integral element of culture', in that they shed such light on contemporary social relations – not just between people but between people and material culture, popular culture and place. However, it is not only folklorists who may need convincing of this but also those other groups who find themselves engaging – quite unexpectantly – with this contemporary folk custom: local authorities, landowners and bridge engineers. These are the focus of the following, and concluding, chapter.

Notes

1. Anonymous, 'St. Trifun and Valentine's Day in Serbia'; Anonymous, 'Najduži poljubac trajao 36 minuta'.

2. Vrnjačka Banja Tourist Organization, Guide (Nd.), 11; Anonymous, 'Bridge of Love'; Anonymous, 'Šta imaju zajedničko Vrnjačka Banja i Rim? Most Ljubavi!'; 'Most Ljubavi', *Wikipedia* (Nd.).

3. Milišić, 'S katancem smo jači'.

4. Pers. comm. (and with many thanks to) Dr Marija Marić, Institute for Cultural Heritage Preservation, Kraljevo, Serbia, 18 November 2019. With many thanks also to Darko Dimitrovski, University of Kragujevac, and Dr Dubravka Juraga, Triton College Library, for their insights into the history of this site.

5. Jokanović, 'Most ljubavi jačii od potopa!'.

6. As I have noted previously, absence of evidence is not always evidence of absence, and I would gladly receive information about this assemblage, either in support of or contradiction to my conclusion.

7. Vrnjačka Banja Tourist Organization, Guide (Nd.), 11. See Graham Dann's work on the 'semiotic ethnography' of tourist brochures: Dann, 'The People of Tourist Brochures', 61–81.

8. 'Most Ljubavi', *TripAdvisor*.

9. Anonymous, 'Valentine's Day in Georgia: Where To Go?'; Day, 'The Lock of Love'.

10. 'Lovelock – Rome', *Love Locks UK*; 'The History of Love Locks', *Love Locks*.

11. 'Lover Locks on Mt. Huangshan – Contemporary Love Stories', *China Odyssey Tours*.

12. Li and Sofield, 'World Heritage Listing', 250–62.

13. Pers. comm. Dr Trevor Sofield, Visiting Professor, Center for Tourism Planning and Research, Sun Yat Sen University, 19/01/2019.

14. Hobsbawm and Ranger, *The Invention of Tradition*, 1.

15. Lowenthal, *The Past is a Foreign Country*, 265. See also Holtorf and Schadla-Hall, writing of 'age-value' (Holtorf and Schadla-Hall, 'Age as Artefact', 232). But for a critique of the notion of authenticity in relation to customs, see Kevin Meethan, who stresses that it is 'predicated on a false dichotomy between the non-modern, viewed as the authentic, and the modern, viewed as the inauthentic' (Meethan, *Tourism in Global Society*, 91).

16. Penrose, *Images of Change*, 13.

17. See, for example, Alessandro Testa's ethnographic exploration of carnivals in Europe today, which are given (largely false) historical roots: 'one can explain the emic usage of adjectives like "very ancient", "antique", "pagan", or even "prehistoric": the equation at work is that the more remote the evoked past is, the more "authentic"' (Testa, '"Fertility" and the Carnival 2', 124). It should, however, be noted that this tactical adaptation of customs and age is not regarded in modern-day scholarship as a necessarily negative process.

18. Kovesi, 'From Ancient China to an Italian Chick Flick'.

19. Said, *Orientalism*, 1; Longxi, 'The Myth of the Other', 130.

20. Pers. comm. Dr Trevor Sofield, Visiting Professor, Center for Tourism Planning and Research, Sun Yat Sen University, 19/01/2019.

21. Andrea, 'Montevideo's Locks Fountain'.

22. Fees, 'Tourism and the Politics of Authenticity in a North Cotswold Town', 131.

23. Pers. comm. Sofield, 19/01/2019.

24. Kolås, 'Tourism and the Making of Place in Shangri-La', 272.

25. Hillman, 'Paradise Under Construction', 176.

26. Selwyn, 'Introduction', 28.

27. Newall, 'The Adaptation of Folklore and Tradition', 146; Hobsbawm and Ranger, *The Invention of Tradition*; Trevor-Roper, 'The Invention of Tradition', 15–41; Sax, 'The Tower Ravens', 231–40.

28. Selwyn, *The Tourist Gaze*, 1–32.

29. Muri, '"The World's Smallest Village"', 53–64; Creighton, 'Consuming Rural Japan', 239–54; Silverman, 'Touring Ancient Times', 881–902.

30. Pers. comm. Paul Cook, Assistant Site Manager, Sherwood Forest National Nature Reserve, 31/10/2017.

31. Jones, 'Authenticity, the Media and Heritage Tourism', 145–54.

32. Ibid., 147.

33. Laycock, 'Mothman', 70–86.

34. Ibid.

35. Ricketts, 'Land of (Re) Enchantment', 257.

36. Bruun, '"When You Have Seen the Yellow Mountains"', 20.

37. Krause, 'Romantic Paris'; Anonymous, 'The 10 Most Romantic Places in Paris'.

38. Samuel, 'Paris to Remove Love Padlocks from Pont des Arts Bridge'.

39. 'About Locking Your Love, An Ancient Chinese Custom', *Lovers Lock*.

40. 'Videos', *Lovers Lock*.

41. Brough, 'Welcoming a Wall of Love to Gretna Green'.

42. Brough, 'Leaving Paris for the World'; 'Gretna Green Love Lock', *Love Locks UK*.

43. 'Love Lock Bridge', *Bakers Ranch*.

44. 'Wedding Gallery', *Statham Lodge*.

45. Anonymous, 'Celebrate Valentine's Day with Love Locks and Mûre Blanche'.

46. Jennifer, 'Love Locks for Valentine's Day Romance in Sparta WI'.

47. See Wallgren, 'Love Locks Tradition Spreads to Utah County'.

48. Anonymous, 'Vision and Mission'.

49. Van der Merwe, 'Bridge of Love Locks in Pretoria'.

50. *Pershing County Chamber of Commerce and Visitors Center*: https://www.pershingchamber
.com/home.html [Accessed 16/02/2019].

51. Richter and Pfeiffer-Kloss describe people standing with sales trays on Most Tumski in Wroclaw, Poland, selling small padlocks for 10 to 20 zloties (Richter and Pfeiffer-Kloss, 'Bridges, Locks
and Love', 188).

52. Goh, 'Locked in Love'; https://www.tripadvisor.co.uk/ShowUserReviews-g294197-d1169465-
r596552953-N_Seoul_Tower-Seoul.html [Accessed 31/01/2019]; https://www.tripadvisor.co.kr/Loc
ationPhotoDirectLink-g294197-d1169465-i330825222-N_Seoul_Tower-Seoul.html [Accessed 31/
01/2019]; https://www.tripadvisor.co.uk/ShowUserReviews-g294197-d554582-r596798194-Namsan_
Park-Seoul.html [Accessed 31/01/2019].

53. O'Neill, '"In Fair [Europe], Where We Lay Our Scene"', 284; Pfister, 'Juliet's Balcony', 43.

54. Steves, 'The Love Story Behind the Via dell'Amore'.

55. Hammond, 'Renegade Ornament and the Image of the Post-Socialist City', 189.

56. 'Forth Road Bridge Love Locks Raise Thousands for Charity', *The Scotsman*; 'Forth Road
Bridge Lovelocks Raise £10,000', *Edinburgh Evening News*; 'Forth Road Bridge Love Lock', *Love Locks
UK*.

57. Pers. comm. Reuben Turner, Creative partner, GOOD Agency, pers. comm. 19/02/2019.

58. Pudelek, 'Case Study'.

59. 'Gifts in Memory', *Liverpool Women's NHS Foundation Trust*; 'Lock in Your Love', *Locks Heath
Shopping Village*; 'Ladysmith Love Locks', *Ladysmith Shopping Centre*.

60. Moss, 'Sculpture at Heart of Love Locks'; 'Love Locks 2015: Care for Children', *Total Giving*.

61. Hull, *Folklore of the British Isles*, 107; Jones, *The Holy Wells of Wales*, pp. 93, 148, 208.

62. Houlbrook, 'The Penny's Dropped', 182–83.

63. Block, 'Wishing-Well Type Coin Collector', 1.

64. Dundes, 'The Folklore of Wishing Wells', 28.

65. Pers. comm. A. Reid (2013) Community Development Manager, intu Trafford Centre, 2
December (email).

66. 'The Mall's Foundation Charity Fund', *Quartet Community Foundation*.

67. Brandt, 'Nagelfiguren', 62–71.

68. Ibid., 62.

69. See Santino, 'Performative Commemoratives, the Personal, and the Public', 366; Preston,
'Panty Trees, Shoe Trees, and Legend', 12.

70. Moss, 'Sculpture at Heart of Love Locks'; 'Love Locks 2015: Care for Children', *Total Giving*.

71. Pudelek, 'Case Study'.

72. Engravables, '40mm Lock, Personalized Engraved Padlock, Large Linked Hearts Image,
Gift Box, Bold Text (LLHrt)', *Amazon*: https://www.amazon.co.uk/Personalized-Engraved-Padlock-
Linked-Hearts/dp/B013KABM8A?ref_=fsclp_pl_dp_1 [Accessed 15/03/2019].

73. 'About Us', *Love Locks UK*.

74. 'Custom Engraved Love Locks', *Love Locks*; *Make Love Locks*: https://www.makelovelocks
.com/; 'About Lock-itz', *Lock-itz*.

75. 'Love Locks Dangle Charm, Clear CZ', *Pandora*: https://us.pandora.net/en/love-locks-dangle-
charm-clear-cz/791807CZ.html [Accessed 15/03/2019].

76. 'Love Lock Necklace', *Tiffany & Co*: https://www.tiffany.co.uk/jewelry/necklaces-pendants/return-to-tiffany-love-lock-necklace-36340282/; 'Gold Colour Padlock Necklace Multipack' [Accessed 15/03/2019].

77. Lockal na Petkovšku, *Facebook*: https://www.facebook.com/Lockal.Petkovsek/ [Accessed 09/07/2019]. Many thanks to Ollie Douglas for the example and photograph.

78. Lloyds Bank, 'My Home's Safe and Sound' (leaflet) (2018).

79. *Smart Love Lock*: http://smartlovelock.com/en/ [Accessed 15/03/2019].

80. Sham Idrees VLOGS, 'WE PLACED A LOCK on THE LOVE BRIDGE'.

81. 'Fast Facts', *Geocaching*.

82. Houlbrook and Parker, 'Finding Love: The Materialities of Love-Locks and Geocaches' (2020).

83. Greenwood, 'Culture by the Pound', 174.

84. Ibid., 180.

85. Boissevain, 'Ritual, Tourism and Cultural Commoditization in Malta', 116.

86. Muri, '"The World's Smallest Village"', 55; Creighton, 'Consuming Rural Japan', 248–49.

87. See Hobsbawm and Ranger, *The Invention of Tradition*.

88. Dorson, 'Folklore and Fake Lore', 335; Dorson, 'Fakelore', 60.

89. Moser, 'Vom Folklorismus in unserer Zeit', 179–80, cited in Buccitelli, 'Paying to Play', 250n.

90. Dorson, 'Folklore and Fake Lore', 336.

91. Hartland, 'The Science of Folk-Lore', 117, quoted by Dorson in Dorson, 'Folklore in the Modern World', 23.

92. Buccitelli, 'Paying to Play'.

93. Dundes, 'Nationalistic Inferiority Complexes and the Fabrication of Folklore', 15.

94. Ibid., 10.

95. Ibid., 15.

96. Yolen, 'Folklore vs. Fakelore, the Epic Battle', 56.

97. Dundes, 'Nationalistic Inferiority Complexes and the Fabrication of Folklore', 15.

CHAPTER 7

UNLOCKING LOVE

Controversy and Heritage

Seventy-two tonnes. This is the estimated weight of the love-locks removed from Paris's Pont des Arts and Pont de l'Archevêché bridges in 2015.[1] To put this into context, the average African elephant weighs between 2.5 and 7 tonnes; so more than ten elephants' combined weight worth of love-locks. This demonstrates two things. Firstly, the immense popularity of the custom, as has been attested to throughout this book: how many people must have participated in love-locking on just those two bridges in order to reach such a vast weight? And secondly, not all love-locks stay locked.

As popular as this custom undoubtedly is, it is also extremely unpopular. I would go so far as to claim love-locking the most widely polarising folk custom today, with people from a diverse range of cultures and backgrounds expressing vehement opinions on it. The bulk of this book has been dedicated to those in favour of the custom: the individuals who choose to participate in it; the writers who incorporate it into their works; the local authorities who integrate it into their identity of place; and the businesses who capitalise on it. This chapter turns to the other side of the debate, to those who oppose the custom, exploring who these individuals and groups are, why they take this stance and what methods they employ. And by tracing the biographies of the love-locks that find themselves removed, this chapter will also consider the contested heritage status of love-locking and what this reveals about our perceptions of heritage 'value'.

As we will be engaging with 'heritage' throughout this chapter, a brief note is needed on how I am approaching a term that seems to elude tight definition, with Peter Larkham observing that heritage is 'all things to all people'.[2] For the purposes of this chapter, an understanding of what heritage actually is stems from the mission of the UN Educational, Scientific and Cultural Organization (UNESCO), whose 1994 'Global Strategy for a Representative, Balanced and

Credible World Heritage List' strove to 'recognize and protect sites that are outstanding demonstrations of human coexistence with the land as well as human interactions, cultural coexistence, spirituality and creative expression'.[3] Therefore to examine where the custom of love-locking sits within our conceptions of heritage, this chapter will consider whether there has been recognition of the practice – and tangible evidence of it in the form of love-lock assemblages – as an outstanding demonstration of human interactions, cultural coexistence, spirituality and creative expression and whether it is protected as such.

Contesting the Custom

The previous chapter outlined the variety of places worldwide that encourage love-locking. This is primarily for commercial reasons – not just for the economic value of selling padlocks on site but also to incorporate the custom into the site's identity. However, it is equally common to find places – often already well-established tourist destinations – that discourage the practice. Florence, Italy, appears to have been the first. In 2006, an article in *Italy Magazine* described how 5,500 love-locks had been removed from the Ponte Vecchio by city officials, following the decision to criminalise the practice. A sign was erected on the bridge stating in both Italian and English, 'IT'S NOT ALLOWED TO PUT LOCKS ON THE RAILING as it is ruled by the Rule of Municipal Police article 112 Fine Euro 50.' The council's cultural affairs chief Simone Siliani is quoted as explaining, 'As well as the aesthetic problem, these locks scratch and dent the metal,'[4] citing the two main reasons referred to by later anti-love-lock campaigners: aesthetics and structural damage. These reasons are discussed further below.

Florence may have been the first, but many other cities were soon following. For example, in 2007, Rome's Mayor Walter Vetroni introduced fines for anyone caught attaching a love-lock to the Ponte Milvio, reportedly wanting to 'free' one of the city's oldest monuments from the custom.[5] Signs began appearing at other locations worldwide, prohibiting the deposition of padlocks. 'All Padlocks fastened to this fence will be cut off and disposed of,' warns a sign on Blackpool's North Pier; while 'NO LOCKS FINE $100' declares another on New York's Brooklyn Bridge.

Although such signs, bans and threats of fines may discourage some potential depositors, they did not – and still do not – put a stop to the practice. Love-locks were still present along Blackpool's North Pier, on the railings on Ponte Vecchio and along Brooklyn Bridge in blatant defiance of the prohibitions. And so, many local authorities resort to love-lock culls, either removing them discretely and periodically, such as on Dublin's Ha'penny Bridge, or in one mass cull. The latter occurred in Melbourne in 2015, when around 20,000 love-locks were removed from Southbank Bridge, and then a mere month later in Paris, when more than one million love-locks were bolt-cut from the Pont des Arts.[6] As was outlined in *Chapter Four: Locking Love*, this has also been occurring in the UK, with love-locks removed from Leeds's Centenary Bridge in 2016 and Newcastle's High Level Bridge in 2019.

Such anti-love-lock campaigns are not, however, just led by city officials. In Paris, two US citizens living in the French capital, Lisa Anselmo and Lisa Taylor Huff, founded the 'No Love Locks' campaign in January 2014, dubbing love-locks a 'destructive force'. Their mission mantra, as stated on the website, is 'Free Your Love. Save Our Bridges', and on their Facebook page, they explain that:

> No Love Locks is a grass-roots effort to create awareness of the damage to cultural heritage sites by the 'love locks' trend . . . over 1 million locks now weigh the city down, putting the previous heritage of Paris at risk, and creating safety issues for the public, as well as pollution in the Seine from discarded keys.[7]

In March 2014, Anselmo and Taylor Huff launched a successful online petition for a citywide ban of love-locks. The fact that 10,963 people signed this petition demonstrates the high level of support it received.[8] Under 'Reasons for signing', the petitioners offered a range of motivators: 'Because tacky doesn't belong in Paris'; 'Because being in love doesn't give you permission to deface beautiful things'; 'Such a shame to ruin the beautiful Paris bridges with the heavy and unsightly locks'; 'This is true vandalism. It should be punished'; 'Paris is a world treasure! This selfish nonsense has to be stopped!'[9]

Similarly in Venice, local writer Alberto Toso Fei instigated the 'Unlock Your Love' campaign in 2014,[10] while in Bristol, UK, local resident Edward Nougat (a pseudonym) fronted an online crowdfunding crusade to 'Lose the Locks' on Pero's Bridge.[11] The aim was to raise enough money to purchase six bolt-cutters so that a team could remove them, but Nougat also wanted to ensure that public opinion was on his side: 'it'd be very curmudgeonly to just make that unilateral decision about things which have genuine meaning to people,' he explained.[12] When asked why he had founded this campaign, he listed a number of reasons: 'They're ugly'; 'They can damage the bridge'; 'Personal opinion, but I find them extremely tacky (lots of the locks are Wilko's branded . . . I mean, expressing your love with a Wilko's padlock? Seriously?)'. The crowdfunding campaign was ultimately unsuccessful, but Nougat estimated that 75 per cent of the reactions to it were positive, with only about 5 per cent of people speaking out against the removal of love-locks.

Reactions to the love-lock custom have been particularly negative in Middle Eastern countries, where few assemblages have grown. Granted, one love-lock bridge (or 'Promise Bridge') purposefully set up in The Yard, a contemporary development in Dubai, in 2018 has proven popular, with an estimated 4,000 locks added in its first month. In March 2018, Sheikh Mohammed bin Rashid Al Maktoum, Vice President of the United Arab Emirates and ruler of Dubai, was photographed seemingly admiring the assemblage. However, elsewhere in the Middle East, the custom has proved less popular.[13]

In 2017, love-locks were quickly removed from the corniche in Jeddah, Saudi Arabia, by authorities 'amid complaints that they are the work of "infidels" copying the West',[14] while in the southern Iraqi province of Dhi Qar, officials reacted negatively to a single love-lock bearing the initials 'H K', appearing on the Bridge of Civilizations in 2017. It was immediately removed, and *Iraqi News* recorded the response of Kadhim al-Obeidi, a civil society activist: 'This exotic phenomenon, which was imported from France, does not suit us as an Islamic society. The beautiful bridge was deformed by one lover, so what happens if his action exacerbates and more lovers show up? . . . Love is at the heart, and not in locks.'[15]

Elsewhere in Iraq, negative reactions have even proven dangerous. In 2015, Ayman Karim, a 26-year-old engineer from Basra, implemented a love-lock bridge on Basra's waterfront, inspired by a new relationship. With permission from local authorities, he attached wire mesh to the sides of the bridge and officially 'launched' the love-lock bridge in September 2015. *The Washington Post* quotes the engineer as saying, 'We were living in the dark [speaking of war-torn Basra] . . . We needed a point of light to make people happy. I was happy, and I wanted to share my love with everyone.' The custom quickly became popular in the city – but with that popularity came backlash. The engineer and his family began receiving death threats, warning them to stay away from the bridge, and one day some Shiite militias removed the locks and threw them into the water below.[16] Perhaps some of the negative reactions stem from the religious nature of the custom of attaching padlocks at shrines and mosques, as detailed in *Chapter Five: Symbolising Love.*

Unlocking the Love-Lock

In the Middle East, reasons behind different groups' negative reactions to the love-lock custom are very context specific: it does not fit within some people's religious or political ideals. However, in the majority of other cases worldwide, the reasons cited are concern for the structural integrity of the bridge or other public structure, and/or the aesthetics of the site. The former is an objective (and objectively legitimate) reason to disapprove of and discourage the custom. There have, after all, been cases of love-lock assemblages damaging bridges, with Paris's Pont des Arts being the most well-known example. On 8 June 2014, a section of the mesh along the footbridge collapsed under the weight of the love-locks, an event that gave the No Love Locks campaign greater impetus and ultimately led to the removal of over one million locks.[17]

The Paris case led to concerns at other sites. Love-locks were removed from a footbridge at the Falls of Feugh, Aberdeenshire, for example, following the Pont des Arts damage.[18] In Chicago, love-locks are systematically removed from their movable downtown bridges: Pete Scales, spokesman for the transportation department, explains, 'It's not for a lack of sentiment, but simply because it's a public safety issue. Our bridges are regularly lifted for boat traffic, and we can't vouch for the security of any of these locks, which are sometimes quite heavy.'[19] In another case, bridge engineers were concerned that the love-locks on the Centenary Bridge in Leeds were increasing the rate of rust on the tensioned galvanised steel cables, which form part of the footbridge parapets. There was also concern that some people were attaching their locks to multiple cables; the locks would consequently hold the cables together, creating gaps large enough for young children to climb through. In such cases, structural integrity and people's safety are deemed higher priorities than the public's freedom of ritual expression.

However, aesthetics is more often cited as a reason to prohibit the practice than safety, and protestors are more likely to show concern about the aesthetics of a historic bridge or a bridge of heritage. Many comments about Paris's bridges focus on this aspect; as the No Love Locks campaign stresses, their efforts are 'mainly focused on protecting the architectural heritage of Paris ... [their aim being to] reclaim the historic bridges and beautiful river views that have been lost due to "love locks"'.[20] Bruno Julliard, Paris's Deputy Mayor, is quoted as saying 'They spoil the aesthetics of the bridge.'[21] A paper in *The Journal* describes love-locks as being an 'eyesore' on Dublin's Ha'penny Bridge, which dates to 1816, and cites this as one of the reasons for their removal.[22] The same expression was used with regard to the love-locks on the Rialto Bridge and the Ponte dell'Accademia in Venice,[23] while in Prague, Kateřina Bártová, who works for the tourism board, has been quoted as saying: 'We get questions from locals who aren't happy to see so many locks on the bridges, gates and other landmarks around Prague.'[24]

As well as local authorities and local residents, members of the media have likewise railed against the aesthetics of the love-lock custom. On the *France Revisited* news website, love-locks are described as having grown 'like cancer',[25] while *The Guardian*'s Jonathan Jones has been particularly disparaging, lamenting that the world's cities are suffering from a 'plague of padlocks', with 'Some of Europe's most beautiful bridges ... being destroyed by rusting clumps of metal', which he describes as 'visually repulsive'. 'Why', Jones asks, 'spoil that perfect moment by desecrating a bridge that is centuries old and laden with the atmosphere of time?'[26]

The Love-Lock as 'Renegade Ornament'

Clearly, with millions of love-locks deposited worldwide, not everyone agrees with Jonathan Jones. And even with the bans, signs, threats of fines and mass removals people are still depositing their love-locks today. Paris officials continue to tackle the custom, despite having replaced the metal mesh on Pont des Arts with acrylic glass panels; people simply moved to other bridges.[27] On High Level

Bridge in Newcastle, love-locks began appearing mere weeks after 5,000 of them were removed in April 2019, in defiance of the signs prohibiting the practice and warning depositors that all locks will be removed.[28] And it is not only depositors who are acting in opposition to the prohibitions.

In 2005, Florence local authorities' criminalisation of the deposition of love-locks on the Ponte Vecchio incited countrywide controversy, sparking what are known as the 'fine wars'. In 2008, right-wing politician Giovanni Donzelli proposed the creation of an alternative monument upon which people could deposit their love-locks, as part of his local elections campaign. In 2007, another political war was sparked in Rome when left-wing Mayor Walter Veltroni introduced fines for people caught depositing love-locks on the Ponte Milvio. Members of his right-wing opponents Forza Italia and the National Alliance accused him of 'trampling lovers' rights'.[29] Granted, these examples of resistance were probably motivated more by political agendas than genuine sentiment, but they still demonstrate the highly contested nature of the love-lock.

Cynthia Hammond has explored the 'multiple tensions' surrounding the love-lock fence in Pécs, Hungary, which was instigated in the 1980s. Hammond believes that 'the locks are a crucial trace of a nexus of oppositional stances in the city, rehearsing, by their very presence and multiple axes of significance, the public-ness of the spaces of Pécs' historic core'.[30] These oppositional stances are understood within the historic context of the Soviet control over the city at the time the love-locks – viewed by Hammond as a political statement of defiance – first began to emerge. However, as has been demonstrated so far in this chapter, even when there is no political agenda behind the custom, love-locks are still contested objects.

When a person deposits a love-lock at a site that prohibits the practice, they are engaging in – to use more of Hammond's words – 'spatial dissent', the love-locks themselves becoming 'renegade ornaments'.[31] This hinges on contrasting perceptions of the love-lock as a ritually deposited token of love or as a piece of vandalism. 'Venice doesn't need your garbage' were the words written on leaflets passed out in Venice as part of the Unlock Your Love campaign, with its founder Alberto Toso Fei explaining that those who deposit love-locks are 'committing an act of vandalism'.[32] The same language was used in Paris's No Love Locks campaign: 'However well-intentioned the locks might be, in fact they are acts of vandalism.'[33] Furthermore, Jonathan Jones compares love-locking to leaving litter at mountain peaks and on beaches: 'It is a wanton and arrogant act of destruction. It is littering.'[34] This calls to mind the term 'ritual litter', often quite indiscriminately applied to contemporary ritual deposits (see below).[35]

In 2013, a *BBC News* article questioned, 'is the growing trend for love locks really a thoughtless act of vandalism, or just a harmless expression of love?'[36] In truth, though, they can be both. Expressions of love and vandalism are not mutually exclusive. Love-hearts, initials and declarations of 'forever' have a long history of being carved into trees, scratched into school desks and spray-painted onto buildings. It cannot be denied that these are expressions of love. However, they can also be viewed as examples of renegade behaviour, in that they defy an authority that prohibits such actions. Whether or not they can also be classified as vandalism, defined by the *Oxford English Dictionary* as 'ruthless destruction or spoiling of anything beautiful or venerable',[37] is entirely subjective.

Any custom is subject to multiple personal interpretations, even amongst its participants. This is evident in numerous anthropological studies in which multiple practitioners have been shown to observe a custom or perform a ritual in homogeneity and yet interpret that ritual and the symbolisms it employs quite differently. To quote anthropologist James Fernandez, there is inevitable 'variation in the individual interpretation of commonly experienced phenomena'.[38] And how we dub a custom is equally dependent upon the interpreter: their personality, age, gender and cultural and educational backgrounds amidst myriad other factors.[39] This subjectivity equates to multiplicity: the love-lock is not a romantic token *or* vandalism but both simultaneously, because it is being interpreted as both simultaneously by the thousands of people – millions even – who have contemplated the custom, even if only in passing.

The Contested Landscape

Just as love-locks are contested objects, love-lock sites have become contested landscapes. To some, a bridge covered with padlocks is a 'love-lock bridge'; a romantic landscape and a destination in its own right by virtue of the ritual assemblage. As Richter and Pfeiffer-Kloss claim, the collective ritual engagement with love-lock bridges grants them the status of monuments.[40] To others, it may be a bridge already with history behind it, one that is already granted the status of a monument, its aesthetics now spoiled by the 'eyesore' of love-locks and its structural integrity threatened by their weight. Unsurprisingly, the more vocal debates tend to surround love-locks on heritage bridges: those that are considered significant landscape features because of their age, history or design, such as the Pont des Arts or Dublin's Ha'penny Bridge. More interestingly, far more debate seems to focus on love-lock bridges than other structures, such as fences or gates. This may tell us something about people's perceptions of bridges, to which, as Lucy Blakstad notes, people tend to respond on an emotional level. Bridges 'have a strange power over us', which Blakstad attributes to the symbolism of unification and separation encapsulated in these structures, already explored in *Chapter Five: Symbolising Love.*[41]

Blakstad explores the shock, grief and anger surrounding the destruction of the Mostar Bridge in Bosnia-Herzegovina. This iconic sixteenth-century Ottoman bridge in the city of Mostar had arched over the Neretva River for 427 years when it was destroyed in 1993 by Croat paramilitary forces during the Croat–Bosniak War. Local residents of Mostar explained to Blakstad that 'Fifty year old men were crying like little children' at the bridge's destruction. 'I could somehow accept that my mother and my husband had been killed in the war. People die. They disappear', said one woman, who had lived through the war, 'but not the Old Bridge which was built in 1566 and had been here for so many years'. 'I felt like a part of my body had been torn off,' explained another Mostarian. 'Men, women and children were killed and raped in the war. But to consciously destroy the Old Bridge which was sacred to all Mostarians. It hurts us to the core.'[42]

Such impassioned responses to the destruction of this bridge highlight our emotional connections to these structures that span our rivers and unite otherwise separate spaces. Bridges often stand at the heart of cities, both geographically and emotionally speaking. It is unsurprising, therefore, that the strongest reactions to the love-lock custom would be motivated by a protectiveness of a city's bridge, both for its aesthetics and its longevity. But the bridge, like any other landscape feature, is polysemic: it is, to use Barbara Bender's words, 'something political, dynamic, and contested, something constantly open to renegotiation'.[43] There is a plurality to what people want from these sites, and therefore an inevitable plurality to how people react to a custom that transforms a bridge into a 'love-lock bridge'.

When an assemblage of love-locks threatens the structural integrity of a bridge, the decision to ban the custom and remove the locks can be seen as an objective one. However, as we have seen in the various campaigns against the practice, descriptions of love-lock assemblages have included the terms: 'ugly', 'tacky', 'unsightly', 'eyesore', 'vandalism' and 'visually repulsive'. These are all subjective words, based on personal preferences rather than fact. One person's 'ugly' is another person's 'beautiful'. This subjectivity is precisely what makes considerations of heritage 'value' so complex.

Erasing a Layer

It has long been recognised that landscapes, and our cultural perceptions of them, are mutable. They have biographies that are complex, non-linear and inalienable to the ebbs and flows of society. Since archaeologist Osbert Crawford first applied the palimpsest metaphor to the 'surface of England', as a 'document that has been written on and erased over and over again', historians, archaeologists and geographers alike have been employing a variety of imagery to illustrate the complex nature of people's relationships with their perpetually changing environments.[44] In the 1970s, geographer Donald Meinig described the landscape as an 'accumulation . . . an enormously rich store of data about the peoples and societies which have created it'.[45] In the 1990s, Simon Schama characterised it as strata of myth and memory, and more recently Alexandra Walsham presented it as 'a porous surface upon which each generation inscribes its own values and preoccupations without ever being able to erase entirely those of the preceding one'.[46]

So, the landscape – whether rural or urban – is a palimpsest. It consists of layers of meaning and memory created and built upon by the generations of people who have lived and moved within it. And, approve or disapprove of them, love-locks are one such layer of meaning and memory. With the ebb and flow of society, this layer will eventually and inevitably be built upon and semi-obscured by new layers, but to remove and dispose of a love-lock assemblage is to delete that layer. It is erasing the tangible evidence of how millions of people have engaged with these landscapes; it is erasing a part of those landscapes' biographies.

This is of course not unusual. Today, such erasures occur frequently for economic reasons, for the purposes of development: when one building is demolished to make space for another. However, erasures are taken more seriously when their aim is to remove a layer of cultural or ritual activity, such as with iconoclasm. This is what was happening when, during the Reformation, attempts were made to remove the structures and symbols of medieval Catholicism from the British and Irish landscapes: a 'holocaust' of hallowed artefacts and buildings, to use Alexandra Walsham's expression.[47] This is what was happening in 2001 when the Taliban destroyed the sixth-century Buddhas of Bamyan in Afghanistan, wilfully 'jettisoning [the statues] from the nation's construction of contemporary identity', to quote Lynn Meskell.[48]

In these cases, many of us look back at these erasures with a sense of loss. Regarding the destruction of the Bamyan Buddhas, the then Director General of UNESCO Koichiro Matsuura described it as a 'crime against culture. It is abominable to witness the cold and calculated destruction of cultural properties which were the heritage of the Afghan people, and, indeed, of the whole of humanity'.[49] We are, on the whole, indignant and angry that these layers of cultural and ritual activity were erased because we see truth in the words of the 1954 Hague Convention: that 'damage to cultural property belonging to any people whatsoever means damage to the cultural heritage of all mankind, since each peoples makes its own contribution to the culture of the world'.[50] Love-locks are an indisputable layer of cultural heritage, meaning, memory and ritual activity – practised by millions. They form part of the palimpsest of a landscape, as pointed out by Simon Sleight in his work on 'vernacular' memorials.[51] With this in mind, therefore, why is the removal of love-lock assemblages any different?

Ritual 'Litter'

Love-locks suffer from the 'ritual litter' mentality. This is a term applied to contemporary ritual deposits, which receive relatively little attention from the heritage industry. For example, Robert Wallis and Jenny Blain employ 'ritual litter' to encompass objects ranging from crystals to tea-light holders deposited by Neo-Pagans at historical sites.[52] Kathryn Rountree notes the derogatory connotations of the term, claiming that those who tend to apply it to contemporary deposits are 'those inclined to disapprove of their deposition'.[53] It is, after all, an unambiguously belittling term, 'litter' being defined as 'rubbish' and a 'disorderly accumulation of things lying about'.[54] And certainly Phillip Lucas demonstrates this mentality by describing how modern-day offerings at megalithic sites in Western Europe 'can become piles of trash over time'.[55]

There are three primary reasons behind the equation of contemporary ritual deposits such as love-locks to 'litter'. Firstly, their unsanctioned nature. Rountree observes that a candle or a written prayer may be deposited in a church without being designated 'ritual litter', a contrast she attributes to the sanctioned statuses of churches as 'sacred places' and of officially allocated receptacles for deposits such as prayer and collection boxes and votive candle stands.[56] Another comparison would be the removal of graffiti in contrast to the protected status of official murals, though both may demonstrate equal artistic merit. The unsanctioned – in some cases, explicitly prohibited – deposition of love-locks is certainly a primary factor in their removal, with the consequent erasure of a layer of meaning and memory from the landscape.

The second reason behind objects such as love-locks being dubbed ritual litter is the nature of many of their depositors: tourists, who I would estimate account for roughly half of love-lock depositors. As Dean MacCannell noted wryly in the 1970s, 'It is intellectually chic nowadays to deride tourists,' while more recently Edward Bruner added that 'being a tourist is deprecated by almost everyone. Even tourists themselves belittle tourism as it connotes something commercial, tacky, and superficial'.[57] Love-locking suffers from these perceptions. In 2007, *The New York Times* reported on how many Italians felt that with the growing popularity of love-locking the custom 'may soon be as touristy as flipping a coin into the Trevi Fountain' and that 'the ritual has lost its appeal and gotten touristy'.[58] Here, 'touristy' is used as an unambiguously derogatory adjective, while many of the anti-love-lock campaigns home in on the non-local nature of the custom: Paris's No Love Locks campaign, for example, attacks love-locking for not being a 'Parisian tradition; they are a recent tourist trend'.[59]

Within heritage, Lois Turner and John Ash observe, as wryly as MacCannell, that 'Tourism is, everywhere, the enemy of authenticity and cultural identity.' Certainly, scholars have a history of being scathing towards 'tourist folklore', quite dismissively designating it 'fakelore'.[60] Fortunately, many scholars now reject the structuralism of tourist versus local and the equation of the tourist with inauthenticity, crass consumption and cultural destruction.[61] As was also argued in *Chapter One: Dating Love*, tourists are a folk-group who perform culture, co-producing as well as co-consuming, and a ritual is no less a ritual if performed by non-local residents. The fact that many love-lockers are tourists should not therefore negate the cultural significance – or heritage 'value' – of the custom and nor should the custom's global nature, with John Storey asserting that folk culture does not need to be bounded by a locality in order to be 'authentic': 'The movement of people and commodities around the globe, bringing the global into the local, clearly challenges the idea that locality can fix the boundaries of a culture.'[62]

The third reason behind the love-lock's perceived lack of heritage 'value' is its contemporaneity. I believe this is the primary factor behind some of the resistance I have encountered towards my own research. In response to a piece on love-locks I had published in *The Conversation*, an academic online news platform, negative comments included: 'This paper is about a nonsensical concept', 'frivolous nonsense' and 'This stupid craze is not only a huge waste of metal (the padlocks) — it also unneccessarily [sic] damages expensive public infrastructure . . .'[63] Would I have received such criticism for studying prehistoric or historic ritual deposits? Unlikely.

The main factor distinguishing love-locks from other ritual objects such as Bronze Age river deposits, votive offerings on the Athenian acropolis or Roman coin hoards is age. Age authenticates; it 'lends it status' and value.[64] To repeat Sefryn Penrose, quoted above, 'the older something becomes the more important it tends to be thought'.[65] This applies to customs, which are viewed by some as only interesting insofar as they are seasoned; insofar as they are 'survivals' from earlier times.[66] Troy Lovata, examining arborglyphs (tree graffiti), notes the heritage value given to historic examples (which are worthy of study and preservation) in contrast to contemporary graffiti, which is prohibited: people, Lovata notes, 'place value on the past while creating a firm disjuncture between past and present behaviors'.[67] This also applies to landscapes and monuments such as the love-lock bridge. Tellingly – and ironically – Hoskins, who wrote of the English language as a perpetually changing palimpsest, opined that 'especially since the year 1914, every single change in the English landscape has either uglified it or destroyed its meaning, or both'.[68] Had he been writing now, he probably would not have approved of the contemporary love-lock bridge.

However, as was demonstrated in *Chapter Three: Excavating Love*, a not insignificant number of scholars have turned their attention to the archaeological value of contemporary ritual deposits,[69] while in recent years, heritage professionals have also begun to challenge the time-centred criterion for heritage 'value'. Contemporary archaeologist and heritage specialist John Schofield has posed the following questions:

> Is there consensus on what we allow into the heritage 'club' and what are the rules of admission? What do we leave at the door because it is thought to be too new or

too everyday – and often both? How and when should its definition be extended into modern times, a period for which we have an abundance of site types, perceptions, experiences and sources?[70]

UNESCO does specify that 'heritage is our legacy from the past, *what we live with today*, and what we pass on to future generations' (emphases added), while English Heritage are just one organisation that has broadened its definition of 'heritage' to challenge the more dated notion that sites only deserve designated protective status once a respectable amount of time has passed.[71] In the early 2000s they began to advocate progressive forward planning, establishing the 'Change and Creation' programme to address the question of whether aspects of the British landscape from 1950–2000 could be considered part of our 'heritage' and should thus be protected.[72]

'Today's landscapes have the potential to become tomorrow's heritage,' notes Schofield.[73] If we begin to record and preserve the monuments of the twenty-first century now, then we can address our own heritage and legacy while it still survives. Should we not, therefore, be doing more to preserve or at least record love-lock assemblages, which – despite many people's negative perceptions of them – certainly fit UNESCO's definition of a site of world cultural heritage: a site 'of Outstanding Universal Value from the historical, aesthetic, ethnological or anthropological point of view'.[74] Surely these love-lock assemblages, which represent what is probably the most widespread ritual deposit of the twenty-first century, constitute sites of outstanding universal value.

The Heritage of the Custom

Although not (yet) recognised as worthy of protection or preservation by the larger heritage organisations, a significant number of places worldwide are engaging with the heritage of love-locks in a variety of ways. For some local authorities, it is a matter of encouraging a practice that benefits their locale – if not economically then in terms of contributing to a sense of place, with those sites newly marketed as romantic destinations, as was demonstrated in *Chapter Six: Selling Love*. The chain-link fence especially installed to invite love-locks in Lovelock, Nevada, is one obvious example.

For other local authorities, it is a case of renegotiating attitudes towards the custom. Returning again to Hammond, she traces how love-locks in Pécs were initially 'renegade ornaments', defiantly deposited in the 1980s and discouraged until 2003. However, as was demonstrated in the previous chapter, by 2007 they had been incorporated into the city's official image. This renegotiation of Pécs's identity, and of what structures within the city contributed to that identity, came amidst their (successful) bid for the title of European Capital of Culture 2010, and tellingly a photograph of the love-lock fence featured in the city's Capital of Culture publication *Borderless City*. 'The message', interprets Hammond, 'is that the locks are no longer an embarrassing oddity, but are now respected and treasured, like the buildings that surround them'.[75]

For many other local authorities, however, love-locks do constitute a problem, for the reasons outlined above. But, despite the fact that in most cases this is a new and unfamiliar problem to be faced with, they do engage with the heritage of the custom by tackling it in a variety of innovative ways. Dispersion is one strategy that has been adopted and adapted to the love-lock 'problem', whereby to alleviate physical pressures of deposition at one site management strategically redirect people's attention to an alternative site.[76] This method is employed when local authorities are concerned for the structural integrity of a bridge but do not wish to stymie the love-locking custom, and so they deflect depositors' ritual attention to a different structure. This has occurred at a number of different locations worldwide, demonstrating a widespread recognition of the value – or perhaps the indomitability – of the custom.

Structures and sculptures have been designed specifically for the purpose of dispersion. In Kobe, Japan, when love-locks were removed from Venus Bridge in 2005, a large metallic dome-like sculpture was installed on Venus Terrace, with cables ideally sized for accommodating love-locks. At the Nomasaki Lighthouse, also in Japan, a heart-shaped monument was built in an attempt to encourage depositors to attach their love-locks there instead of to the lighthouse itself.[77] In Los Gatos, California, when local authorities began prohibiting love-locking on the Main Street Bridge, they made an arrangement with the Los Gatos Museum of Art to provide a 'love-lock fence', which launched on Valentine's Day 2013.[78] In Vancouver, steel sculptures of four couples embracing under umbrellas, entitled 'Love in the Rain', were installed in Queen Elizabeth Park in 2016 – along with a drop box for padlock keys – to deflect love-locking from Burrard Bridge.[79] In Toronto, a nine-metre long installation spelling out the word 'love' was erected in 2014 in the Distillery District to discourage love-lock deposition on the Humber Bridge.[80] And in Moscow, several iron trees span the Luzhkov Bridge, densely populated with love-locks and keeping the bridge's railings relatively love-lock free (Illustration 7.1.).

In the UK, father–daughter team Ken and Caroline Massingham have designed a 'Love Lock Tree' that they are selling as self-assembly kits and promoting as a potential dispersal strategy for local authorities or land managers. This is a sculpture of cylindrical shape with eight stainless steel profile tubes, high enough to walk inside, surrounded by inner and outer stainless steel mesh display panels, which would accommodate love-locks (Illustration 7.2.). As Ken is an engineer, much pragmatic thought went into the sculpture's design: it is structurally safe, strong, durable in adverse weather, able to accommodate an estimated

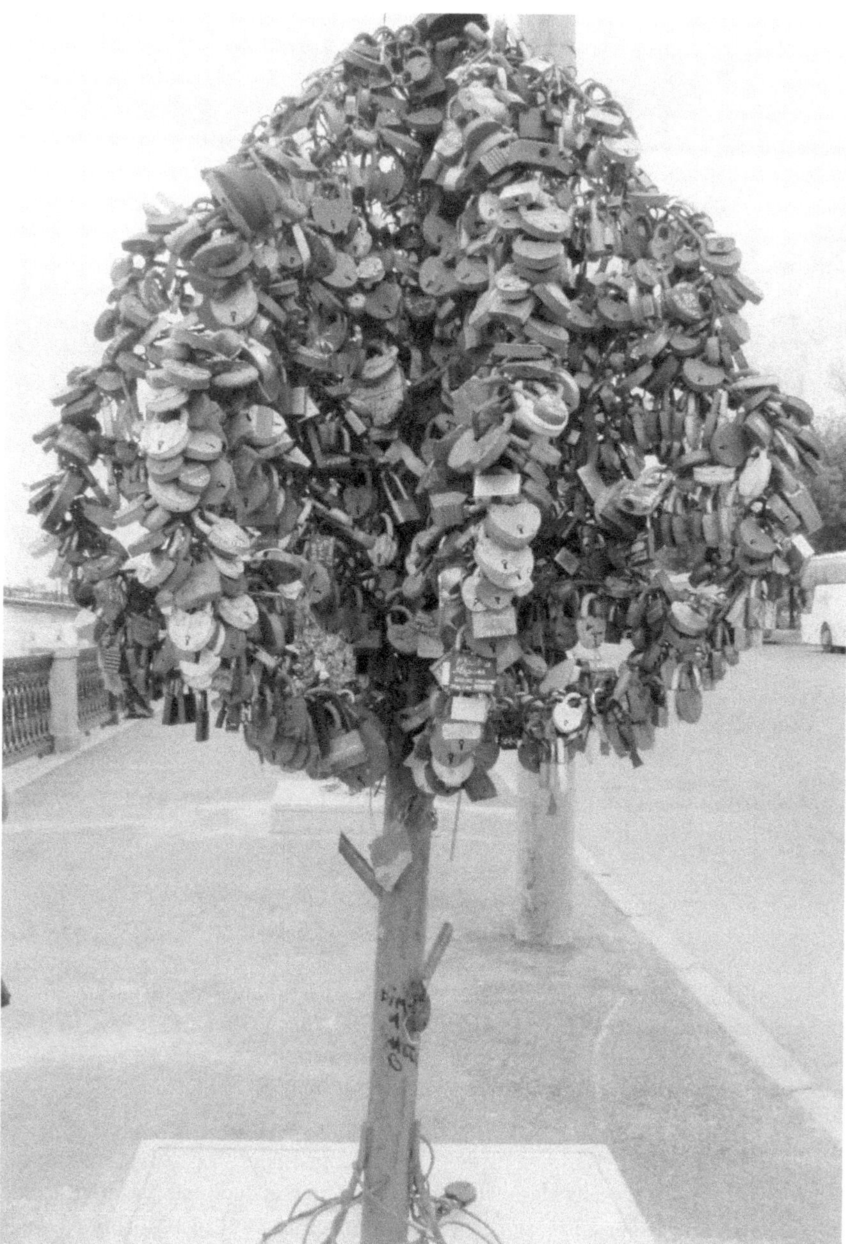

Illustration 7.1. One of several heavily populated love-lock trees on and close to Luzhkov Bridge, Moscow. Photograph by the author.

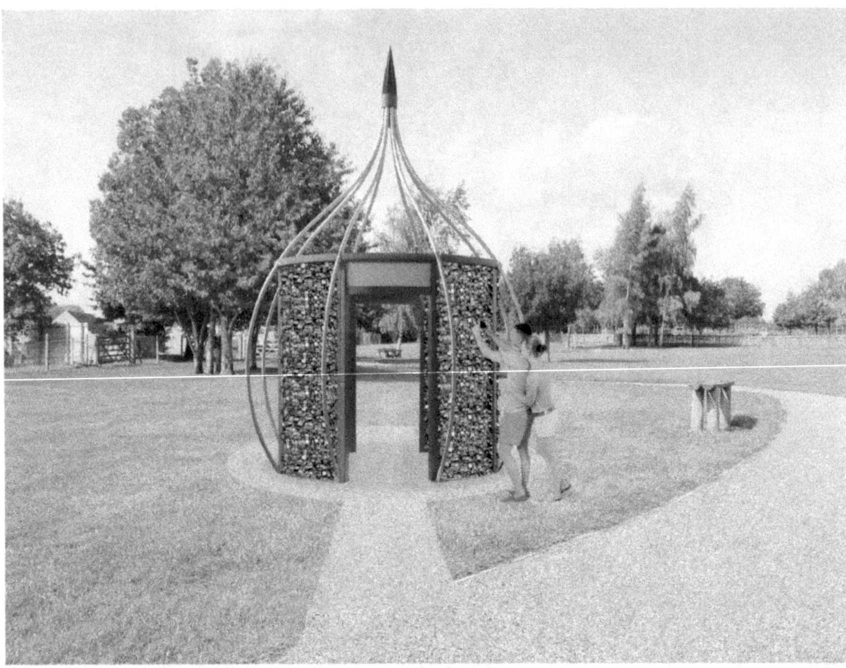

Illustration 7.2. A digitally populated large-size 'Love Lock Tree'. Image courtesy of Love Lock Trees: www.lovelocktrees.com.

26,000 love-locks, child-friendly and accessible to wheelchair users.[81] In their brochure, they explain:

> We took this potential love lock issue and came up with a solution and, better still, an opportunity. We conceived, designed and developed the 'Love Lock Tree', a permanent, universal tree shaped structure, for the sole purpose of hanging locks onto, so that tourists can still place their love locks at these sites without damaging the very thing that makes these places special . . . Love them or hate them, love locks displayed properly are a recognised and impressive attraction for tourists. We can help you to make the most of this growing phenomenon.[82]

Some local authorities have attempted to adapt the custom, encouraging romantic gestures on their bridges while discouraging the deposition of love-locks. For instance, in 2014, City Hall in Paris implemented a 'Love Without Locks' social media campaign, with public notices in key spots inviting lovers to take 'selfies' on the city's bridges and post them to Twitter, Facebook and Instagram with the hashtag #lovewithoutlocks. Posts with this hashtag feed onto the 'Love Without Locks' website.[83] A similar attempt was made at the Falls of Feugh, Aberdeenshire. To deflect love-locking attention from a footbridge, the local council commissioned a wooden sculpture adorned with a heart and two salmon and encouraged lovers to take 'selfies' in front of this rather than deposit a love-lock.[84] Whether successful or not, such dispersion strategies are engendering a swathe of sculptural art, altering the fabric of these landscapes and producing another layer of meaning and memory.

The Love-Lock as Art Object

There is clearly some engagement with the intangible cultural heritage of love-locking; recognition that even when the custom should be discouraged, people have the right to continue participating in a (perhaps adapted) romantic ritual. There is also engagement with the tangible cultural heritage of the love-lock, as demonstrated by some local authorities' treatment of removed locks. While in some cases when assemblages are bolt-cut from their bridges they are disposed of or recycled, often local authorities give past depositors the opportunity to collect their love-lock. Notices tend to be placed on bridges warning people that the assemblages are going to be removed and inviting the public to contact the local authority if they wish to reclaim theirs. This has happened in Munich, Melbourne, York and Leeds, to name only a few examples, and as was demonstrated in *Chapter Four: Locking Love*, people do go to the effort of collecting their locks.

What is significant for this chapter, however, is that some local authorities go to the effort of making this easy for them. In Leeds, people sent photographs of their love-locks to the bridge engineers, who searched for them while they were being removed from the Centenary Bridge. Once found, they set them aside ready for collection, and in a couple of cases – where the depositors lived further afield – they posted them out. The bridge engineers also permitted me to catalogue all of the removed love-locks, welcoming me enthusiastically to their offices on the outskirts of Leeds, where I compiled a photographic record of over 600 locks (see below).[85] These considerate actions demonstrate a level of respect for the custom, its participants and its recording, the latter having been identified by UNESCO as an important measure in ensuring the viability of intangible cultural heritage.[86]

Although many removed love-locks do find themselves reclaimed by their depositors, most do not. Some local authorities dispose of or recycle those unclaimed locks, and others keep them in storage indefinitely, but there are others who conceive of more creative and altruistic uses for them. Melbourne is a prime example of this. In 2015, around 20,000 love-locks were removed from the Southbank Footbridge (also known as the Evan Walker Bridge) by the City of Melbourne, following concerns that the assemblage was compromising the bridge's structural integrity. Then, innovatively, City of Melbourne began working with arts organisation Craft Victoria to implement the 'Love Locks Project', commissioning five local artists to incorporate the removed assemblage into the creation of new artwork.

Sculptor and bell designer Anton Hasell was one of these artists. Noting in personal communication with me that the brief from City of Melbourne had made it 'clear that the artwork using the locks should be respectful of the loving act', he selected some of the removed locks that were being held in storage and smelted them down, using the metal to create a bell. 'I really loved the idea of the cries and whispers of lovers, in confident intimacy, clasping shut their lock's clasp, and their murmurs being squeezed from the metal of the locks in the form of a bell,' Anton explained. 'The poetry of Lovers with the pitch clarity of a harmonic bell's breath.' This sculpture, he added, worked well within his work ethic of aiming 'to create site experiences with architectures that allow, encourage and celebrate the joy of individuals playing creatively together and building identity based in shared communal activity' (Illustrations 7.3.–7.4.).[87]

Jeweller Elise Sheehan was another of the artists. She recalled that Craft Victoria had requested projects fulfilling key ideas: 'Memorial of love and commitment, Celebrating individuality within the greater community, Embracing spontaneity'. Following this mandate, Elise created two sculptural pieces. The first, entitled 'An Enduring Gesture', was a chain fabricated from the shanks of the locks, starting out thick and dark and gradually becoming thinner and lighter until reconnecting to the beginning. This was intended to symbolise 'that everything can be cyclical and have the ability to remain strengthened or have the ability for a new beginning.' The second piece was entitled 'Heavy Memories',

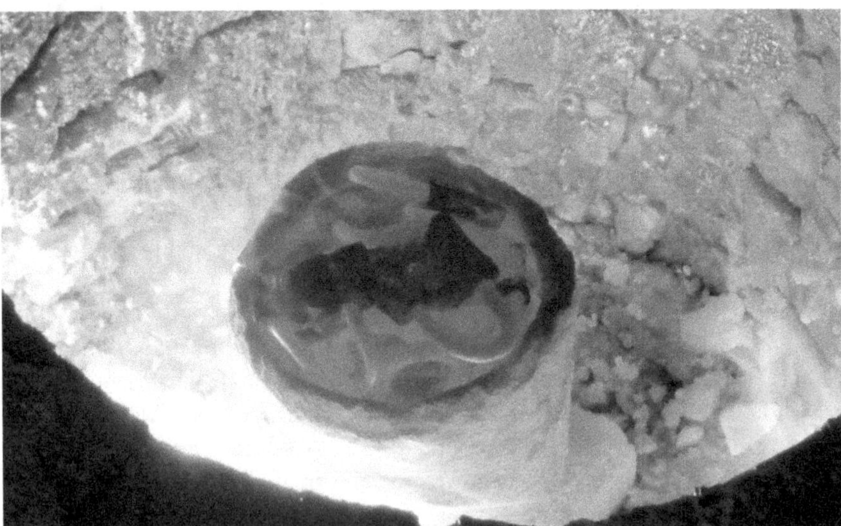

Illustration 7.3. Anton Hasell smelting love-locks to create his bell. Photograph by Dr Anton Hasell Director Australian Bell p/l.

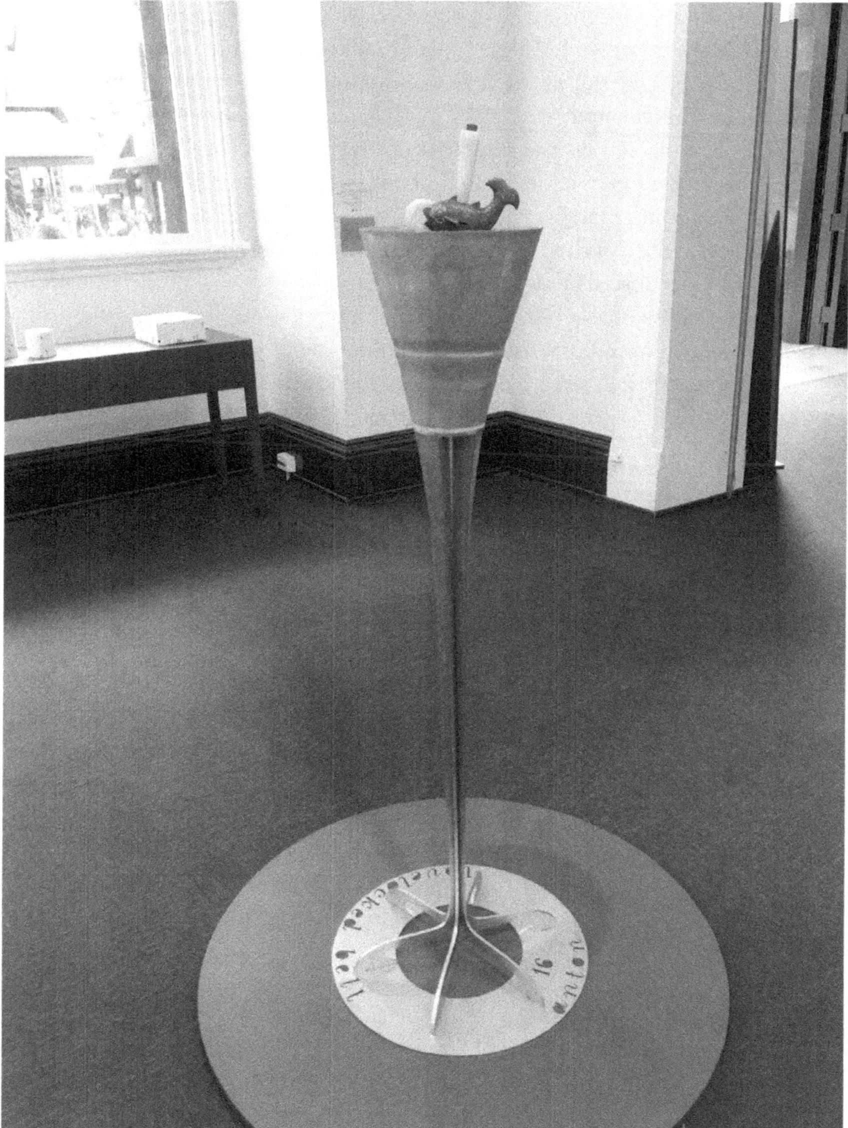

Illustration 7.4. Anton Hasell's Love-Lock Bell. Photograph by Dr Anton Hasell Director Australian Bell p/l.

and for this Elise filed down some of the locks and combined the particles and fragments with plaster to create a solid mass. This piece, she explained, 'acts as a memento for love lost. A catharsis for those who may no longer feel their gesture is relevant or enduring'.[88]

Another jeweller, Katheryn Leopoldseder, was also chosen to work with the love-locks. Katheryn recalled that 'themes of love and inclusiveness were expected to be a part of the finished artwork. And an opportunity for the public to come and interact with the locks in their new form was a very important outcome.' She reflected on the similarity of love-locks to jewellery: 'Jewellery is all about honouring people, and often about our identity in a relational sense. The locks are a similar language.' With this in mind, Katheryn decided to create a large-scale necklace of the locks, drawing on inspiration from the convict coin tradition, whereby inscribed pennies were given as love tokens (Illustration 7.5.). To create the coins of the necklace, she melted down the locks bearing no inscriptions – 'They were unidentifiable, so I didn't feel that I was violating something sacred when they were melted down' – and then selected the locks with interesting engravings to incorporate unaltered into the piece. Reflecting on the

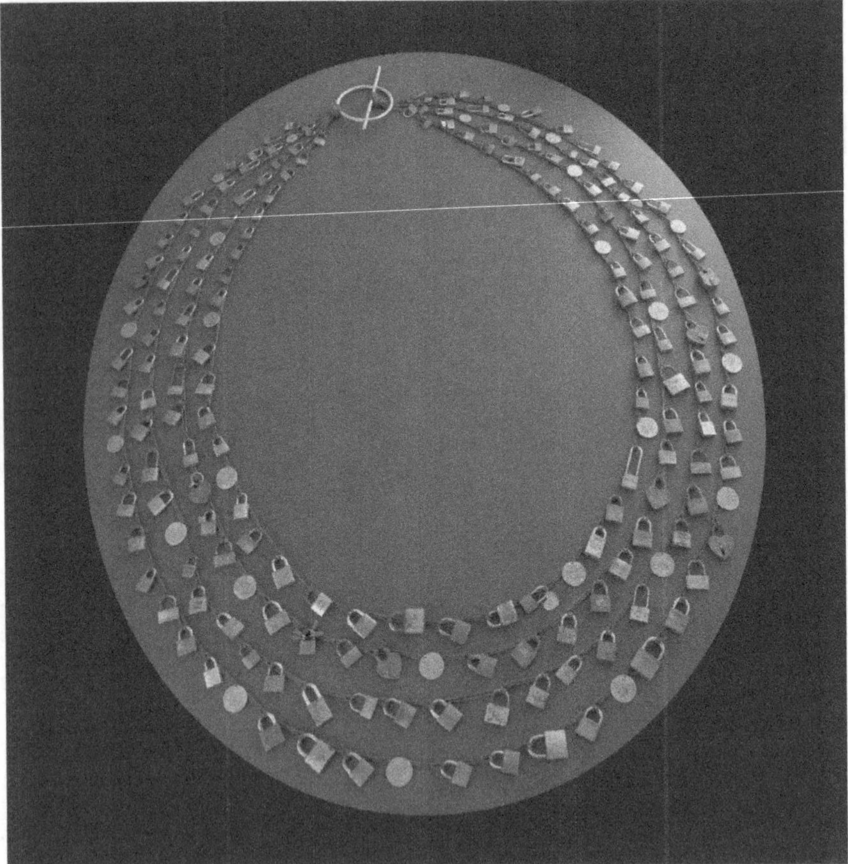

Illustration 7.5. 'Devotion' by Katheryn Leopoldseder, 2016. Materials: repurposed engraved love-locks, cast brass from love-locks, nylon rope. 300 x 250cm. Photograph by Fred Kroh.

project, Katheryn explained, 'I feel more like it completed some ideas that I had been carrying for a long time; about the nature of devotional objects . . . I'm really pleased with how the two streams of the Love Locks and the Convict Coins came together. It brought a distinctly Australian interpretation to the project.'[89]

The other artists drew on their own expertise and sentiments to create diverse and unique pieces. Louiseann King smelted the locks to create a sculpture text piece reading 'Always Forever' and photographer Kirsty Macafee produced a series of porcelain locks. These pieces were then displayed in the City Gallery in August 2016. King's 'Always Forever' sculpture was selected as a permanent piece for the City of Melbourne's collection, while the remaining five were entered into a public lottery. The proceeds raised went to the Lord Mayor's Charitable Fund, and the winners of the lottery acquired the sculptures. The winner of Hasell's bell, Victoria Goodridge, keeps the sculpture in her garden 'where it can be rung by all that pass it . . . The bell is beautiful, sounds magnificent and I just love its history; my own bit of Melbourne's love life!' (Illustration 7.6.)[90]

A similar project was initiated in Paris following the removal of over one million love-locks. Paris City Hall chose a number of the locks – 'We selected the locks that seemed the most beautiful, the ones that were colourful, full of fantasy,' according to auctioneer Mathilde Belcour-Cordelier – and divided them into 150 bunches, which were then mounted on stands made from wood or recycled paving stone. Then, on 13 May 2017, an auction was held at the Crédit Municipal de Paris, which also included fifteen sections of the removed Pont des Arts railings, still adorned with love-locks. The proceeds were earmarked

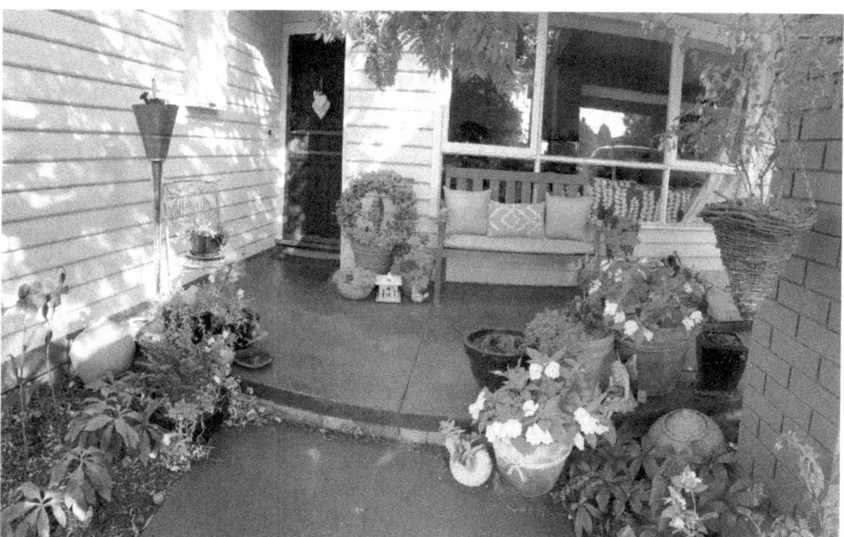

Illustration 7.6. Winner of Hasell's love-lock bell, Victoria Goodridge, keeps the sculpture in her garden. Photograph by Victoria Goodridge.

for three migrant and refugee charities: Solipam, the Salvation Army and Emmaüs Solidarité. The auction was unexpectedly successful, with some of the bunches selling for over €1,000, one of the railings selling for €17,000, and the total amount raised reaching €250,000. First Deputy Mayor of Paris Bruno Juiliard, who organised the auction and admitted he had expected three times less, reflected, 'It is beautiful . . . that declarations of love can be transformed into an act of kindness and humanity towards refugees.'[91]

Returning to the object biographical approach of *Chapter Four: Locking Love*, the biographies of these love-locks have continued, but they have entered new life stages. They have transitioned from ritual deposits to pieces of art, passing out of the possession of the depositor, briefly through the possession of the local authorities and the artists, and into the possession of their new owners, who no doubt value them as pieces of their respective cities' heritage. 'It's a way to have a small souvenir of Paris,' auctioneer Belcour-Cordelier is quoted as saying, while Victoria Goodridge, the winner of the Melbourne love-lock bell, is excited to be 'a part of its love lock history' and to have her 'own bit of Melbourne's love life!'.[92] In this way, the love-lock has become akin to the myriad other fragments of a city taken as souvenirs, as synecdoche of the city as a whole. The Berlin Wall is one notable comparison, with sections of the structure hacked away (or purchased) by local residents and tourists alike, wanting to take home 'fragments of a historical object imbued with historical significance', to use Frederick Baker's words.[93] This is precisely what love-locks are.

In all of the above examples, the prohibition of the love-lock custom has engendered something new. Not only have the tangible locks been physically transformed into artworks but the concepts and emotions behind the custom have been creatively reinterpreted. Particularly in the case of Melbourne, each artist has approached the love-locks via their own expertise and sentiments and then presented them to the public coloured by their own perceptions. Then the public in turn view them differently – no longer renegade objects on bridges but as art, as concept, as valuable (and coveted) pieces of heritage.

The Love-Lock as Curated Artefact

There is another life stage the removed love-lock can enter: that of the curated artefact. This course is far rarer and dependent upon interested researchers and museum curators. An example of this is the Leeds Centenary Bridge assemblage, which I catalogued following its removal. With 600 love-locks arranged in neat columns on a table before me in the Highways and Transportation offices of Leeds City Council, I was struck by the tangibility of their transition from ritual deposit to what is essentially an excavated artefact (Illustration 7.7.). They lay flat on the table's surface, peculiarly lifeless now that they no longer hung in

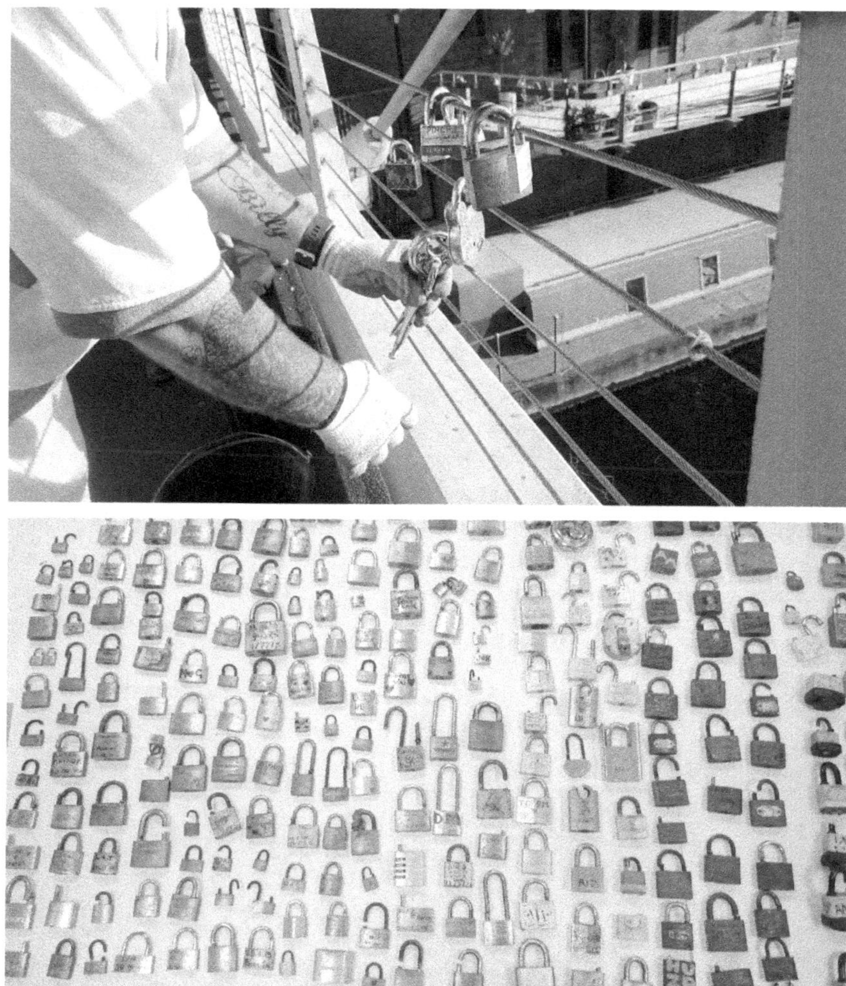

Illustration 7.7. Cataloguing the removed Leeds Centenary Bridge love-locks. Photographs by the author.

dense clusters from the bridge; now that they were separated by miles from their respective keys, no doubt still resting on the bed of the River Aire. Their shackles were broken, evidence of their removal. I aligned each one with a photography scale before taking a picture, a very different experience to the shots taken by depositors of their love-locks in situ to be shared on social media (compare to Illustrations 4.4.–4.5. above). Each love-lock was assigned a catalogue number and a row on a spreadsheet. Each also had its inscription transcribed and was then returned to storage.

This was not the end for the Leeds love-locks, for many of them entered yet another life stage: exhibited artefact. From 2017–18, I was an Associate Curator for an exhibition at the Ashmolean Museum, Oxford, entitled 'Spellbound: Magic, Ritual & Witchcraft'. The curatorial team wanted to demonstrate, through material culture, that magical thinking was prevalent today as well as in the past. Love-locks, so widely recognisable, were the ideal objects. And so, in a gallery dedicated to the cosmos and medieval love magic, the love-locks adorned an entire wall, each one glued to a miniature shelf. Projected above them were the inscriptions from the locks interspersed with Latin and French inscriptions from medieval love tokens: 'Mon desir me vaille', 'Amor vincit omnia', 'Married 08.08.15', 'LOCKED OUR LOVE ONTO LEEDS 05.07.16' (Illustration 7.8.). This latter inscription featured on a love-lock that found itself centre stage in the introductory cabinet.

Just as love-locks are a polarising feature of landscapes, so too are they within a museum environment – adding a layer of meaning and memory to another type of landscape. Some visitors were baffled by their presence in the Ashmolean, no doubt due to their contemporaneity; others even seemed angry. I overheard one woman bemusedly remark to her companion, 'I know what they are, but I don't know why they're *here*.' Other visitors, however, appreciated the modern

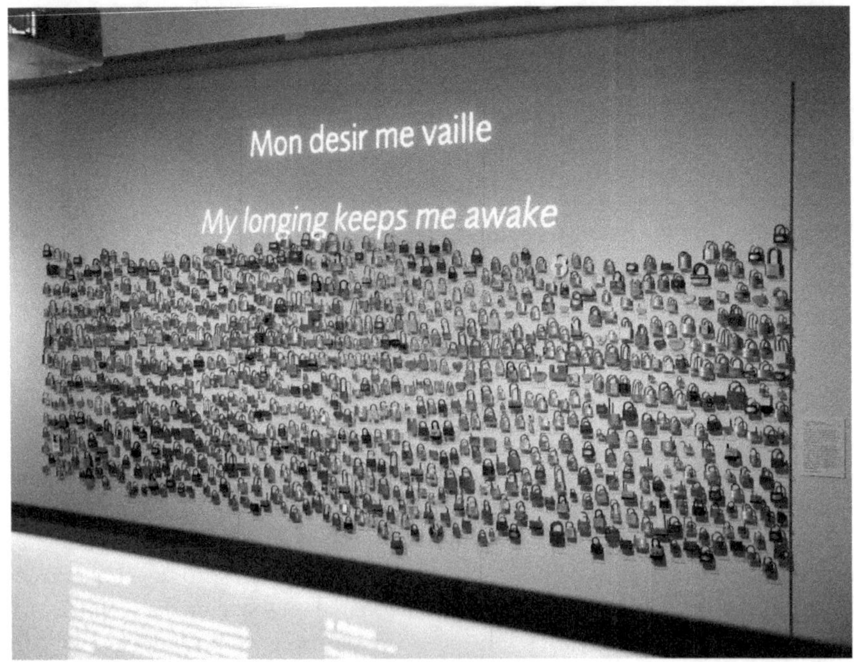

Illustration 7.8. Love-locks curated and displayed in the Ashmolean Museum, Oxford. Photograph by James Brown. Image © Ashmolean Museum, University of Oxford.

comparison, and children particularly enjoyed examining the love-locks, reading the inscriptions aloud. Of particular interest was one young girl's request to touch the love-locks, which were not protected behind glass. Her mother's 'No, of course not' was instant and sharp. I witnessed similar interactions over the course of the exhibition, between August 2018 and January 2019, with guardians admonishing children for trying to touch the love-locks. This is in contrast to how people engage with the same objects while they are still attached to bridges, touching them, lifting them, angling them for photographs. Clearly we engage with the love-lock as ritual deposit far differently than the love-lock as exhibited artefact.

This is unsurprising considering what Barbara Kirshenblatt-Gimblett terms the 'museum effect'.[94] The placing of an object into a museum, even if only temporarily, results in 'the loss of environmental context', as observed by historian David Lowenthal.[95] 'Museumizing' is the process of physically removing an object from its typical place of use and group of users, thus limiting or prohibiting access to it. In the case of the 'Spellbound' love-locks, these became exhibited museum artefacts; they had transitioned into something to be looked at and studied from a safe distance. However, accessioned objects undergo more than physical displacement. They are also conceptually altered. Place an object in a gallery or within a glass cabinet and it becomes something 'other', something 'special'. This is an issue that has occupied many museologists, with Crispin Paine noting a parallel between 'museumification' and 'sacralization': when an object becomes a 'museum artefact' it 'acquires a new meaning, a new value, a new personality'.[96]

And now that 'Spellbound' has come to an end? The love-locks have entered yet another life stage, having been accessioned into teaching collections at University College London and the University of Hertfordshire. At the latter they are used in a final-year undergraduate History module on the material culture of everyday ritual, where they are handled by students seeking to understand how the materiality of an object shapes its ritual purposes, and vice versa. And so these particular love-locks have undergone numerous recontextualisations: from padlocks to ritual deposits, to exhibited artefacts and now to teaching tools, demonstrating once more the mutability of the object and the longevity of its biography beyond its original purpose.

Conclusion

This chapter has explored the polarising nature of love-locks, demonstrating that the custom is as unpopular as it is popular. Many people – local residents, members of the press, local authorities – have spoken up against the practice, citing concern over structural damage caused by love-locks and the (in their view) unappealing aesthetics of the assemblages. Love-locks have been dubbed 'ugly', 'tacky', 'unsightly', 'eyesore', 'vandalism' and 'visually repulsive'. Campaigns have been instigated to prohibit love-locking, petitions signed, notices declaring bans erected on bridges, fines threatened and whole assemblages culled. Often, these assemblages are set in direct contrast to the heritage of the sites they adorn/tarnish; Paris's No Love Locks campaign, for example, aims to 'create awareness of the damage to cultural heritage sites by the "love locks" trend'.[97] According to these approaches, love-locks therefore damage cultural heritage – they are not cultural heritage themselves.

However, if we return to UNESCO's aim to 'recognize and protect sites that are outstanding demonstrations of human coexistence with the land as well as human interactions, cultural coexistence, spirituality and creative expression', how can we not situate love-locking within the context of cultural heritage?[98] As the bulk of this book has surely demonstrated, love-locking is probably the most widespread and democratic ritualised custom of the twenty-first century, and therefore constitutes an outstanding demonstration of all of the above: human interactions with their landscapes and with each other, cultural coexistence, spirituality and creative expression. It is, therefore, according to UNESCO's mandate, worthy of recognition and protection.

This chapter is not suggesting that we encourage the practice, especially where it poses a risk of structural damage or danger. Nor is it suggesting that heritage organisations enshrine love-lock assemblages, fixing them permanently in place so that nobody adds to or removes them. It is the participatory nature of love-locking that makes the custom what it is, and a concern over preservation can have the effect of stymying deposition and fossilising the ritual identity of a site. As Lowenthal observes, 'Protection can debase the ambience of antiquities even when their fabric remains intact'. Protection may keep the structures standing, but it does not keep them 'alive'.[99]

The transformation of a landscape through preservation attempts has occurred elsewhere, such as at Stonehenge, access to which has been a contested subject for over a century now, with archaeologist Barbara Bender lamenting: 'Roped off, fenced in, set in their polite green sward, the stones today are viewed by the visitor in isolation.' They have been removed from their environment, designated a 'museum piece' rather than a 'living site'.[100] Anthropologist Ahmed Skounti has likewise demonstrated how preservation attempts impacted on Place Jemaâ El Fna, a market square in Marrakech, which has been an open area of performance and trade for almost a millennium. With the restrictions of preservation in place, the individuals bound up in the cultural heritage of this site, from snake charmers to henna artists, were denied the freedom to engage with the space as they had done previously, and many locals complained that it had 'lost its nature'.[101]

At the very centre of love-locking is public participation, be it encouraged, tolerated or prohibited, and so preserving the love-lock assemblages would suppress the custom, fossilising the assemblages at one particular point in time.[102]

As Dawson Munjeri, who has worked for and with UNESCO in a number of roles, including Deputy Secretary-General for Zimbabwe, maintains, 'intangible heritage does not survive under overly interventionist and or restrictive conditions.'[103] There are, however, some solutions that would recognise the cultural heritage value of this custom without freezing it. One would be the creation of an archive of love-lock videos.

Elisa Giaccardi has recognised the 'profound and transformative impact of social media on our understanding and experience of heritage', editing a multi-contributor volume that explores the various ways in which new digital technologies have altered how both tangible and intangible cultural heritages are engaged with.[104] Such developments within heritage scholarship and industries have positive implications for the custom of love-locking. For instance, Sheenagh Pietrobruno has identified YouTube as a participatory and interactive archive of intangible heritage. Whenever somebody publishes a video of an event, an activity, a ceremony, a dance, a ritual, they are contributing to an unofficial on-line social archive of primary visual sources, stored and transmitted through this video-hosting service. 'Social archiving', notes Pietrobruno, 'could potentially capture intangible heritage as an ongoing process'.[105] More than this, it can 'safeguard expressions by communities that are not officially recognized'[106] – such as love-lockers, who because of their geographical and cultural disparity and the fact that many of them are tourists are not officially recognised as a community whose heritage is worthy of preservation.

It was demonstrated in *Chapter Four: Locking Love* that YouTube already stores thousands of videos of people participating in the love-lock custom. The producers of these videos probably did not intend for their work to constitute documentation, but they have inadvertently created an archive of love-locking.[107] This archive is dynamic, continuously growing and therefore able to capture any changes or diversity in the custom. On the other hand, however, it is also unstable; as Pietrobruno notes, YouTube cannot guarantee that videos uploaded will be conserved or protected.[108] Google can remove them, as can their creators. Of the 100 love-lock YouTube videos sampled, eleven have been removed over the course of writing this monograph and are no longer available. To counterbalance this impermanence, a heritage agency could archive some videos themselves as UNESCO does for other examples of intangible cultural heritage. Their 'Digitizing Our Shared UNESCO Heritage' project, for instance, has made available videos of events, ceremonies, speeches and so on in their digital archives as well as on their YouTube channel, which has over 222,000 subscribers.[109] Alongside videos entitled 'Knon, masked dance drama in Thailand', 'Chakan, embroidery art in the Republic of Tajikistan', 'Nativity scene (szopka) tradition in Krakow' and 'Ritual and festive expressions of the Congo culture', would a video on 'Love-locking, a ritual of the twenty-first century' be so out of place?

Before this could happen, heritage agencies would need to recognise love-locking as a demonstration of 'human coexistence with the land as well as human interactions, cultural coexistence, spirituality and creative expression'.[110] To go some way towards achieving this, there are a number of smaller steps we can take. Local authorities should be working with local heritage specialists and art organisations in engaging with love-lock sites on a case by case basis. Photographic records should be made of these folk assemblages as they are growing. Contemporary archaeologists should be cataloguing these ritual deposits before they are disposed of – preferably in situ, but this can also be accomplished post-removal. And curators should be contemplating love-locks as cultural artefacts, deserving of preservation and exhibition. Rather than waiting for love-locks to develop the heritage 'value' that comes with age, we should be engaging with this custom now, while it is still thriving.

Notes

1. Lewis, 'Paris is Selling Old Love Locks to Raise Money for Refugees'.
2. Larkham, 'Heritage as Planned and Conserved', 85. See Lowenthal, *The Heritage Crusade and the Spoils of History*, 9; Harvey, 'Heritage Pasts and Heritage Presents', 319–38.
3. 'Global Strategy', *UNESCO*.
4. 'Florence Tries to Stamp Out Locks of Love', *Italy Magazine*.
5. Enulescu, 'Rome Mayor in "Love Padlock" Row'.
6. Safi, 'Melbourne Bridge's 20,000 "Love Locks" to be Removed'; 'Paris "Love Locks" Removed from Bridges', *BBC News*.
7. 'No Love Locks', *Facebook*.
8. 'Ban "Love Locks" in Paris Now! Save Our Historic Sites!' *Change.org*.
9. See Gravari-Barbas and Jacquot, 'No Conflict?' 44–61. Gravari-Barbas and Jacquot examine the campaigns against the Paris love-locks as an example of mobilisation within discourses of tourism-related tensions. See also Borraz, 'Love and Locks', 10.
10. 'Venice Launches New Campaign Against "Love Locks"', *Gazzetta del Sud*.
11. 'Lose the Locks', *Fundsurfer*.
12. Pers. comm. Edward Nougat (pseudonym), 12/10/2016.
13. Holtham, 'You Can Now Hang Your Own Love Lock on This Dubai Bridge'; Dhanwani, 'Dubai's Promise Bridge is a Huge Hit'; Downes, 'Sheikh Mohammed was Spotted Admiring Dubai's Love Lock Bridge'.
14. Trew, 'Saudi Crusade over "Infidel" Love Padlocks'. See also Toumi, 'Love Padlocks in Jeddah Cause Stir'.
15. Mostafa, 'Southern Iraq Bridge Sees Rare Streak of Romance With Love Lock, Officials Offended'.
16. Morris, 'How Militias Doomed an Iraqi's Attempt to Replicate Paris's "Love Locks" Bridge'.
17. Lichfield, 'Part of Paris Bridge Collapses Under Weight of "Love Locks" Left by Tourists'.
18. Pers. comm. Councillor Ingleby, Aberdeenshire Council, 05/02/2016.
19. Schiffman Tufano, 'Love Locks on Chicago Bridges Don't Have the Staying Power of Paris'.
20. 'About', *No Love Locks*.
21. 'Paris "Love Locks" Removed from Bridges'.
22. Bohan, 'Where's the Love?'.

23. Squires, 'Venice Cracks Down on "Love Locks"'.

24. Scallon, 'No Love for the Locks'.

25. 'Paris Love Locks Sold for Charity', *France Revisited: Museum and Exhibition News*.

26. Jones, 'Love Locks are the Shallowest, Stupidest, Phoniest Expression of Love Ever – Time to Put a Stop to It'.

27. 'Paris Won't Fine 'Love Lock' Lovebirds . . but Struggles to Solve the Problem', *The Local*.

28. Hutchinson, 'Love Locks Return to the High Level Bridge as Defiant Romantics Ignore Warning'.

29. Enulescu, 'Rome Mayor in "Love Padlock" Row'.

30. Hammond, 'Renegade Ornament and the Image of the Post-Socialist City', 181–82.

31. Ibid., 182.

32. 'Campaign to Reduce "Love Locks" on Venice Bridges', *BBC News*.

32. 'Venice Launches New Campaign Against "Love Locks"', *Gazzetta del Sud*.

33. 'FAQ', *No Love Locks*.

34. Jones, 'Love Locks are the Shallowest, Stupidest, Phoniest Expression of Love Ever'.

35. See Wallis and Blain, 'Sites, Sacredness, and Stories', 310; Rountree, 'Performing the Divine', 100; Lucas, 'Constructing Identity with Dreamstones', 49–50.

36. Lowbridge, 'Are Love Locks on Bridges Romantic or a Menace?'.

37. 'Vandalism, n.', *Oxford English Dictionary*.

38. Fernandez, 'Symbolic Consensus in a Fang Reformative Cult', 906. When Fernandez interviewed members of the Bwiti cult of the Fang peoples of northern Gabon, it soon became apparent that identical ritual actions do not necessarily indicate identical ritual perceptions or motivations. Despite the night-long ritual, which Fernandez studied, being intended to promote the unity – or nlem-mvore, 'one-heartedness' – of the cult, there were vast discrepancies within the various personal interpretations of the ritual's key symbols and actions. See also Leach, *Political Systems of Highland Burma*, 281; Jordan, 'The Jiaw of Shigaang (Taiwan): An Essay in Folk Interpretation', 81–107; Stromberg, 'Consensus and Variation in the Interpretation of Religious Symbolism', 544–59; Bowman, 'Christian Ideology and the Image of a Holy Land', 98–121; Sallnow, 'Pilgrimage and Cultural Fracture in the Andes', 137–53; Reader, 'Dead to the World', 107–36.

39. Honko, 'Memorates and the Study of Folk Beliefs', 14. See also Brück, 'Monuments, Power and Personhood in the British Neolithic', 649–67.

40. Richter and Pfeiffer-Kloss, 'Bridges, Locks and Love', 200.

41. Blakstad, *Bridge*, 6.

42. Blakstad, *Bridge*, 172–73.

43. Bender, *Landscape*, 276.

44. Crawford, *Archaeology in the Field*, 51.

45. Meinig, 'The Beholding Eye', 44.

46. Schama, *Landscape and Memory*, 7; Walsham, *The Reformation of the Landscape*, 6.

47. Walsham, 'Sacred Topography and Social Memory', 32.

48. Meskell, 'Negative Heritage and Past Mastering in Archaeology', 561.

49. UNESCO, 'Convention Concerning the Protection of the World Cultural and Natural Heritage', 8.

50. UNESCO, 'Convention for the Protection of Cultural Property in the Event of Armed Conflict with Regulations for the Execution of the Convention 1954'.

51. Sleight, 'Memory in the City', 139.

52. Wallis and Blain, 'Sites, Sacredness, and Stories', 310.

53. Rountree, 'Performing the Divine', 100.

54. 'Litter, n.' *Oxford English Dictionary*.

55. Lucas, 'Constructing Identity with Dreamstones', 49–50.

56. Rountree, 'Performing the Divine', 100.

57. MacCannell, *The Tourist*, 9; Bruner, *Culture on Tour*, 7.

58. Fisher, 'In Rome, a New Ritual on an Old Bridge'.

59. 'No Love Locks', *Facebook*.

60. Turner and Ash, *The Golden Hordes*, 197. See Leslie Grinsell's treatment of the folklore surrounding the prehistoric sites in Menorca and Tony Mitchell's examination of Maori ritual in the 1982 New Zealand film *Utu*: Grinsell, 'The Popular Names and Folklore of Prehistoric Sites in Menorca', 95; Mitchell, '"Utu" – A New Zealand Revenge Tragedy', 47–53.

61. See Lanfant, Allcock and Bruner, *International Tourism*; Bruner, *Culture on Tour*; Picard and Robinson, 'Remaking Worlds', 1–31.

62. Storey, *Inventing Popular Culture*, 117.

63. Houlbrook, 'The Lock of Love'.

64. Lowenthal, *The Past is a Foreign Country*, 265. See also Holtorf and Schadla-Hall, writing of 'age-value' (Holtorf and Schadla-Hall, 'Age as Artefact', 232). But for a critique of the notion of authenticity in relation to customs, see Kevin Meethan, who stresses that it is 'predicated on a false dichotomy between the non-modern, viewed as the authentic, and the modern, viewed as the inauthentic' (Meethan, *Tourism in Global Society*, 91). See also Spooner, 'Weavers and Dealers', 195–235; Macdonald, 'On "Old Things"', 89–106.

65. Penrose, *Images of Change*, 13.

66. See Testa, '"Fertility" and the Carnival 2', 124.

67. Lovata, 'Marked Trees', 95.

68. Hoskins, *The Making of the English Landscape*, 238.

69. See Hulse, 'A Modern Votive Deposit at a North Welsh Holy Well', 31–42; Finn, 'Leaving More Than Footprints', 169–78; Wallis and Blain, 'Sites, Sacredness, and Stories', 307–21; Beattie, 'A Most Peculiar Memorial', 215–24.

70. Schofield, 'Editorial', 2.

71. Penrose, *Images of Change*, 9.

72. Bradley et al. *Change and Creation*.

73. Schofield, 'Editorial', 2.

74. UNESCO, 'Policies Regarding CREDIBILITY of the World Heritage List'.

75. Hammond, 'Renegade Ornament', 189.

76. See Timothy and Boyd, *Heritage Tourism*, 174–75.

77. Ryall, 'Japan's Young Couples Risking Death in "Love Padlock" Ritual'.

78. 'Los Gatos Museum Offers Space for "Love Locks" Amid City Crackdown', *KPIX CBS BayArea*.

79. Scobie, 'Love Locks Sculpture Unveiled in Vancouver's Queen Elizabeth Park'.

80. Graham, 'Love Lock Installation Opens in Distillery District'.

81. Pers. comm. Ken Massingham and Caroline Massingham, 10/04/2018.

82. Love Lock Trees, 'Introducing the Love Lock Tree . . . in Detail', 2; Love Lock Trees: www.lovelocktrees.com [Accessed 30/07/2019].

83. *Love Without Locks*: http://www.lovewithoutlocks.paris.fr/ [Accessed 09/07/2019].

84. Pers. comm. Councillor Ingleby, Aberdeenshire Council, 05/02/2016.

85. I have previously advocated the recording of contemporary ritual deposits as a measure of ensuring the viability of the intangible cultural heritage of the practice of deposition. See Houlbrook, 'The Penny's Dropped', 173–89; Houlbrook, 'Lessons from Love-Locks', 214–38.

86. UNESCO, 'Convention for the Safeguarding of the Intangible Cultural Heritage', 2.3.

87. Pers. comm. Dr Anton Hasell, RMIT University Melbourne, 03/04/2017.

88. Pers. comm. Elise Sheehan, 13/04/2017.

89. Pers. comm. Katheryn Leopoldseder, 20/04/2017.

90. Pers. comm. Victoria Goodridge, 06/04/2017.

91. Samuel, 'Paris to Auction Off "Love Locks" and Give Proceeds to Migrant Charities'; Jacob, 'Paris "Love Locks" Raise Thousands at Auction'; Vente aux Enchères, *Vente Solidaire des Cadenas d'Armour de la Ville de Paris.*

92. Samuel, 'Paris to Auction Off "Love Locks"'; pers. comm. Victoria Goodridge, 06/04/2017.

93. Baker, 'The Berlin Wall', 720.

94. Kirshenblatt-Gimblett, 'Objects of Ethnography', 410.

95. Lowenthal, *The Past is a Foreign Country*, 286.

96. Paine, *Religious Objects in Museums*, 2.

97. 'No Love Locks', *Facebook*.

98. UNESCO, 'Global Strategy'.

99. Lowenthal, *The Past is a Foreign Country*, 276.

100. Bender, *Stonehenge*, 6–9.

101. Skounti, 'The Authentic Illusion', 87.

102. Jones, '"They Made It A Living Thing Didn't They . . ."', 107–26.

103. Munjeri, 'Following the Length and Breadth of the Roots', 148.

104. Giaccardi, 'Introduction', 1.

105. Pietrobruno, 'YouTube and the Social Archiving of Intangible Heritage', 1260.

106. Ibid., 1272.

107. See Lange, 'Video-Mediated Nostalgia and the Aesthetics of Technical Competencies', 29; Kaplan, 'Curation and Tradition on Web 2.0', 123–48.

108. Pietrobruno, 'YouTube and the Social Archiving', 1261.

109. UNESCO, 'Films and Videos'; UNESCO, 'Videos'.

110. UNESCO, 'Global Strategy'.

CONCLUDING THOUGHTS
A Final Case-Study

Back in April 2010, fifteen- and sixteen-year-old students across Ontario will have sat in their classrooms and opened their Ontario Secondary School Literacy Test (OSSLT) papers. These exams, now sat by every student wanting their Secondary School Diploma, test their reading and writing skills by presenting them with a piece of text and a series of questions, designed to measure their understanding of the information and concepts communicated in that text. In the particular case of April 2010, the students will have turned to the first piece of text to find it accompanied by a photograph of a lamp post adorned with clusters of padlocks and a heading that read 'Romans Putting a Lock on Love'.[1] What followed was an adapted version, just over 200 words, of journalist Alessandra Rizzo's *Toronto Star* article from March 2007, which briefly outlined the history of love-locks on the Ponte Milvio, the impact of Moccia's novels and the local authority's uncertainty over its practical sustainability.[2]

Five multiple choice questions followed this short piece, including: '"Milvio" is the name of a: a. river / b. bridge / c. city official / d. Roman emperor' and 'Which event occurred first in the development of the ritual? a. Couple threw keys into the river / b. Two popular novels were published / c. A Roman city official made a statement / d. Many tourists chose to visit the ancient bridge.' The sixth question of this section required a written answer and asked 'Should city officials in Rome be worried or pleased about the fad of putting locks on the lamp post? Explain your answer using details from the selection [the text piece] and your own ideas.'

Nine years later, my own piece on love-locks in *The Conversation* was adapted for inclusion on the digital reading platform *Actively Learn*. The assignment directions preceding the text instruct the student: 'As you read, think about whether the author appears to support love locking and whether you agree with her opinions. It will be helpful to highlight text that indicates an opinion and make note [sic.] about how strong the evidence is and whether you agree.'[3] Multiple choice questions, scattered throughout the text, include: 'What dangerous problem do the locks potentially create?' and 'Why would the author choose to mention The United Nations Educational, Scientific, and Cultural Organisation's view on love locks?' In addition, there are suggestions for how a teacher might use this text: 'to begin an analysis of symbols' or 'as a springboard into examining the nature of beauty and what people consider to be beautiful or artistic'.

These two examples highlight a number of the themes explored throughout this book. Firstly, the 2007 Rizzo piece adapted for the 2010 OSSLT demonstrates how the custom was being perceived at the time. The test paper identifies love-locking as a 'new ritual' and a 'padlock fad' that had been 'adopted' by the Romans following 'two best-selling novels (with combined sales of 2.5 million copies) and their movie adaptations'. It was therefore being perceived as a new trend sparked by the success of Moccia's novels, with no reference to the custom already well established elsewhere, such as in Pécs, Hungary. Evidently, research had not reached that far back yet.

By tracing the history of the 'Love lock' page on free online encyclopaedia *Wikipedia* – which folklorist Lynne McNeill identifies as a 'good source for emic definitions of informal culture'[4] – we can see how knowledge of this custom developed throughout the 2000s. As each entry is created, edited and perpetually updated by numerous volunteers, each *Wikipedia* page is a palimpsest of knowledge on that particular subject. By digging beneath those layers, we can see that the first 'Love lock' page was written on 7 September 2006 and – in contrast to Rizzo's 2007 piece in the *Toronto Star*, which referred only to the Rome assemblage – focused only on the Pécs assemblage, described as a 'unique site', and comparative examples in Latvia, which the writer believes came later. The word 'unique' had been deleted by another contributor by 11 September and a sentence added about the Ponte Vecchio assemblage in Florence. The entry remained largely the same for about a year, and then in 2008 information was added about assemblages in Guam and Montevideo. In 2009, further examples were contributed: in Seoul, Tokyo, Cologne, Kiev, Seville and Huangshan, to name only some.

Interestingly, it was not until 8 August 2010 that Federico Moccia appeared on the page, with the introductory sentence edited to read that the custom 'first start[ed] at the bridge Ponte Milvio in Rome, Italy. It is inspired by an [sic.] fictional event in the book *I Want You* by Italian author Federico Moccia'. Vrnjačka Banja's Most Ljubavi was then added to the page on 6 October 2010, but not as the origin of the custom; the description consisted only of a statement that this site was where love-locks could be found and that the bridge is 'in one of the oldest spa towns in Serbia'. Clearly, information about which love-lock assemblages predate others is inconsistently presented and shifted sporadically over time depending upon who the writers were – hence why seeking the origins of a custom is often fruitless (and why *Chapter One: Dating Love* proved so difficult to write).

The 2010 test paper not only shows us the level of knowledge about the custom at the time but also the process of the dissemination of that knowledge. This was an article written in a Canadian newspaper for a Canadian audience, adapted for Canadian students, about an *Italian* custom. This demonstrates that as early as 2007 there was international interest in a seemingly European practice, with people in North America learning about a 'new ritual' in Rome. And with the dissemination of knowledge comes the dissemination of practice; while the process may have taken a few years, by the early 2010s Canadians were not only reading about the custom but were implementing and participating in it themselves, with assemblages emerging in their own towns and cities.

What the 2019 *Actively Learn* teaching resource also demonstrates is the assumed establishment of knowledge about love-locking. Tessa Polizzi, who adapted the *Conversation* article for the online learning platform, explained that she chose the piece because: 'I've seen love locks around before, and I am guessing that many students have probably seen them or even done one themselves, so I thought that it would be meaningful and relevant to them.'[5] Polizzi has assumed that most people are aware of the love-lock custom and may have participated in the custom themselves, giving the topic relevance. This assumption indicates widespread familiarity with love-locking, which links us back to our early consideration of the love-lock as *seme* and stock image, appearing without need for explanation in popular culture, in advertisements and in photo frames: the love-lock has become an instantly recognisable icon connoting romance.

This also links back to the adaptability of this custom. Love-locking has been widely commodified, commercialised and marketed. Padlocks have been sold at love-lock assemblages for monetary gain, both officially and unofficially, or for charitable causes. Their symbolism has been harnessed in the creation of new products – Pandora charms, chocolates, Louis Vuitton handbags – or in the advertisement for other products or services, from dating events to home insurance. They have been integrated into site identity via processes of place-marketing and place-making, such as in Vrnjačka Banja, Pécs, Gretna Green and Lovelock, Nevada. And also, they have been reutilised as a topic appropriate for literacy test papers. Clearly the adaptability of this custom knows few bounds – which is no doubt a significant contributing factor to its continued growth.

Both test pieces also demonstrate the ambiguity of such terms as 'heritage value', 'beauty' and 'vandalism'. The 2010 paper instructs students to consider whether 'city officials in Rome [should] be worried or pleased about the fad of putting locks on the lamp post?' while the 2019 online test asks, 'What do you think about vandalism (destruction of someone else's property)?' and 'Do you support the author's claim that love locks should be preserved for future generations?' Polizzi focused on this element in her explanation for why she chose this particular piece: because it presents 'the idea that new things can constitute culture' and 'an interesting view on valuing things based on age that I think students can probably identify with because they experience ageism themselves'.[6]

As we saw in the last chapter, the heritage 'value' of love-locking is a polarising topic, transforming love-lock assemblages into contested landscapes. Just as the custom is still hugely popular at the time of writing in 2019, with love-lock assemblages sustaining themselves and continuing to appear worldwide, it also remains hugely *unpopular*, and contestations persist. As these test papers demonstrate, the custom of love-locking is providing people – in particular, young people – with a point of reference, something they are familiar with, through which they can comprehend the polysemic complexities of their cultural landscapes and contemplate the issues at the heart of the debate: What is vandalism? What is beauty? What is culture? What is worth saving for future generations? And who gets to decide?

Notes

1. Education Quality and Accountability Office. 2010. *Ontario Secondary School Literacy Test: Session 1*, April 2010. Booklet 1, Section 1: Reading, 2–4.

2. Rizzo, 'Romans Putting a Lock on Love'.

3. *Actively Learn*: https://read.activelylearn.com/#teacher/reader/authoring/preview/895619/notes [Accessed 12/03/2019].

4. McNeill, 'Real Virtuality', 86.

5. Pers. comm. Tessa Polizzi, *Actively Learn*, 11/02/2019.

6. Ibid.

BIBLIOGRAPHY

'About'. *No Love Locks*: https://nolovelocks.com/about/ [Accessed 02/06/2019].

'About Locking Your Love, An Ancient Chinese Custom'. *Love Lock*: http://loverslock.com/about-locking-your-love-an-ancient-chinese-custom/ [Accessed 13/02/2019].

'About Lock-itz'. *Lock-itz*: https://lock-itz.com/about-lock-itz/ [Accessed 15/03/2019].

'About Us'. *Love Locks UK*: https://www.lovelocksuk.com/about-us.html [Accessed 15/03/2019].

Actively Learn: https://read.activelylearn.com/#teacher/reader/authoring/preview/895619/notes [Accessed 12/03/2019].

Adrian. 'Locks of Love: Why N Seoul Tower is Romantic'. *HELLOKPOP* (3 January 2016): https://www.hellokpop.com/korea-joa/locks-of-love-why-n-seoul-tower-is-romantic/ [Accessed 01/12/2018].

Aitchison, N.B. 'Roman Wealth, Native Ritual: Coin Hoards With and Beyond Roman Britain'. *World Archaeology* 20(2) (1988), 270–84.

'Aku Cinta Kamu'. *Shadowhunters: The Mortal Instruments* [television programme] Netflix, Season 3, Episode 19, 22 April 2019.

Andrea. 'Montevideo's Locks Fountain'. *Inspiring Travellers* (3 May 2011): https://inspiringtravellers.com/montevideos-locks-fountain/ [Accessed 31/01/2019].

Anonymous. 'The 10 Most Romantic Places in Paris'. *Come to Paris* (Nd.): https://www.cometoparis.com/paris-guide/the-10-most-romantic-places-in-paris-s910 [Accessed 13/02/2019].

Anonymous. 'Vision and Mission'. *Marriage Week*: http://www.mymarriage.co.za/index.php?option=com_content&view=article&id=394&Itemid=541 [Accessed 14/06/2019].

Anonymous. 'Bridge of Love'. *Vrnjačka Banja* (Nd.): http://www.vrnjackabanja.co.rs/en/index.php?option=com_content&view=article&id=87&Itemid=40 [Accessed 31/01/2019].

Anonymous. 'Šta imaju zajedničko Vrnjačka Banja i Rim? Most Ljubavi!'. *Vrnjačka Banja* (Nd.): https://www.vrnjacka-banja.co.rs/sta-imaju-zajednicko-vrnjacka-banja-i-rim/ [Accessed 31/01/2019].

Anonymous. 'The Moccia Phenomenon, Italian Love Boom!' Blogspot (2010): http://comeniuson.blogspot.com/2010/01/moccia-phenomenon-italian-love-boom.html [Accessed 04/12/2018].

Anonymous. 'Rome's Ponte Milvio Bridge: "Padlocks of Love" Removed'. *BBC News* (10 September 2012): https://www.bbc.co.uk/news/world-europe-19545942 [Accessed 13/08/2018].

Anonymous. 'St. Trifun and Valentine's Day in Serbia'. *Serbia* (14 February 2016): http://www.serbia.com/st-trifun-and-valentines-day-in-serbia/ [Accessed 31/01/2019].

Anonymous. 'The Triumph of Love Novels that Desperate Critics'. *Spain's News* (2018): https://spainsnews.com/the-triumph-of-love-novels-that-desperate-critics-culture/ [Accessed 04/12/2018].

Anonymous. 'Celebrate Valentine's Day with Love Locks and Mûre Blanche'. *Wine and Stile* (9 February 2018): https://www.fencestile.com/wine-and-stile/celebrate-valentines-day-with-love-locks-and-mure-blanche [Accessed 14/02/2019].

Anonymous. 'Namsan Tower AKA Seoul Tower'. *Korean Dramaland* (2018): https://koreandramal and.com/listings/namsan-tower-aka-n-seoul-tower/ [Accessed 01/12/2018].

Anonymous. 'Valentine's Day in Georgia: Where to Go?' *CBW* (14 February 2018): http://cbw.ge/ georgia/valentines-day-georgia-go/ [Accessed 20/12/2018].

Anonymous. 'Najduži poljubac trajao 36 minuta'. *PTC* (14 February 2019): http://www.rts.rs/page/ magazine/sr/story/511/zanimljivosti/3420894/najduzi-poljubac-trajao-36-minuta.html [Accessed 18/02/2019].

Apoh, W., and K. Gavua. 'Material Culture and Indigenous Spiritism: The Katamansu Archaeological "Otutu" (Shrine)'. *African Archaeological Review* 27(3) (2010), 211–35.

Armit, I. *Headhunting and the Body in Iron Age Europe*. Cambridge: Cambridge University Press, 2012.

Asad, T. *Genealogies of Religion: Discipline and Reasons of Power in Christianity and Islam*. Baltimore and London: The John Hopkins University Press, 1993.

Bacchilega, C. 'Folklore and Literature', in R.F. Bendix and G. Hasan-Rokem (eds), *A Companion to Folklore* (Hoboken, NJ: Wiley & Sons, 2012), 447–63.

Badon, E., and S.R. Roseman (eds). *Intersecting Journeys: The Anthropology of Pilgrimage and Tourism*. Urbana: University of Illinois Press, 2004.

Baker, F. 'The Berlin Wall: Production, Preservation and Consumption of a 20th-Century Monument'. *Antiquity* 67 (1993), 709–33.

'Ban "Love Locks" in Paris Now! Save Our Historic Sites!' *Change.org*: https://www.change.org/p/ anne-hidalgo-ban-love-locks-in-paris-now-save-our-historic-sites [Accessed 10/09/2017].

Bascom, W.R. 'Four Functions of Folklore', in A. Dundes (ed.), *The Study of Folklore* (Englewood Cliffs: Prentice-Hall, 1965), 279–98.

Beattie, M. 'A Most Peculiar Memorial: Cultural Heritage and Fiction', in J. Schofield (ed.), *Who Needs Experts? Counter-mapping Cultural Heritage* (Farnham: Ashgate, 2014), 215–24.

Becker, K. 'Media and The Ritual Process'. *Media, Culture & Society* 17 (1995), 629–46.

Bell, T., and P. Spikins, 'The Object of My Affection: Attachment Security and Material Culture'. *Time & Mind* 11(1) (2018), 23–39.

Beloved Padlocks: http://www.belovedpadlocks.com.au/engraving-text-ideas/ [Accessed 19/06/2018].

Bender, B. *Stonehenge: Making Space*. Oxford and New York: Berg, 1998.

Bender, B. (ed.). *Landscape: Politics and Perspectives*. Providence and Oxford: Berg, 1993.

Bender, B., S. Hamilton and C. Tilley. 'Leskernick: Stone Worlds; Alternative Narratives; Nested Landscapes'. *Proceedings of the Prehistoric Society* 63 (1997), 147–78.

Bendix, R.F., and G. Hasan-Rokem (eds). *A Companion to Folklore*. Hoboken, NJ: John Wiley & Sons, 2012.

Berger, H.A., and D. Ezzy. *Teenage Witches: Magical Youth and the Search for the Self*. New Brunswick: Rutgers University Press, 2007.

Bergiato, J. 'Moving Objects: Emotional Transformation, Tangibility, and Time Travel', in S. Downes, S. Holloway and S. Randles (eds), *Feeling Things: Objects and Emotions through History* (Oxford: Oxford University Press, 2018), 229–42.

Berton, E. '"Love Locks" Scourge of Bridges Worldwide'. *USA Today* (5 June 2015): https://eu.usato day.com/story/news/world/2015/06/05/paris-love-locks/28532155/ [Accessed 10/08/2018].

Betlyon, J.W. 'Guide to Artifacts: Numismatics and Archaeology'. *The Biblical Archaeologist* 48(3) (1985), 162–65.

Bird, S.E. 'Cultural Studies as Confluence: The Convergence of Folklore and Media Studies', in H.E. Hinds, M.F. Motz and A.M.S. Nelson (eds), *Popular Culture Theory and Methodology: A Basic Introduction* (Madison: University of Wisconsin Press, 2006), 344–55.

Blacker, C. 'Other World Journeys in Japan', in H.R.E. Davidson (ed.), *The Journey to the Other World* (Cambridge: Mistletoe Press, 1975), 66–68.

Blain, J., and R.J. Wallis. 'Representing Spirit: Heathenry, New-Indigenes and the Imaged Past', in I. Russell (ed.), *Images, Representation and Heritage: Moving beyond Modern Approaches to Archaeology* (New York: Springer, 2006), 89–108.

Blakstad, L. 'Introduction', in L. Blakstad (ed.), *Bridge: The Architecture of Connection* (London: Augusta Media, 2002), 6–7.

Blakstad, L. (ed.). *Bridge: The Architecture of Connection*. London: Augusta Media, 2002.

Blank, T.J. 'Introduction: Toward a Conceptual Framework for the Study of Folklore and the Internet', in T.J. Blank (ed.), *Folklore and the Internet: Vernacular Expression in a Digital World* (Logan: Utah State University Press, 2009), 1–20.

Blank, T.J. (ed.). *Folk Culture in the Digital Age: The Emergent Dynamics of Human Interaction*. Utah State University Press, 2012.

Block, E.L. 'Wishing-Well Type Coin Collector'. *United States Patent Office* 2,991,932 (patented 11 July 1961).

Bocock, R. *Ritual in Industrial Society: A Sociological Analysis of Ritualism in Modern England*. London: George Allen & Unwin Ltd., 1974.

Bohan, C. 'Where's the Love? Council Removes "Love Padlocks" from Dublin's Ha'penny Bridge'. *The Journal* (13 January 2012): https://www.thejournal.ie/wheres-the-love-council-removes-love-padlocks-from-dublins-hapenny-bridge-327300-Jan2012/ [Accessed 04/07/2019].

Boissevain, J. 'Ritual, Tourism and Cultural Commoditization in Malta: Culture by the Pound?', in T. Selwyn (ed.), *The Tourist Gaze: Myths and Myth Making in Tourism* (Chichester: Wiley, 1996), 105–18.

Bord, J., and C. Bord. *Sacred Wells: Holy Wells and Water Lore in Britain and Ireland*. London: Paladin Books, 1985.

Bordwell, D., K. Thompson and J. Smith. *Film Art: An Introduction*. New York: McGraw-Hill Education, 2017.

Borraz, S. 'Love and Locks: Consumers Making Pilgrimages and Performing Love Rituals'. *Consumer Culture Theory* 20 (2019), 7–21.

Bowman, G. 'Christian Ideology and the Image of a Holy Land', in J. Eade and M.J. Sallnow (eds), *Contesting the Sacred: The Anthropology of Christian Pilgrimage* (London and New York: Routledge, 1991), 98–121.

Bradbury, M. 'Forget Me Not: Memorialisation in Cemeteries and Crematoria', in J. Hockey, J. Katz and N. Small (eds), *Grief, Mourning and Death Ritual* (Buckingham and Philadelphia: Open University Press, 2001), 218–25.

Bradley, A., et al. *Change and Creation: Historic Landscape Character 1950–2000*. London: English Heritage, 2004.

Bradley, R. *The Passage of Arms: Archaeological Analysis of Prehistoric Hoards and Votive Deposits*. Oxford: Oxbow, 1990.

———. *The Significance of Monuments: On the Shaping of Human Experience in Neolithic and Bronze Age Europe*. London and New York: Routledge, 1998.

Brandt, S. 'Nagelfiguren: Nailing Patriotism in Germany 1914–18', in N.J. Saunders (ed.), *Matters of Conflict: Material Culture, Memory and the First World War* (London and New York: Routledge, 2004), 62–71.

Breidenbach, J., and P. Nyíri. '"Our Common Heritage": New Tourist Nations, Post-"Socialist" Pedagogy, and the Globalization of Nature'. *Current Anthropology* 48(2) (2007), 322–30.

Brendan Brady (Emmett J. Scanlan) Fan Thread! *Digital Spy*: https://forums.digitalspy.com/discussion/2070543/brendan-brady-emmett-j-scanlan-fan-thread-part-196/p552 [Accessed 19/12/2018].

British Museum. Brooch, 1978,1002.612: http://www.britishmuseum.org/research/collection_online/collection_object_details.aspx?objectId=78153&partId=1&searchText=1978,1002.612&page=1 [Accessed 19/01/2018].

———. Locket, 2010,8023.1: http://www.britishmuseum.org/research/collection_online/collection_object_details.aspx?objectId=3335914&partId=1&searchText=2010,8023.1&page=1 [Accessed 19/01/2018].

Brough, A. 'Leaving Paris for the World: The Lovelock Story'. *Gretna Green* (24 July 2015): https://www.gretnagreen.com/leaving-paris-for-the-world-the-lovelock-story-a935 [Accessed 14/02/2019].

———. 'Welcoming a Wall of Love to Gretna Green'. *Gretna Green* (15 October 2015): https://www.gretnagreen.com/welcoming-a-wall-of-love-to-gretna-green-a947 [Accessed 14/02/2019].

Brück, J. 'Monuments, Power and Personhood in the British Neolithic'. *The Journal of the Royal Anthropological Institute* 7(4) (2001), 649–67.

———. 'Material Metaphors: The Relational Construction of Identity in Early Bronze Age Burials in Ireland and Britain'. *Journal of Social Archaeology* 4(3) (2004), 307–33.

———. 'Fragmentation, Personhood and the Social Construction of Technology in Middle and Late Bronze Age Britain'. *Cambridge Archaeological Journal* 16(3) (2006), 297–315.

———. 'Ritual and Rationality: Some Problems of Interpretation in European Archaeology', in T. Insoll (ed.), *The Archaeology of Identities: A Reader* (Oxon and New York: Routledge, 2007), 281–307.

Bruner, E.M. *Culture on Tour: Ethnographies of Travel*. Chicago and London: University of Chicago Press, 2005.

Bruun, O. '"When You Have Seen the Yellow Mountains": Approaches to Nature, Essence and Ecology in China'. *Worldviews* 18 (2014), 1–29.

Buccitelli, A.B. 'Performance 2.0: Observations toward a Theory of the Digital Performance of Folklore', in T.J. Blank (ed.), *Folk Culture in the Digital Age: The Emergent Dynamics of Human Interaction* (Utah State University Press, 2012), 60–84.

———. 'Paying to Play: Digital Media, Commercialization, and the Scholarship of Alan Dundes'. *Western Folklore* 73(2–3) (2014), 235–56.

Buchli, V., and G. Lucas (eds). *Archaeologies of the Contemporary Past*. London and New York: Routledge, 2001.

Buchmann, A., K. Moore and D. Fisher. 'Experiencing Film Tourism: Authenticity and Fellowship'. *Annals of Tourism Research* 37(7) (2010), 229–48.

Burns, T. 'Folklore in the Mass Media: Television'. *Folklore Forum* 2(4) (1969), 90–106.

Butler, K. 'Romantic Couples Demonstrate their Love with Specially Designed Padlocks on Manchester City Centre Bridge'. *Manchester Evening News* (4 August 2015): https://www.manchestereveningnews.co.uk/news/greater-manchester-news/romantic-couples-demonstrate-love-specially-9789839.

———. 'Love Locks in Manchester to Get a Special City Centre Location'. *Manchester Evening News* (9 August 2015): http://www.manchestereveningnews.co.uk/news/greater-manchester-news/love-locks-manchester-special-city-9816918.

Calabrese, O. 'The Bridge: Suggestions about the Meaning of a Pictorial Motif'. *Journal of Art Historiography* 5 (2011), 1–14.

Cameron, L.J. 'Patterns of Metaphor Use in Reconciliation Talk'. *Discourse & Society* 18(2) (2007), 197–222.

'Campaign to Reduce "Love Locks" on Venice Bridges'. *BBC News* (28 August 2014): https://www.bbc.co.uk/news/blogs-news-from-elsewhere-28967549 [Accessed 03/07/2019].

Campbell, A. 'That's Amore! But Lovers' Locks are Littering the Brooklyn Bridge'. *Brooklyn Paper* (27 April 2010): https://www.brooklynpaper.com/stories/33/18/all_brooklynbridgelocks_2010_04_30_bk.html [Accessed 13/08/2018].

Campbell, J.F. *Popular Tales of the West Highlands*. Volume I. London: Alexander Gardner, 1890.

Cerdá, J.F., D. Delabastita and K. Gregor (eds). *Romeo and Juliet in European Culture*. Amsterdam and Philadelphia: John Benjamins, 2017.

Chandler, D. *Semiotics: The Basics*. London and New York: Routledge, 2007.

Chapman, J. *Fragmentation in Archaeology: People, Places and Broken Objects in the Prehistory of South-Eastern Europe*. London and New York: Routledge, 2000.

Cherry, J. 'The Medieval Jewellery from the Fishpool, Nottinghamshire, Hoard'. *Archaeologia; or, Miscellaneous Tracts Relating to Antiquity* 104 (1973), 307–21.

'Clean Skin'. *Homeland* [television programme], Showtime, Season 1, Episode 3, 16 October 2011.

Coffey, H. 'Lyra's Oxford: New Philip Pullman-Inspired Walking Tour Launches to Celebrate Book of Dust Trilogy'. *The Independent* (19 October 2017): https://www.independent.co.uk/travel/uk/lyras-oxford-walking-tour-philip-pullman-book-of-dust-trilogy-la-belle-sauvage-northern-lights-his-a8005131.html [Accessed 10/08/2018].

Cool, H.E.M., and J.E. Richardson. 'Exploring Ritual Deposits in a Well at Rothwell Haigh, Leeds'. *Britannia* 44 (2013), 1–27.

Cooley, T.J. 'Folk Festival as Modern Ritual in the Polish Tatra Mountains'. *The World of Music* 41(3) (1999), 31–55.

Couldry, N. 'The View from Inside the "Simulacrum": Visitors' Tales from the Set of Coronation Street'. *Leisure Studies* 17(2) (1998), 94–107.

Crawford, O.G.S. *Archaeology in the Field*. London: Phoenix House Ltd., 1953.

Creighton, M. 'Consuming Rural Japan: The Marketing of Tradition and Nostalgia in the Japanese Travel Industry'. *Ethnology* 36(3) (1997), 239–54.

Crouch, D., and N. Lübbern (eds). *Visual Culture and Tourism*. Oxford and New York: Berg, 2003.

Cushing, F.H. 'The Cock and the Mouse', in A. Dundes (ed.), *The Study of Folklore* (Englewood Cliffs: Prentice-Hall, Inc., 1965), 269–76.

'Custom Engraved Love Locks'. *Love Locks*: https://lovelocksonline.com/ [Accessed 15/03/2019].

Danielson, L. 'Folklore and Film: Some Thoughts on Baughman Z500–599'. *Western Folklore* 38 (1979), 209–19.

Dann, G. 'The People of Tourist Brochures', in T. Selwyn (ed.), *The Tourist Gaze: Myths and Myth Making in Tourism* (Chichester: Wiley, 1996), 61–81.

David, G. 'Camera Phone Images, Videos and Live Streaming: A Contemporary Visual Trend'. *Visual Studies* 25(1) (2010), 89–98.

Davidsen, M.A. 'Fiction-Based Religion: Conceptualising a New Category against History-Based Religion and Fandom'. *Culture and Religion* 14(4) (2013), 378–95.

Davies, O. 'The Material Culture of Post-Medieval Domestic Magic in Europe: Evidence, Comparisons and Interpretations', in D. Boschung and J.N. Bremmer (eds), *The Materiality of Magic* (Paderborn: Wilhelm Fink, 2015), 379–417.

Day, E. 'The Lock of Love: Padlocks on Bridges'. *The Guardian* (14 February 2016): https://www.theguardian.com/lifeandstyle/2016/feb/14/the-lock-of-love-padlocks-on-bridges [Accessed 20/12/2018].

Day, J.W. *Archaic Greek Epigram and Dedication: Representation and Reperformance*. Cambridge: Cambridge University Press, 2010.

Deetz, J. *In Small Things Forgotten*. New York: Doubleday, 1996.

Dégh, L., and A. Vázsonyi. 'Does the Word "Dog" Bite? Ostensive Action: A Means of Legend-Telling'. *Journal of Folklore Research* 20(1) (1983), 5–34.

Deloitte. *Global Mobile Consumer Survey 2017: UK Cut*. London: Deloitte, 2017.

Denby, P. 'Folklore in the Mass Media'. *Folklore Forum* 4(5) (1971), 113–25.

Dhanwani, S. 'Dubai's Promise Bridge is a Huge Hit'. *Gulf News* (21 February 2018): https://gulfnews.com/uae/dubais-promise-bridge-is-a-huge-hit-1.2177290 [Accessed 16/08/2019].

Domokos, M. 'Towards Methodological Issues in Electronic Folklore'. *Slovak Ethnology* 2(62) (2014), 283–95.

Doolittle, J. *Social Life of the Chinese: With Some Account of Their Religious, Governmental, Educational, and Business Customs and Opinions*. Volume II. London: Sampson Low, Son & Marston, 1866.

Dorson, R.M. 'Folklore and Fake Lore'. *The American Mercury* 70 (1950), 335–43.

———. *American Folklore*. Chicago: University of Chicago Press, 1959.

———. 'Fakelore'. *Zeitschrift für Volkskunde* 65 (1969), 56–64.

———. 'Folklore in the Modern World', in R.M. Dorson (ed.), *Folklore in the Modern World* (The Hague: Mouton Publishers, 1978), 12–51.

Douglas, M. *The World of Goods: Towards an Anthropology of Consumption*. London and New York: Routledge, 1979.

Dowd, M. 'Bewitched by an Elf Dart: Fairy Archaeology, Folk Magic and Traditional Medicine in Ireland'. *Cambridge Archaeological Journal* 28(3) (2018), 451–73.

Dowden, K. *European Paganism: The Realities of Cult from Antiquity to the Middle Ages*. London and New York: Routledge, 2000.

Downes, S. 'Sheikh Mohammed Was Spotted Admiring Dubai's Love Lock Bridge'. *What's On* (11 March 2018): https://whatson.ae/dubai/2018/03/sheikh-mohammed-love-lock-bridge/ [Accessed 16/08/2019].

Downes, S., S. Holloway and S. Randles (eds). *Feeling Things: Objects and Emotions through History*. Oxford: Oxford University Press, 2018.

Duda, M. *Four Centuries of Silver: Personal Adornment in the Qing Dynasty and After*. Singapore: Times Editions, 2002.

Dundes, A. 'The Folklore of Wishing Wells'. *American Imago* 19(1) (1962), 27–34.

———. 'The Study of Folklore in Literature and Culture: Identification and Interpretation'. *Journal of American Folklore* 78 (1965), 136–43.

———. 'Nationalistic Inferiority Complexes and the Fabrication of Folklore: A Reconsideration of Ossian, the *Kinder- und Hausmärchen*, the *Kalevala*, and Paul Bunyan'. *Journal of Folklore Research* 22(1) (1985), 5–18.

———. 'Folkloristics in the Twenty-First Century (AGS Invited Presidential Plenary Address, 2004)'. *The Journal of American Folklore* 118(470) (2005), 385–408.

Dundes, A. (ed.). *The Study of Folklore*. Englewood Cliffs: Prentice-Hall, 1965.

Eade, J., and M.J. Sallnow (eds). *Contesting the Sacred: The Anthropology of Christian Pilgrimage*. London and New York: Routledge, 1991.

Eckardt, H., and H. Williams. 'Objects Without a Past? The Use of Roman Objects in Early Anglo-Saxon Graves', in H. Williams (ed.), *Archaeologies of Remembrance: Death and Memory in Past Societies* (New York: Kluwer Academic/Plenum Publishers, 2003), 141–70.

Eco, U. 'Critique of the Image', in V. Burgin (ed.), *Thinking Photography* (Basingstoke and London: Macmillan, 1990), 32–38.

Education Quality and Accountability Office. 2010. *Ontario Secondary School Literacy Test: Session 1, April 2010. Booklet 1, Section 1: Reading*, 2–4.

Edwards, D. et al. 'Ambassadors of Knowledge Sharing: Co-produced Travel Information through Tourist-Local Social Media Exchange'. *International Journal of Contemporary Hospitality Management* 29(2) (2017), 690–708.

Eliade, M. *Shamanism: Archaic Techniques of Ecstasy*. Princeton, NJ: Princeton University Press, 1964.

'Emmett Fans'. *Tumblr* (2014): http://emmettfans.tumblr.com/post/47703848840/here-is-the-ste-and-brendan-love-lock-from [Accessed 19/12/2018].

Engravables. '40mm Lock, Personalized Engraved Padlock, Large Linked Hearts Image, Gift Box, Bold Text (LLHrt)'. *Amazon*: https://www.amazon.co.uk/Personalized-Engraved-Padlock-Linked-Hearts/dp/B013KABM8A?ref_=fsclp_pl_dp_1 [Accessed 15/03/2019].

Enulescu, D. 'Rome Mayor in "Love Padlock" Row'. *BBC News* (1 March 2007): http://news.bbc.co.uk/1/hi/6408635.stm [Accessed 10/09/2017].

Eras, V.J.M. *Locks and Keys throughout the Ages*. Folkestone: Bailey Bros and Swinfen Ltd., 1974.

'FAQ'. *No Love Locks*: https://nolovelocks.com/faq/ [Accessed 04/07/2019].

'Fast Facts'. *Geocaching*: https://newsroom.geocaching.com/fast-facts/ [Accessed 25/05/2018].

Fees, C. 'Tourism and the Politics of Authenticity in a North Cotswold Town', in T. Selwyn (ed.), *The Tourist Gaze: Myths and Myth Making in Tourism* (Chichester: Wiley, 1996), 121–46.

Fernandez, J.W. 'Symbolic Consensus in a Fang Reformative Cult'. *American Anthropologist* 67(4) (1965), 902–29.

Finn, C. '"Leaving More Than Footprints": Modern Votive Offerings at Chaco Canyon Prehistoric Site'. *Antiquity* 71 (1997), 169–78.

Fisher, I. 'In Rome, a New Ritual on an Old Bridge'. *The New York Times* (6 August 2007): https://www.nytimes.com/2007/08/06/world/europe/06rome.html [Accessed 26/07/2018].

Fletcher, G. 'Sentimental Value'. *Journal of Vale Inquiry* 43 (2009), 55–65.

'Florence Tries to Stamp out Locks of Love'. *Italy Magazine* (1 May 2006): https://www.italymagazine.com/italy/tuscany/florence-tries-stamp-out-locks-love [Accessed 10/09/2017].

Foley, R. 'Performing Health in Place: The Holy Well as a Therapeutic Assemblage'. *Health and Place* 17 (2011), 470–79.

Fontijn, D.R. *Sacrificial Landscapes: Cultural Biographies of Persons, Objects and 'Natural' Places in the Bronze Age of the Southern Netherlands, c.2300–600 BC.* Leiden: Analecta Praehistorica Leidensia, 2002.

Forlong, J.G.R. *Faiths of Man: A Cyclopaedia of Religions.* Volume I. London: B. Quaritch, 1906.

'Forth Road Bridge Love Lock'. *Love Locks UK*: https://www.lovelocksuk.com/lovelocks-projects/LL09.html [Accessed 14/02/2019].

'Forth Road Bridge Lovelocks Raise £10,000'. *Edinburgh Evening News* (7 April 2015): https://www.edinburghnews.scotsman.com/news/forth-road-bridge-lovelocks-raise-10-000-1-3740145 [Accessed 14/02/2019].

'Forth Road Bridge Love Locks Raise Thousands for Charity'. *The Scotsman* (15 September 2015): https://www.scotsman.com/news/odd/forth-road-bridge-love-locks-raise-thousands-for-charity-1-3886956 [Accessed 14/02/2019].

Foster, M.D. 'Introduction: The Challenge of the Folkloresque', in M.D. Foster and J.A. Tolbert (eds), *The Folkloresque: Reframing Folklore in a Popular Culture World* (Logan: Utah State University Press, 2015).

Foster, M.D., and J.A. Tolbert (eds). *The Folkloresque: Reframing Folklore in a Popular Culture World.* Logan: Utah State University Press, 2015.

Fowler, C. *The Archaeology of Personhood: An Anthropological Approach.* London and New York: Routledge, 2005.

Fox, C. *A Find of the Early Iron Age from Llyn Cerrig Bach, Anglesey.* Cardiff: National Museum of Wales, 1946.

Frederick, U.K., and A. Clarke. 'Signs of the Times: Archaeological Approaches to Historical and Contemporary Graffiti'. *Australian Archaeology* 78(1) (2016), 54–57.

Fritsch, A., and K. Johannsen. *Ecotourism in Appalachia.* Lexington: University Press of Kentucky, 2004.

Frosh, P. *The Image Factory: Consumer Culture, Photography and the Visual Content Industry.* Oxford and New York: Berg, 2003.

Frost, W. 'Braveheart-ed Ned Kelly: Historic Films, Heritage Tourism and Destination Image'. *Tourism Management* 27 (2006), 247–54.

Fulford, M. 'Links with the Past: Pervasive "Ritual" Behaviour in Roman Britain'. *Britannia* 32 (2001), 199–218.

Gamble, C. *Origins and Revolutions: Human Identity in Earliest Prehistory.* Cambridge: Cambridge University Press, 2007.

Garrow, D. 'Odd Deposits and Average Practice: A Critical History of the Concept of Structured Deposition'. *Archaeological Dialogues* 19(2) (2012), 85–115.

Gell, A. *Art and Agency: An Anthropological Theory.* Oxford: Clarendon Press, 1998.

Giaccardi, E. 'Introduction', in E. Giaccardi (ed.), *Heritage and Social Media: Understanding Heritage in a Participatory Culture* (Abingdon: Routledge, 2012), 1–10.

Giaccardi, E. (ed.). *Heritage and Social Media: Understanding Heritage in a Participatory Culture*. Abingdon: Routledge, 2012.

Gibbs, J. *Mise-en-scène: Film Style and Interpretation*. London and New York: Wallflower, 2012.

'Gifts in Memory'. *Liverpool Women's NHS Foundation Trust*: https://www.liverpoolwomens.nhs.uk/charity/get-involved/gifts-in-memory/ [Accessed 14/02/2019].

'Glaciator'. *Miraculous: Tales of Ladybug and Cat Noir* [television programme] Netflix, Season 2, Episode 9, 14 January 2018.

'Global Strategy'. *UNESCO*: https://whc.unesco.org/en/globalstrategy/ [Accessed 09/07/2019].

Goh, S. 'Locked in Love'. *Asia One* (8 June 2015): https://www.asiaone.com/women/locked-love [Accessed 31/01/2019].

González-Ruibal, A. 'The Past is Tomorrow: Towards an Archaeology of the Vanishing Present'. *Norwegian Archaeological Review* 39(2) (2006), 110–25.

———. 'Time to Destroy: An Archaeology of Supermodernity'. *Current Anthropology* 49(2) (2008), 247–79.

Gould, R.A., and M.B. Schiffer (eds). *Modern Material Culture: The Archaeology of Us*. New York and London: Academic Press, 1981.

Graham. 'Love Lock Installation Opens in Distillery District'. *The Star* (7 August 2014): https://www.thestar.com/entertainment/2014/08/07/love_lock_installation_opens_in_distillery_district.html [Accessed 03/08/2018].

Gravari-Barbas, M., and S. Jacquot. 'No Conflict? Discourses and Management of Tourism-Related Tensions in Paris', in C. Colomb and J. Novy (eds), *Protest and Resistance in the Tourist City* (Oxon and New York: Routledge, 2017), 44–61.

Graves-Brown, P.M. (ed.). *Matter, Materiality and Modern Culture*. London and New York: Routledge, 2000.

Greenhill, P. 'Folklore and/on Film', in R.F. Bendix and G. Hasan-Rokem (eds), *A Companion to Folklore* (Hoboken, NJ: John Wiley & Sons, 2012), 483–99.

Greenwood, D. 'Culture by the Pound: An Anthropological Perspective on Tourism', in V. Smith (ed.), *Hosts and Guests: The Anthropology of Tourism* (Philadelphia: The University of Pennsylvania Press, 1989).

'Gretna Green Love Lock'. *Love Locks UK*: https://www.lovelocksuk.com/gretna/gretna-green-love-lock.html [Accessed 14/02/2019].

Grinsell, L.V. 'The Popular Names and Folklore of Prehistoric Sites in Menorca'. *Folklore* 95(1) (1984), 90–99.

Gruner, E. 'Replicating Things, Replicating Identity: The Movement of Chacoan Ritual Paraphernalia Beyond the Chaco World', in R.M. Van Dyke (ed.), *Practicing Materiality* (Tucson: University of Arizona Press, 2015), 56–78.

Gye, L. 'Picture This: The Impact of Mobile Camera Phones on Personal Photographic Practices'. *Continuum* 21(2) (2007), 279–388.

Gymnich, M., and K. Sheunemann. 'The "*Harry Potter* Phenomenon": Forms of World Building in the Novels, the Translations, the Film Series and the Fandom', in M. Gymnich, H. Birk and D. Burkhard (eds), *"Harry – Yer a Wizard!": Exploring J. K. Rowling's Harry Potter Universe* (Baden-Baden: Tectum Verlag, 2017), 11–36.

Hammond, C.I. 'Renegade Ornament and the Image of the Post-Socialist City: The Pécs "Love Locks", Hungary', in T. Kovács (ed.), *Halb-Vergangenheit: Städtische Räume und urbane Lebenswelten vor und nach der Wende* (Berlin: Lukas Verlag, 2010), 181–95.

Hammond, J.D. 'The Tourist Folklore of Pele: Encounters with the Other', in B. Walker (ed.), *Folklore and the Supernatural* (Boulder: University Press of Colorado, 1995), 159–79.

Handelman, D. *Models and Mirrors: Towards an Anthropology of Public Events*. Cambridge: Cambridge University Press, 1990.

Hannerz, U. *Transnational Connections: Culture, People, Places*. London and New York: Routledge, 1996.

Harris, J. 'A Gold Hoard from Corinth'. *American Journal of Archaeology* 43(2) (1939), 268–77.

Harris, O. 'Agents of Identity: Performative Practice at the Etton Causewayed Enclosure', in D. Hofmann, J. Mills and A. Cochrane (eds), *Elements of Being: Mentalities, Identities and Movements*. BAR International Series 1437 (Oxford: Archaeopress, 2005), 40–49.

Harrison, R. 'Surface Assemblages: Towards an Archaeology *in* and *of* the Present'. *Archaeological Dialogues* 18(2) (2011), 141–61.

Harrison, R., and J. Schofield. *After Modernity: Archaeological Approaches to the Contemporary Past*. Oxford: Oxford University Press, 2010.

Hartland, E.S. 'The Science of Folk-Lore'. *The Folk-Lore Journal* 3(2) (1885), 97–121.

———. 'Pin-Wells and Rag-Bushes'. *Folklore* 4(4) (1893), 451–70.

Harvey, D.C. 'Heritage Pasts and Heritage Presents: Temporality, Meaning and the Scope of Heritage Studies', in S. Watson, A.J. Barnes and K. Bunning (eds), *A Museum Studies Approach to Heritage* (Abingdon: Routledge, 2009), 319–38.

Hastings, J. *Encyclopaedia of Religion and Ethics*. Volume II. Edinburgh, T. & T. Clark, 1909.

Herbert, D.T. (ed.). *Heritage, Tourism and Society*. London: Mansell, 1995.

Hicks, D. 'The Material-Cultural Turn: Event and Effect', in D. Hicks and M.C. Beaudry (eds), *The Oxford Handbook of Material Culture Studies* (Oxford: Oxford University Press, 2010), 25–98.

Hicks, D., and M.C. Beaudry (eds). *The Oxford Handbook of Material Culture Studies*. Oxford: Oxford University Press, 2010.

Hilliard, M. '"Love Locks" to be Removed from Ha'penny Bridge'. *The Irish Times* (21 June 2013): https://www.irishtimes.com/news/love-locks-to-be-removed-from-ha-penny-bridge-1.1438002 [Accessed 13/08/2018].

Hillman, B. 'Paradise Under Construction: Minorities, Myths and Modernity in Northwest Yunnan'. *Asian Ethnicity* 4(2) (2003), 175–88.

Hinds, H.E., M.F. Motz and A.M.S. Nelson (eds). *Popular Culture Theory and Methodology: A Basic Introduction*. Madison: University of Wisconsin Press, 2006.

Hobsbawm, E., and T. Ranger (eds). *The Invention of Tradition*. Cambridge: Cambridge University Press, 1983.

Hodder, I. 'Bow Ties and Pet Foods: Material Culture and the Negotiation of Change in British Industry', in I. Hodder (ed.), *The Archaeology of Contextual Meanings* (Cambridge: Cambridge University Press, 1987), 11–19.

———. *Entangled: An Archaeology of the Relationships between Humans and Things*. Chichester: Wiley-Blackwell, 2012.

Hodder, I. (ed.). *The Archaeology of Contextual Meanings*. Cambridge: Cambridge University Press, 1987.

Hoggard, B. 'The Archaeology of Counter-Witchcraft and Popular Magic', in O. Davies and W. de Blécourt (eds), *Beyond the Witch Trials: Witchcraft and Magic in Enlightenment Europe* (Manchester and New York: Manchester University Press, 2004), 167–86.

Holloway, S. 'Materializing Maternal Emotions: Birth, Celebration, and Renunciation in England, c.1688–1830', in S. Downes, S. Holloway and S. Randles (eds), *Feeling Things: Objects and Emotions through History* (Oxford: Oxford University Press, 2018), 154–71.

Hollyoaks [television programme]. Channel 4, 19 December 2012.

Holtham, A. 'You Can Now Hang Your Own Love Lock on This Dubai Bridge'. *What's On* (30 January 2018): https://whatson.ae/dubai/2018/01/theres-now-love-locks-bridge-dubais-al-khawaneej-the-yard/ [Accessed 16/08/2019].

Holtorf, C., and A. Piccini (eds). *Contemporary Archaeologies: Excavating Now*. Frankfurt am Main: Peter Lang, 2011.

Holtorf, C., and T. Schadla-Hall. 'Age as Artefact: On Archaeological Authenticity'. *European Journal of Archaeology* 2(2) (1999), 229–47.

Honko, L. 'Memorates and the Study of Folk Beliefs'. *Journal of the Folklore Institute* 1 (1/2), 5–19.

Hope, R.C. *The Legendary Lore of the Holy Wells of England: Including Rivers, Lakes, Fountains, and Springs*. London: Elliot Stock, 1893.

Hornby, J. 'Rumors of Maggie: Outlaw News in Folklore', in P. Narváez and M. Laba (eds), *Media Sense: The Folklore-Popular Culture Continuum* (Bowling Green, OH: Bowling Green State University Popular Press, 1986), 99–115.

Horniman Museum. Love Token, 16.111: https://www.horniman.ac.uk/collections/browse-our-collections/object/62761 [Accessed 19/01/2018].

Hoskins, W.G. *The Making of the English Landscape*. London: Hodder and Stoughton, 1955.

Houlberg, M.H. 'Notes of Egungun Masquerades among the Oyo Yoruba'. *African Arts* 11(3) (1978), 51–66, pp. 99.

Houlbrook, C. 'Ritual, Recycling, and Recontextualisation: Putting the Concealed Shoe in Context'. *Cambridge Archaeological Journal* 23 (2013), 99–112.

———. 'The Mutability of Meaning: Contextualising the Cumbrian Coin-Tree'. *Folklore* 125(1) (2014), 40–59.

———. 'Possession through Deposition: The "Ownership" of Coins in Contemporary British Coin-Trees', in C. Hedenstierna-Jonson and A.M. Klevnas (eds), *Own and Be Owned: Archaeological Approaches to the Concept of Possession* (Stockholm: Stockholm Studies in Archaeology, Stockholm University, 2015), 189–214.

———. 'Small Change: Economics and the British Coin-Tree'. *Post-Medieval Archaeology* 4(1) (2015), 114–30.

———. 'The Penny's Dropped: Renegotiating the Contemporary Coin Deposit'. *Journal of Material Culture* 20(2) (2015), 173–89.

———. 'The Lock of Love: How Leaving Padlocks Became a Modern-Day Romantic Ritual'. *The Conversation* (10 February 2017): https://theconversation.com/the-lock-of-love-how-leaving-padlocks-became-a-modern-day-romantic-ritual-72140.

———. *The Roots of a Ritual: The Magic of Coin-Trees from Religion to Recreation*. Basingstoke: Palgrave Historical Studies in Witchcraft and Magic Series, 2018.

———. 'Lessons from Love-Locks: The Archaeology of the Contemporary Assemblage'. *Journal of Material Culture* 23(2) (2018), 214–38.

———. 'Des pieces de monnaie au cadenas: Un spectre des dépôts contemporains'. *Techniques & Culture* 70 (2019), Matérialiser les désirs: Techniques votives, 241–59.

Houlbrook, C., and A. Parker. 'Finding Love: The Materialities of Love-Locks and Geocaches'. *Journal of Material Culture* (2020).

Hughes, R. *Heaven and Hell in Western Art*. London: Weidenfeld and Nicolson, 1968.

Hukantaival, S. '"For a Witch Cannot Cross Such a Threshold!" Building Concealment Traditions in Finland c.1200–1950'. *Archaeologia Medii Aevie Finlandiae* 23. Turku: University of Turku, 2016.

Hull, E. *Folklore of the British Isles*. London: Methuen & Co., 1928.

Hulse, T.G. 'A Modern Votive Deposit at a North Welsh Holy Well'. *Folklore* 106 (1995), 31–42.

Hutchinson, L. 'Love-Locks are Being Removed from High Level Bridge and it is Causing Outrage'. *Chronicle Live* (28 March 2019): https://www.chroniclelive.co.uk/news/north-east-news/love-locks-removed-high-level-16042122 [Accessed 04/04/2019].

———. 'Love Locks Return to the High Level Bridge as Defiant Romantics Ignore Warning'. *ChronicleLive* (11 May 2019): https://www.chroniclelive.co.uk/news/north-east-news/love-locks-return-high-level-16254306 [Accessed 04/07/2019].

Hutton, R. (ed.). *Physical Evidence for Ritual Acts, Sorcery and Witchcraft in Christian Britain: A Feeling for Magic*. Basingstoke: Palgrave Historical Studies in Witchcraft and Magic Series, 2015.

Insoll, T. 'Introduction: Ritual and Religion in Archaeological Perspective', in T. Insoll (ed.), *The Oxford Handbook of the Archaeology of Ritual and Religion* (Oxford: Oxford University Press, 2011), 1–5.

Insoll, T. (ed.). *The Archaeology of Identities: A Reader*. Oxon and New York: Routledge, 2007.

———. *The Oxford Handbook of the Archaeology of Ritual and Religion*. Oxford: Oxford University Press, 2011.

Italian Charts. 'Tiziano Ferro – Ti scatterò una foto (Song)'. *Italiancharts.com*: https://italiancharts .com/showitem.asp?interpret=Tiziano+Ferro&titel=Ti+scatter%F2+una+foto&cat=s [Accessed 23/11/2018].

Italian Film Festival. *Love 14* (2010): https://www.italianfilmfestival.com.au/2010/films/love14/ [Accessed 23/11/2018].

Ivanow, W. *Kalāmi Pīr: A Treatise of Ismaili Doctrine, also (Wrongly) Called Haft-Babi Shah Sayyid Nasir*. Bombay: A.A.A. Fyzee, 1935.

Iwashita, C. 'Media Representation of the UK as a Destination for Japanese Tourists: Popular Culture and Tourism'. *Tourist Studies* 6(1) (2006), 59–77.

Jackson, B. 'A Film Note'. *Journal of American Folklore* 102 (1989), 388–89.

Jacob, P. 'Paris "Love Locks" Raise Thousands at Auction'. *The Connexion* (14 May 2017): https:// www.connexionfrance.com/French-news/Paris-love-locks-raise-thousands-at-auction [Accessed 07/07/2018].

James, B.T. 'Ciki and Jiki: The Inner and Outer Layers of Healers' Workspaces in Madina, Accra', in C. Houlbrook and N. Armitage (eds), *The Materiality of Magic: An Artefactual Investigation into Ritual Practices and Popular Beliefs* (Oxford: Oxbow, 2015), 143–69.

Jennifer. 'Love Locks for Valentine's Day Romance in Sparta WI'. *Franklin Victoria Bed and Breakfast* (27 January 2016): https://www.franklinvictorianbb.com/blog/love-locks-for-valentine-s-day-romance-in-sparta-wi [Accessed 14/02/2019].

Ji-yun, P. 'Seoul Tower Locked in Everlasting Love'. *Korea Times* (12 November 2008): http://www .koreatimes.co.kr/www/news/special/2011/03/181_34302.html [Accessed 13/08/2018].

Johnson, R. 'Love Locks in Memoriam?'. *FLS News* 85 (June 2018), 11.

Jokanović, J. 'Most ljubavi jačii od potopa!' *Alo!* (29 May 2014): http://arhiva.alo.rs/vesti/reportaza-srbija/most-ljubavi-jacii-od-potopa/56523 [Accessed 31/01/2019].

Jones, A., and G. MacGregor (eds). *Colouring the Past: The Significance of Colour in Archaeological Research*. Oxford and New York: Berg, 2002.

Jones, F. *The Holy Wells of Wales*. Cardiff: University of Wales Press, 1954.

Jones, J. 'Love Locks are the Shallowest, Stupidest, Phoniest Expression of Love Ever – Time to Put a Stop to It'. *The Guardian* (2 June 2015): https://www.theguardian.com/artanddesign/jonathan jonesblog/2015/jun/02/love-locks-removal-paris-rome-florence-stupidest-phoniest-time-to-stop [Accessed 02/07/2016].

Jones, R. 'Authenticity, the Media and Heritage Tourism: Robin Hood and Brother Cadfael as Midlands Tourist Magnets', in E. Waterton and S. Watson (eds), *Culture, Heritage and Representation: Perspectives on Visuality and the Past* (Farnham: Ashgate Publishing, 2010), 145–54.

Jones, S. '"They Made it a Living Thing Didn't They. . .': The Growth of Things and the Fossilisation of Heritage', in R. Layton, S. Shennan and P. Stone (eds), *A Future for Archaeology: The Past in the Present* (London: UCL Press, 2006), 107–26.

Jordan, D.K. 'The Jiaw of Shigaang (Taiwan): An Essay in Folk Interpretation', *Asian Folklore Studies* 35(2) (1976), 81–107.

Kaplan, M. 'Curation and Tradition on Web 2.0', in T.J. Blank and R.G. Howard (eds), *Tradition in the Twenty-First Century: Locating the Role of the Past in the Present* (University Press of Colorado, Utah State University Press, 2013), 123–48.

Karate Kid [film], dir. by Harald Zwart (US: Sony Pictures, 2010).

Kim, S.S. 'Extraordinary Experience: Re-enacting and Photographing at Screen Tourism Locations'. *Tourism and Hospitality Planning and Development* 7(1) (2010), 59–75.

Kindberg, T. et al. 'The Ubiquitous Camera: An In-Depth Study of Camera Phone Use'. *IEEE Pervasive Computing* 4(2) (2005), 42–50.

Kirshenblatt-Gimblett, B. 'Objects of Ethnography', in I. Karp and S.D. Lavine (eds), *Exhibiting Cultures: The Poetics and Politics of Museum Display* (Washington, DC and London: Smithsonian Institution Press, 1991), 386–443.

Kirshenblatt-Gimblett, B. 'The Electronic Vernacular', in G.E. Marcus (ed.), *Connected: Engagements with Media* (Chicago and London: University of Chicago Press, 1996), 21–65.

Kolås, A. 'Tourism and the Making of Place in Shangri-La'. *Tourism Geographies* 6(3) (2004), 262–78.

Kopytoff, I. 'The Cultural Biography of Things: Commoditization as Process', in A. Appadurai (ed.), *The Social Life of Things: Commodities in Cultural Perspective* (Cambridge: Cambridge University Press, 1986), 64–91.

Koven, M.J. 'Folklore Studies and Popular Film and Television: A Necessary Critical Survey'. *The Journal of American Folklore* 116(460) (2003), 176–95.

———. 'Most Haunted and the Convergence of Traditional Belief and Popular Television'. *Folklore* 118(2) (2007), 183–202.

Kovesi, C. 'From Ancient China to an Italian Chick Flick: The Story Behind Venice's Love Lock Burden'. *The Conversation* (29 September 2014): https://theconversation.com/from-ancient-china-to-an-italian-chick-flick-the-story-behind-venices-love-lock-burden-32182 [Accessed 01/02/2019].

Kozinets, R.V. *Netnography: Doing Ethnographic Research Online*. London: Sage, 2010.

Krause, R. 'Romantic Paris: Our 6 Favourite Activities for Romance'. *Travel? Yes Please* (2013): https://www.travelyesplease.com/travel-blog-romantic-paris/ [Accessed 13/02/2019].

Laba, M. 'Popular Culture and Folklore: The Social Dimension', in P. Narváez and M. Laba (eds), *Media Sense: The Folklore-Popular Culture Continuum* (Bowling Green, OH: Bowling Green State University Popular Press, 1986), 9–18.

Lady Gregory. *Cuchulain of Muirthemne: The Story of the Men of the Red Branch of Ulster*. London: Facsimile Publisher, 1902.

'Ladysmith Love Locks'. *Ladysmith Shopping Centre*: https://www.ladysmithshoppingcentre.com/Article/Ladysmith-Love-Locks?AspxAutoDetectCookieSupport=1 [Accessed 14/02/2019].

Laing, L.R. *Coins and Archaeology*. London: Weidenfeld and Nicolson, 1969.

Lanfant, M, J.B. Allcock and E.M. Bruner (eds), *International Tourism: Identity and Change*. London: SAGE Studies in International Sociology 47, 1995.

Lange, P. 'Video-Mediated Nostalgia and the Aesthetics of Technical Competencies'. *Visual Communication* 10(1) (2011), 25–44.

Larkham, P.J. 'Heritage as Planned and Conserved', in D.T. Herbert (ed.), *Heritage, Tourism and Society* (London: Mansell, 1995), 85–116.

Lavrinec, J. 'Urban Scenography: Emotional and Bodily Experience'. *LIMES: Borderland Studies* 6(1), (2013), 21–31.

Laycock, J. 'Mothman: Monster, Disaster and Community'. *Fieldwork in Religion* 3(1) (2008), 70–86.

Leach, E.R. *Political Systems of Highland Burma*. London: Athlone Press, 1964.

Leins, I. 'Coins in Context: Coinage and Votive Deposition in Iron Age South-East Leicestershire'. *The British Numismatic Journal* 77 (2007), 22–48.

Le Week-End [film], dir. by Roger Michell (UK: Curzon Film World, 2013).

Lewis. 'Paris is Selling Old Love Locks to Raise Money for Refugees'. *Smithsonian.com* (6 December 2016): https://www.smithsonianmag.com/smart-news/paris-selling-old-love-locks-raise-money-refugees-180961315/ [Accessed 18/06/2018].

Lexhagen, M., M. Larson and C. Lundberg. 'The Virtual Fan(G) Community: Social Media and Pop

Culture Tourism', in A.M. Munar, S. Gyimóthy and C. Liping (eds), *Tourism Social Media: Transformations in Identity, Community and Culture* (Bingley: Emerald Group, 2013), 133–57.

Li, F.M.S., and T.H.B. Sofield. 'World Heritage Listing: The Case of Huangshan (Yellow Mountain), China', in A. Leask and A. Fyall (eds), *Managing World Heritage Sites* (London and New York: Routledge, 2006), 250–62.

Lichfield, J. 'Part of Paris Bridge Collapses under Weight of "Love Locks" Left by Tourists'. *Independent* (9 June 2014): https://www.independent.co.uk/news/world/europe/part-of-paris-bridge-collapses-under-weight-of-love-locks-left-by-tourists-9512594.html [Accessed 04/07/2019].

Light, D. 'Performing Transylvania: Tourism, Fantasy and Play in a Liminal Place'. *Tourist Studies* 9(3) (2009), 240–58.

Lindsay, K. 'Woman's Heartache after Love-Lock in Memory of Husband is Cut from High Level Bridge'. *Chronicle Live* (31 March 2019): https://www.chroniclelive.co.uk/news/north-east-news/womans-heartache-after-love-lock-16051715?utm_source=twitter.com&utm_medium=social&utm_campaign=sharebar_[Accessed 04/04/2019].

Lloyds Bank. 'My Home's Safe and Sound' (leaflet) (2018).

'Lock in Your love'. *Locks Heath Shopping Village*: http://locksheathshoppingvillage.co.uk/news/title/lock-in-your-love [Accessed 14/02/2019].

Lockal na Petkovšku. *Facebook*: https://www.facebook.com/Lockal.Petkovsek/ [Accessed 09/07/2019].

Lock-Itz: http://lock-itz.com/ [Accessed 19/06/2018].

Lollymcd. 'SERIOUSLY! The Ha'penny Bridge is not The Love Lock Bridge'. *Tripadvisor* (2013): https://www.tripadvisor.co.uk/ShowTopic-g186605-i90-k6637516-o50-SERIOUSLY_The_Ha_penny_Bridge_is_not_The_Love_Lock_Bridge-Dublin_County_Dublin.html [Accessed 19/12/2018].

Longxi, Z. 'The Myth of the Other: China in the Eyes of the West'. *Critical Enquiry* 15(1) (1988), 108–31.

Loomis, H. *Adventures in the Middle Ages: A Memorial Collection of Essays and Studies*. New York: Burt Franklin.

'Los Gatos Museum Offers Space for "Love Locks" Amid City Crackdown'. *KPIX CBS BayArea* (1 February 2013): https://sanfrancisco.cbslocal.com/2013/02/01/los-gatos-museum-offers-space-for-love-locks-amid-city-crackdown/ [Accessed 09/07/2019].

'Lose the Locks: Cut the Padlocks Off Pero's Bridge'. *Fundsurfer* (2016): https://www.fundsurfer.com/project/lose-the-locks-cut-the-padlocks-off-peros-bridge [Accessed 09/10/2016].

Lovata, T. 'Marked Trees: Exploring the Context of Southern Rocky Mountain Arborglyphs', in T. Lovata and E. Olton (eds), *Understanding Graffiti: Multidisciplinary Studies from Prehistory to the Present* (Walnut Creek, CA: Left Coast Press, 2015), 91–104.

Lovata, T., and E. Olton (eds). *Understanding Graffiti: Multidisciplinary Studies from Prehistory to the Present*. Walnut Creek, CA: Left Coast Press, 2015.

'Love Lock Bridge'. *Bakers Ranch*: https://www.bakersranch.com/love-lock-bridge/ [Accessed 14/02/2019].

'Love Lock Necklace'. *Tiffany & Co.*: https://www.tiffany.co.uk/jewelry/necklaces-pendants/return-to-tiffany-love-lock-necklace-36340282/ [Accessed 15/03/2019].

'Lovelock – Rome'. *Love Locks UK*: https://www.lovelocksuk.com/travel-destinations/lovelock-rome.html [Accessed 01/02/2019].

Love Locks [film], dir. by Martin Woods (US: Hallmark, 2017).

'Love Locks Dangle Charm, Clear CZ'. *Pandora*: https://us.pandora.net/en/love-locks-dangle-charm-clear-cz/791807CZ.html [Accessed 15/03/2019].

'Love Locks Drop Earrings'. *Pandora*: https://uk.pandora.net/en/earrings/drop-earrings/love-locks-drop-earrings/296575.html [Accessed 15/03/2019].

'Love Locks 2015: Care for Children'. *Total Giving*: https://www.totalgiving.co.uk/appeal/lovelocks [Accessed 14/02/2019].

Love Locks UK: https://www.lovelocksuk.com/romance.html [Accessed 19/06/2018].

Love Lock Trees. *'Introducing the Love Lock Tree . . . in Detail'* (leaflet) (2018).

Love Lock Trees: www.lovelocktrees.com [Accessed 30/07/2019].

'Lover Locks on Mt. Huangshan – Contemporary Love Stories'. *China Odyssey Tours*: https://www.chinaodysseytours.com/special-topic-about-china/huangshan-lover-locks.html [Accessed 01/02/2019].

Love Without Locks: http://www.lovewithoutlocks.paris.fr/ [Accessed 09/07/2019].

Lowbridge, C. 'Are Love Locks on Bridges Romantic or a Menace?' *BBC News* (5 May 2014): https://www.bbc.co.uk/news/uk-england-27221707 [Accessed 04/07/2019].

Lowenthal, D. *The Past is a Foreign Country*. Cambridge: Cambridge University Press, 1985.

———. *The Heritage Crusade and the Spoils of History*. Cambridge: Cambridge University Press, 1998.

Lucas, G. *Understanding the Archaeological Record*. Cambridge: Cambridge University Press, 2012.

Lucas, P.C. 'Constructing Identity with Dreamstones: Megalithic Sites and Contemporary Nature Spirituality'. *Nova Religio: The Journal of Alternative and Emergent Religions* 11(1) (2007), 31–60.

MacCannell, D. *The Tourist: A New Theory of the Leisure Class*. Berkeley: University of California Press, 1976 [2013].

Macdonald, S. 'On "Old Things": The Fetishization of Past Everyday Life', in N. Rapport (ed.), *British Subjects: An Anthropology of Britain* (Oxford and New York: Berg, 2002), 89–106.

MacDowall, L. 'Graffiti, Street Art and Theories of Stigmergy', in J. Lossau and Q. Stevens (eds), *The Uses of Art in Public Spaces* (New York and London: Routledge, 2015), 33–48.

Maiwald, K. 'An Ever-Fixed Mark? On the Symbolic Coping with the Fragility of Partner Relationships by Means of Padlocking'. *Forum: Qualitative Social Research* 17(2) (2016).

Make Love Locks: https://www.makelovelocks.com/ [Accessed 15/03/2019].

Marcus, M.I. 'Dressed to Kill: Women and Pins in Early Iran'. *Oxford Art Journal* 17(2) (1994), 3–15.

Margolin, V. 'Introduction: How Do I Love Thee? Objects of Endearment in Contemporary Culture', in A. Moran and S. O'Brien (eds), *Love Objects: Emotion, Design and Material Culture* (London: Bloomsbury, 2014), 15–21.

Markham, A., and E. Buchanan. 'Ethical Decision-Making and Internet Research Version 2: Recommendations from the AoIR Ethics Working Committee'. *Association of Internet Researchers*, 2012.

Mason, R. *The Economics of Conspicuous Consumption*. Cheltenham: Edward Elgar Publishing, 1998.

McNeill, L.S. 'Portable Places: Serial Collaboration and the Creation of a New Sense of Place'. *Western Folklore* 66(3/4) (2007), 281–99.

———. 'Real Virtuality: Enhancing Locality by Enacting the Small World Theory', in T.J. Blank (ed.), *Folk Culture in the Digital Age: The Emergent Dynamics of Human Interaction* (Utah State University Press, 2012), 85–97.

Meethan, K. *Tourism in Global Society: Place, Culture, Consumption*. Basingstoke: Palgrave Macmillan, 2001.

Meinig, D.W. 'The Beholding Eye: Ten Versions of the Same Scene', in D.W. Meinig and J. Brinckerhoff Jackson (eds), *The Interpretation of Ordinary Landscapes: Geographical Essays* (New York: Oxford University Press, 1979), 33–48.

Meinig, D.W., and J. Brinckerhoff Jackson (eds). *The Interpretation of Ordinary Landscapes: Geographical Essays*. New York: Oxford University Press, 1979.

Merrifield, R. *The Archaeology of Ritual and Magic*. London: B.T. Batsford Ltd, 1987.

Meskell, L. 'Negative Heritage and Past Mastering in Archaeology'. *Anthropological Quarterly* 75(3) (2002), 557–74.

Milišić, M. 'S katancem smo jači: Most ljubavi u Vrnjačkoj banji, mesto stogodišnje "magije"'. *Glas Javnosti* (15 June 2006): http://arhiva.glas-javnosti.rs/arhiva/2006/06/15/srpski/R06061403.shtml [Accessed 01/02/2019].

Miller, 'Face-to-Face with the Digital Folk: The Ethics of Fieldwork on Facebook', in T.J. Blank (ed.), *Folk Culture in the Digital Age: The Emergent Dynamics of Human Interaction* (Utah State University Press, 2012), 212–32.

Mills, B.J. 'Remembering While Forgetting: Depositional Practices and Social Memory at Chaco', in B.J. Mills and W.H. Walker (eds), *Memory Work: Archaeologies of Material Practices* (Santa Fe: School for Advanced Research Press, 2008), 81–108.

Mills, B.J., and W.H. Walker (eds). *Memory Work: Archaeologies of Material Practices*. Santa Fe: School for Advanced Research Press, 2008.

Mitchell, T. '"Utu" – A New Zealand Revenge Tragedy'. *Film Criticism* 8(3) (1984), 47–53.

Moccia, F. *Ho voglia di te* [*I Want You*]. Milan: Feltrinelli Traveller, 2006.

Moore, S.F., and B.G. Myerhoff (eds). *Secular Ritual*. Assen: Van Gorcum, 1997.

Moran, A., and S. O'Brien (eds). *Love Objects: Emotion, Design and Material Culture*. London: Bloomsbury, 2014.

Morris, L. 'How Militias Doomed an Iraqi's Attempt to Replicate Paris's "Love Locks" Bridge'. *The Washington Post* (30 January 2015): https://www.washingtonpost.com/world/middle_east/how-mi litias-doomed-an-iraqis-attempt-to-replicate-pariss-love-locks-bridge/2015/01/30/32fd94fc-cbd7-4844-a641-40c99c3f1711_story.html?utm_term=.36a574675cdf [Accessed 20/03/2019].

Morris, R.C. 'A Room with a Voice: Mediation and Mediumship in Thailand's Information Age', in F.D. Ginsburg, L. Au-Lughod and B. Larkin (eds), *Media Worlds: Anthropology on a New Terrain* (Berkeley: University of California Press, 2002), 383–99.

Morrison, R. 'Some Account of Charms, Talismans, and the Felicitous Appendages Worn about the Person, or Hung Up in the House, &c. Used by the Chinese'. *Transactions of the Royal Asiatic Society of Great Britain and Ireland* 3(2) (1833), 285–90.

Moser, H. 'Vom Folklorismus in unserer Zeit'. *Volkskunde* 58 (1962), 177–209.

Moss, M. 'Sculpture at Heart of Love Locks'. *Dayton Daily News* (16 May 2015): https://www.day tondailynews.com/entertainment/arts--theater/sculpture-heart-love-locks/EMsZzn7e9icyRD9ls GpJ4I/ [Accessed 14/02/2019].

'Most Ljubavi'. *TripAdvisor*: https://www.tripadvisor.co.uk/Attraction_Review-g304103-d8492844-Reviews-Most_Ljubavi-Vrnjacka_Banja_Central_Serbia.html [Accessed 31/01/2019].

'Most Ljubavi'. *Wikipedia* (Nd.): https://en.wikipedia.org/wiki/Most_Ljubavi [Accessed 31/01/2019].

Mostafa, M. 'Southern Iraq Bridge Sees Rare Streak of Romance with Love Lock, Officials Offended'. *Iraqi News* (29 May 2017): https://www.iraqinews.com/features/southern-iraq-bridge-sees-rare-streak-romance-love-lock-officials-offended/ [Accessed 20/03/2019].

Munar, A.M., S. Gyimóthy and C. Liping (eds), *Tourism Social Media: Transformations in Identity, Community and Culture*. Bingley: Emerald Group, 2013.

Munjeri, D. 'Following the Length and Breadth of the Roots: Some Dimensions of Intangible Heritage', in L. Smith and N. Akagawa (eds), *Intangible Heritage* (London and New York: Routledge, 2009), 131–50.

Muri, G. '"The World's Smallest Village": Folk Culture and Tourism Development in an Alpine Context'. *Traditional Dwellings and Settlements Review* 13(1) (2001), 53–64.

Museum of Witchcraft and Magic. 1702 Amulet: Padlock: https://museumofwitchcraftandmagic.co .uk/object/amulet-padlock/ [Accessed 17/06/2019].

Myerhoff, B.G. 'We Don't Wrap Herring in a Printed Page: Fusion, Fictions and Continuity in Secular Ritual', in S.F. Moore and B.G. Myerhoff (eds), *Secular Ritual* (Assen: Van Gorcum, 1997), 199–224.

Mykytenko, O. 'Padlock and Key as Attributes of the Wedding Ceremony: Traditional Symbolism and Contemporary Magic (on the Material of the Slavic Tradition)', in T. Minniyakhmetova and K. Velkoborská (eds), *The Ritual Year 10: Magic in Rituals and Rituals in Magic* (Innsbruck and Tartu: ELM Scholarly Press, 2015), 487–96.

Narváez, P. (ed.). *The Good People: New Fairylore Essays*. New York: Garland Publishing, 1991.

Narváez, P., and M. Laba. 'Introduction: The Folklore-Popular Culture Continuum', in P. Narváez and M. Laba (eds), *Media Sense: The Folklore-Popular Culture Continuum* (Bowling Green, OH: Bowling Green State University Popular Press, 1986), 1–8.

National Museum Wales. Lovespoon, 53.101.15: https://museum.wales/collections/online/object/fe8fc6e8-f701-3a40-a64b-181bc3e2ad1e/Lovespoon/?field0=string&value0=lovespoon&field1=with_images&value1=on&page=2&index=14 [Accessed 23/03/2019].

National Museum Wales. Lovespoon, 01.374.3: https://museum.wales/collections/online/object/0d5d5437-1a0d-399b-bcf9-e87224c60e85/Lovespoon/?field0=string&value0=lovespoon&field1=with_images&value1=on&page=2&index=15 [Accessed 23/03/2019].

Needham, S.P. 'Selective Deposition in the British Early Bronze Age'. *World Archaeology* 20(2) (1988), 229–48.

Neighbours [television programme]. Channel 5, Episode 6819, 13 February 2014.

Neighbours [television programme]. Channel 5, Episode 6820, 14 February 2014.

Neighbours [television programme]. Channel 5, Episode 6823, 19 February 2014.

Neighbours [television programme]. Channel 5, Episode 7292, 2 February 2016.

Neighbours [television programme]. Channel 5, Episode 7710, 13 October 2017.

Neighbours [television programme]. Channel 5, Episode 7714, 19 October 2017.

Neighbours [television programme]. Channel 5, Episode 7717, 24 October 2017.

Newall, V.J. 'The Adaptation of Folklore and Tradition'. *Folklore* 98(2) (1987), 131–51.

'No Love Locks'. *Facebook* (23 January 2019): https://www.facebook.com/pg/NoLoveLocks/about/?ref=page_internal [Accessed 04/07/2019].

Now You See Me [film], dir. by Louis Leterrier (US: Summit Entertainment, 2013).

O'Neal, S. 'Some Jerkface Stole the Parks and Recreation "Leslie And Ben" Lock from Paris'. *AV News* (2 June 2014): https://news.avclub.com/some-jerkface-stole-the-parks-and-recreation-leslie-an-1798265993 [Accessed 19/12/2018].

O'Neill, S. '"In Fair [Europe], Where We Lay Our Scene": *Romeo and Juliet*, Europe and Digital Cultures', in J.F. Cerdá, D. Delabastita and K. Gregor (eds), *Romeo and Juliet in European Culture* (Amsterdam and Philadelphia: John Benjamins, 2017), 283–300.

Opie, I., and P. Opie. 'Certain Laws of Folklore', in V.J. Newall (ed.), *Folklore Studies in the Twentieth Century: Proceedings of the Centenary Conference of the Folklore Society* (Woodbridge: D. S. Brewer, 1978), 64–75.

O'Reilly, K. *Ethnographic Methods* (London: Routledge, 2005).

Orr, A. 'Plotting Jane Austen: Heritage Sites as Fictional Worlds in the Literary Tourist's Imagination'. *International Journal of Heritage Studies* 24(3) (2018), 243–55.

Osborne, R. 'Hoards, Votives, Offerings: The Archaeology of the Dedicated Object'. *World Archaeology* 36(1) (2004), 1–10.

Otnes, C.C., and E.H. Pleck. *Cinderella Dreams: The Allure of the Lavish Wedding*. Berkeley and Los Angeles: University of California Press, 2003.

Owen, J. 'Rome: City of Love'. *Telegraph: Travel* (30 September 2007): https://www.telegraph.co.uk/travel/destinations/europe/italy/rome/738422/Rome-city-of-love.html [Accessed 13/08/2018].

Page, S. 'Love in the Time of Demons: Magic and the Medieval Cosmos', in Ashmolean Museum, *Spellbound: Magic, Ritual & Witchcraft* (Oxford: Ashmolean Museum, 2018), 19–63.

Paine, C. *Religious Objects in Museums: Private Lives and Public Duties*. London and New York: Bloomsbury, 2013.

'Paris "Love Locks" Removed from Bridges'. *BBC News* (1 June 2015): https://www.bbc.co.uk/news/world-europe-32960470 [Accessed 03/03/2016].

'Paris Love Locks Sold for Charity'. *France Revisited: Museum and Exhibition News* (8 May 2017): http://francerevisited.com/2017/05/paris-love-locks-sold-charity/ [Accessed 09/07/2019].

'Paris Won't Fine "Love Lock" Lovebirds . . . but Struggles to Solve the Problem'. *The Local* (4 May 2018): https://www.thelocal.fr/20180504/paris-wont-fine-love-lock-lovebirds-but-struggles-to-solve-problem [Accessed 04/07/2019].

Patch, H.R. *The Other World: According to Descriptions in Medieval Literature*. Cambridge, MA: Harvard University Press, 1950.

Penrose, S. (ed.), *Images of Change: An Archaeology of England's Contemporary Landscape*. Swindon: English Heritage, 2007.

Perse, E.M. *Media Effects and Society*. Mahwah and London: Lawrence Erlbaum Associates, 2008.

Pershing County Chamber of Commerce and Visitors Center: https://www.pershingchamber.com/home.html [Accessed 16/02/2019].

Petts, D. 'Memories in Stone: Changing Strategies and Contexts of Remembrance in Early Medieval Wales', in H. Williams (ed.), *Archaeologies of Remembrance: Death and Memory in Past Societies* (New York: Kluwer Academic/Plenum Publishers, 2003), 193–213.

Pfister, M. 'Juliet's Balcony: The Balcony Scenes from Shakespeare's Romeo and Juliet across Cultures and Media', in J.F. Cerdá, D. Delabastita and K. Gregor (eds), *Romeo and Juliet in European Culture* (Amsterdam and Philadelphia: John Benjamins, 2017), 37–59.

Picard, D., and M. Robinson. 'Remaking Worlds: Festivals, Tourism and Change', in D. Picard and M. Robinson (eds), *Festivals, Tourism and Social Change: Remaking Worlds* (Bristol: Channel View Publications, 2006), 1–31.

———. *Festivals, Tourism and Social Change: Remaking Worlds*. Bristol: Channel View Publications, 2006.

Pietrobruno, S. 'Scale and the Digital: The Miniaturizing of Global Popular Knowledge'. *International Journal of Cultural Studies* 15(2) (2012), 101–16.

———. 'YouTube and the Social Archiving of Intangible Heritage'. *New Media & Society* 15(8) (2013), 1259–76.

Pintoro, B. *Love Lock*. Kindle Edition, 2017.

Pitt Rivers Museum. Amulet in the Form of a Padlock, 1985.51.738: http://objects.prm.ox.ac.uk/pages/PRMUID221770.html [Accessed 16/08/2019].

———. Charm Made from a Tin Dish Containing a Padlock Set in an Earthen Pack with Feathers, Hair and Plant Stems at One Edge, 1891.40.1: http://objects.prm.ox.ac.uk/pages/PRMUID27373.html [Accessed 16/08/2019].

———. 'Charm' Necklet of Twisted Cotton with Strung Magical Items (Padlock, Tree Seed, 2 Small Horns etc.), 1925.12.1: http://objects.prm.ox.ac.uk/pages/PRMUID27434.html [Accessed 16/08/2019].

———. Part of a Native Sorcerer's Outfit: Bird Skull with Metal Padlock through the Top, Bound to a Pointed Stick, 1933.93.44: http://objects.prm.ox.ac.uk/pages/PRMUID190633.html [Accessed 16/08/2019].

———. Silver Padlock & Chain for a Child to Wear as Protection against Spirits, 1909.32.45: http://objects.prm.ox.ac.uk/pages/PRMUID45335.html [Accessed 17/06/2019].

———. St Valentine Key, Italy, 1985.52.459: http://web.prm.ox.ac.uk/amulets/index.php/keys-amulet2/index.html [Accessed 23/03/2019].

Poignant, R. *Oceanic Mythology: The Myths of Polynesia, Micronesia, Melanesia, Australia*. London: Hamlyn, 1967.

'Poll: Should "Love Locks" Be Allowed on Bridges?' *The Journal.ie*: https://www.thejournal.ie/love-locks-poll-on-bridges-1947130-Feb2015/ [Accessed 19/12/2018].

Pontas Literary Agency. 'Grand Central Publishing to Publish the #1 Italian Bestselling Author Federico Moccia'. *Pontas Agency*: https://www.pontas-agency.com/grand-central-publishing-to-publish-the-1-italian-bestselling-author-federico-moccia/ [Accessed 23/11/2018].

Preston, C. 'Panty Trees, Shoe Trees, and Legend'. *FOAFTALE News: News Letter of the International Society for Contemporary Legend Research* 67 (May 2007), 11–12.

Priest, V., P. Clay and J.D. Hill. 'Iron Age Gold from Leicestershire'. *Current Archaeology* 188 (2003), 358–60.

Primiano, L.N. 'Oprah, Phil, Geraldo, Barbara and Things That Go Bump in the Night', in E.M. Mazur and K. McCarthy (eds), *God in the Details: American Religion in Popular Culture* (London: Routledge, 2001), 47–63.

'Princess Fragrance'. *Miraculous: Tales of Ladybug and Cat Noir* [television programme] Netflix, Season 1, Episode 23, 6 April 2016.

Pudelek, J. 'Case Study: British Heart Foundation'. *Third Sector* (26 March 2013): https://www .thirdsector.co.uk/case-study-british-heart-foundation/fundraising/article/1176282 [Accessed 14/ 02/2019].

Raj, S.J., and C.G. Dempsey. 'Introduction: Ritual Levity in South Asian Traditions', in S.J. Raj and C.G. Dempsey (eds), *Sacred Play: Ritual Levity and Humor in South Asian Religions* (Albany: State University of New York Press, 2010), 1–20.

Randles, S. 'Signs of Emotion: Pilgrimage Tokens from the Cathedral of Notre-Dame of Chartres', in S. Downes, S. Holloway and S. Randles (eds), *Feeling Things: Objects and Emotions through History* (Oxford: Oxford University Press, 2018), 43–57.

Rappaport, R.A. *Ecology, Meaning, and Religion.* Berkeley: North Atlantic Books, 1979.

Rathje, W.L. 'Modern Material Culture Studies'. *Advances in Archaeological Method and Theory* 2 (1979), 1–37.

———. 'A Manifesto for Modern Material Culture Studies', in R.A. Gould and M.B. Schiffer (eds), *Modern Material Culture: The Archaeology of Us* (New York and London: Academic Press, 1981), 51–56.

Reader, I. 'Dead to the World: Pilgrims in Shikoku', in I. Reader and T. Walter (eds), *Pilgrimage in Popular Culture* (Basingstoke: Macmillan Press Ltd., 1993), 107–36.

Richards, C., and J. Thomas. 'Ritual Activity and Structured Deposition in Later Neolithic Wessex', in R. Bradley and J. Gardiner (eds), *Neolithic Studies: A Review of Some Current Research* (Oxford: BAR British Series 133, 1984), 189–218.

Richardson, M. 'The Gift of Presence: The Act of Leaving Artifacts at Shrines, Memorials, and Other Tragedies', in P.C. Adams, S. Hoelscher and K.E. Till (eds), *Textures of Place* (Minneapolis: University of Minnesota Press, 2001), 257–72.

Richter, F., and V. Pfeiffer-Kloss. 'Bridges, Locks and Love: Most Tumski in Wroclaw and Thousands of Love Bridges Worldwide: New Secular Sanctuaries in Today's Public Space?', in M. Kowalewski and A. Malgorzata Królikowska (eds), *Transforming Urban Sacred Places in Poland and Germany* (Baden-Baden: Nomos Verlagsgesellschaft, 2017), 187–202.

Ricketts, J.R. 'Land of (Re) Enchantment: Tourism and Sacred Space at Roswell and Chimayó, New Mexico'. *Journal of the Southwest* 53(2) (2011), 239–61.

Rider, C. *Magic and Impotence in the Middle Ages.* Oxford: Oxford University Press, 2006.

Rizzo, A. 'Romans Putting a Lock on Love'. *The Star* (13 March 2007): https://www.thestar.com/ news/2007/03/13/romans_putting_a_lock_on_love.html [Accessed 15/07/2019].

Roach, C.M. *Happily Ever After: The Romance Story in Popular Culture.* Bloomington and Indianapolis: Indiana University Press, 2016.

Rock, J.F. 'Studies in Na-Khi Literature'. *Bulletin de l'Ecole française d'Extrême-Orient* 37 (1937), 50.

Rostas, S. 'From Ritualization to Performativity: The Concheros of Mexico', in F. Hughes-Freeland (ed.), *Ritual, Performance, Media* (London: Routledge, 1998), 85–103.

Rountree, K. 'Performing the Divine: Neo-Pagan Pilgrimages and Embodiment at Sacred Sites'. *Body & Society* 12(4) (2006), 95–115.

Rouse, W.L. 'Charmed Lives: Charms, Amulets, and Childhood in Urban America, 1870–1940'. *The Journal of American Culture* 40(1) (2017), 21–33.

Rowlands, M. 'The Role of Memory in the Transmission of Culture'. *World Archaeology* 25(2) (1993), 141–51.

Ryall, J. 'Japan's Young Couples Risking Death in "Love Padlock" Ritual'. *The Telegraph* (17 April 2009): https://www.telegraph.co.uk/news/worldnews/asia/japan/5168563/Japans-young-couples-risking-death-in-love-padlock-ritual.html [Accessed 13/08/2018].

Safi, M. 'Melbourne Bridge's 20,000 "Love Locks" to be Removed'. *The Guardian* (18 May 2015): https://www.theguardian.com/australia-news/2015/may/18/melbourne-bridges-20000-love-locks-to-be-removed-amid-structural-concerns [Accessed 03/03/2016].

Said, E. *Orientalism*. Harmondsworth: Penguin Books, 1978.

Sallnow, M.J. 'Pilgrimage and Cultural Fracture in the Andes', in J. Eade and M.J. Sallnow (eds), *Contesting the Sacred: The Anthropology of Christian Pilgrimage* (London and New York: Routledge, 1991), 137–53.

Salvato, N. 'Out of Hand: YouTube Amateurs and Professionals'. *Drama Review* 53(3) (2009), 67–83.

Samuel, H. 'Paris to Remove Love Padlocks from Pont des Arts Bridge'. *The Telegraph* (4 May 2010): https://www.telegraph.co.uk/news/worldnews/europe/france/7677377/Paris-to-remove-love-pad locks-from-Pont-des-Arts-bridge.html [Accessed 13/08/2018].

———. 'Love Padlocks Vanish from Paris Bridge'. *The Telegraph* (13 May 2010): https://www.tele graph.co.uk/news/worldnews/europe/france/7720365/Love-padlocks-vanish-from-Paris-bridge .html [Accessed 13/08/2018].

———. 'Paris to Auction Off "Love Locks" and Give Proceeds to Migrant Charities'. *The Telegraph* (4 May 2017): https://www.telegraph.co.uk/news/2017/05/04/paris-auction-love-locks-give-pro ceeds-charity/ [Accessed 07/07/2018].

Santino, J. 'Performative Commemoratives, the Personal, and the Public: Spontaneous Shrines, Emergent Ritual, and the Field of Folklore'. *Journal of American Folklore* 117 (2004), 363–72.

Saraçoğlu Çelik, S. 'Lost Treasures: Locks'. *International Journal of Science Culture and Sport* 3(1) (2015), 96–112.

Sargent, A. 'The Darcy Effect: Regional Tourism and Costume Drama'. *The International Journal of Heritage Studies* 4(3/4) (1998), 177–86.

Sax, B. 'The Tower Ravens: Invented Tradition, Fakelore, or Modern Myth?' *Storytelling, Self, Society* 6(3) (2010), 231–40.

Scallon, A. 'No Love for the Locks'. *Expats.cz* (9 February 2015): https://news.expats.cz/community/ no-love-for-the-locks/ [Accessed 04/07/2019].

Scarborough Museums & Gallery. Clarke Charms Collection 1946.48.

———. Clarke Charms Collection 1946.289.

Schama, S. *Landscape and Memory*. London: Fontana Press, 1996.

Schiffman Tufano, L. 'Love Locks on Chicago Bridges Don't Have the Staying Power of Paris'. *DNA Info* (25 August 2014): https://www.dnainfo.com/chicago/20140825/downtown/love-locks-on-chicago-bridges-dont-have-staying-power-of-paris/ [Accessed 04/07/2019].

Schofield, J. 'Editorial: Modern Times'. *Conservation Bulletin English Heritage* 56 (2007), 2.

Schwartz, O. 'Praying with a Camera Phone: Mediation and Transformation in Jewish Rituals'. *Culture and Religion* 11(3), 177–94.

Scobie, P. 'Love Locks Sculpture Unveiled in Vancouver's Queen Elizabeth Park'. *CBC News* (8 September 2016): http://www.cbc.ca/news/canada/british-columbia/love-locks-sculpture-unveiled-in-vancouver-1.3751968 [Accessed 03/08/2018].

Score, V. 'Ritual, Hoards and Helmets: A Ceremonial Meeting Place for the Corieltavi'. *The Leicestershire Archaeological and Historical Society* 80 (2006), 197–207.

———. 'Hallaton: Sacred Space in Context', in V. Score (ed.), *Hoards, Hounds and Helmets: A Conquest-Period Ritual Site at Hallaton, Leicestershire* (Leicester: Leicester Archaeology Monograph 21, 2011), 152–64.

Scott, A. *The Cornuta Curse*. CreateSpace Independent Publishing Platform, 2014.

'Second Chunce'. *Parks and Recreation* [television programme] NBC, Season 6, Episode 10, 9 January 2014.

Selwyn, T. 'Introduction', in T. Selwyn (ed.), *The Tourist Gaze: Myths and Myth Making in Tourism* (Chichester: Wiley, 1996).

Selwyn, T. (ed.). *The Tourist Gaze: Myths and Myth Making in Tourism*. Chichester: Wiley, 1996.

Shafer, S.S. '"Love Locks" Banned on Ky. Bridge'. *USA Today* (9 August 2013): https://eu.usatoday .com/story/news/nation/2013/08/09/love-locks-banned-on-ky-bridge/2634509/ [Accessed 13/08/ 2018].

Sham Idrees VLOGS. 'WE PLACED A LOCK on THE LOVE BRIDGE'. *YouTube* (23 April 2018): https://www.youtube.com/watch?v=_i620ymURKg [Accessed 16/03/2019].

Shanks, M., and C. Tilley. *Re-Constructing Archaeology: Theory and Practice*. Cambridge: Cambridge University Press, 1987.

'She's Not There'. *Chanel: Coco Mademoiselle* [television advertisement], 2013.

Shils, E. 'Ritual and Crisis'. *Philosophical Transactions of Royal Society of London*, Series B, 251(772) (1966), A Discussion on Ritualization of Behaviour in Animals and Man, 447–50.

Shopkins: World Vacation [film], dir. by Richard Bailey (UK/US: Universal, 2017).

Silverman, H. 'Touring Ancient Times: The Present and Presented Past in Contemporary Peru'. *American Anthropologist* 104(3) (2002), 881–902.

Singh, S. 'Secular Pilgrimages and Sacred Tourism in the Indian Himalayas'. *GeoJournal* 64 (2005), 215–23.

Skounti, A. 'The Authentic Illusion: Humanity's Intangible Cultural Heritage, the Moroccan Experience', in L. Smith and N. Akagawa (eds), *Intangible Heritage* (London and New York: Routledge, 2009), 74–92.

Sleight, S. 'Memory in the City', in A. Maerker, S. Sleight and A. Sutcliffe (eds), *History, Memory and Public Life: The Past in the Present* (London and New York: Routledge, 2018), 126–58.

Smart Love Lock: Share your Moments: http://smartlovelock.com/en/ [Accessed 15/03/2019].

Smith, P. 'Contemporary Legends and Popular Culture: "It's the Real Thing"', in H.E. Hinds, M.F. Motz and A.M.S. Nelson (eds), *Popular Culture Theory and Methodology: A Basic Introduction* (Madison: University of Wisconsin Press, 2006), 318–43.

Snodgrass, A. 'The Economics of Dedication at Greek Sanctuaries', in A. Snodgrass (ed.), *Archaeology and the Emergence of Greece: Collected Papers on Early Greece and Related Topics (1965–2002)* (Edinburgh: Edinburgh University Press, 2006), 258–68.

Sotiriadis, M.D., and C. van Zyl. 'Electronic Word-of-Mouth and Online Reviews in Tourism Services: The Use of Twitter by Tourists'. *Electronic Commerce Research* 13(1) (2013), 103–24.

Spooner, B. 'Weavers and Dealers: The Authenticity of an Oriental Carpet', in A. Appadurai (ed.), *The Social Life of Things: Commodities in Cultural Perspective* (Cambridge: Cambridge University Press, 1986), 195–235.

Squires, N. 'Venice Cracks Down on "Love Locks"'. *The Telegraph* (24 August 2011): https://www .telegraph.co.uk/news/worldnews/europe/italy/8719307/Venice-cracks-down-on-love-locks.html [Accessed 04/07/2019].

Stead, I.M. *The Salisbury Hoard*. Gloucestershire: Tempus, 1998.

Steves, R. 'The Love Story Behind the Via dell'Amore'. *Smithsonian* (30 September 2009): https:// www.smithsonianmag.com/travel/the-love-story-behind-the-via-dellamore-12224656/ [Accessed 14/02/2019].

Stewart, S. *On Longing: Narratives of the Miniature, the Gigantic, the Souvenir, the Collection*. Durham and London: Duke University Press, 1993.

Stokes, P. *Ferocious*. New York: Tor Teen, 2017.

Stolarz, S. 'Cologne Gets a Lock on Love'. *DW* (2 February 2009): https://www.dw.com/en/cologne-gets-a-lock-on-love/a-4008316 [Accessed 26/07/2018].

Storey, J. *Inventing Popular Culture: From Folklore to Globalization*. Oxford: Blackwell, 2003.

Stromberg, P. 'Consensus and Variation in the Interpretation of Religious Symbolism: A Swedish Example'. *American Ethnologist* 8(3) (1981), 544–59.

Styles, J. *Threads of Feeling: The London Foundling Hospital's Textile Tokens, 1740–1770*. London: The Foundling Museum, 2010.

Tanavoli, P., and J.T. Wertime. *Locks from Iran: Pre-Islamic to Twentieth Century*. Washington, DC: Smithsonian Institution, 1976.

Taylor, J. 'Pikinini in Paradise: Photography, Souvenirs and the "Child Native" in Tourism', in K. Alexeyeff and J. Taylor (eds), *Touring Pacific Culture* (Canberra: ANU Press, 2016), 361–78.

Testa, A. '"Fertility" and the Carnival 2: Popular Frazerism and the Reconfiguration of Tradition in Europe Today'. *Folklore* 128 (2017), 111–32.

Thames and Field. *River Finds*: http://www.thamesandfield.com/river-finds-1 [Accessed 18/06/2019].

The Gentle Author. 'Love Tokens from the Thames'. *Spitalfields Life* (23 October 2017): http://spital fieldslife.com/2017/10/23/love-tokens-from-the-thames-x/ [Accessed 13/03/2018].

'The History of Love Locks'. *Love Locks*: http://lovelocksonline.com/history/ [Accessed 01/02/2019].

'The Hurt Stalker'. *iZombie* [television programme] Netflix, Season 2, Episode 8, 1 December 2015.

'The Mall's Foundation Charity Fund'. *Quartet Community Foundation*: https://quartetcf.org.uk/fund holders/the-malls-fountain-charity-fund/ [Accessed 21/03/2018].

Thomas, J. *Understanding the Neolithic*. London and New York: Routledge, 1999.

Thomas, N. *Entangled Objects: Exchange, Material Culture, and Colonialism in the Pacific*. Cambridge MA: Harvard University Press, 1991.

Thompson, M. *Rubbish Theory: The Creation and Destruction of Value*. Oxford: Oxford University Press, 1979.

Thompson, S. *The Folktale*. Berkeley: University of California, [1946] 1977.

Thompson, T. 'Netizens, Revolutionaries, and the Inalienable Right to the Internet', in T.J. Blank (ed.), *Folk Culture in the Digital Age: The Emergent Dynamics of Human Interaction* (Utah State University Press, 2012).

Tilley, C. 'Objectification', in C. Tilley, W. Keane, S. Küchler, M. Rowlands and P. Spyer (eds), *Handbook of Material Culture* (London: Sage Publications, 2006), 60–73.

Tilley, C. et al. (eds). *Handbook of Material Culture*. London: Sage Publications, 2006.

Timothy, J.D., and S.W. Boyd. *Heritage Tourism*. Harlow: Prentice Hall, 2003.

Tinkler, P. 'A Fragmented Picture: Reflections on the Photographic Practices of Young People'. *Visual Studies* 23(3) (2008), 255–66.

Toumi, H. 'Love Padlocks in Jeddah Cause Stir'. *Gulf News* (26 February 2017): https://gulfnews .com/world/gulf/saudi/love-padlocks-in-jeddah-cause-stir-1.1984322 [Accessed 16/08/2019].

Trevor-Roper, H. 'The Invention of Tradition: The Highland Tradition of Scotland', in E. Hobsbawm and T. Ranger (eds), *The Invention of Tradition* (Cambridge: Cambridge University Press, 1983), 15–41.

Trew, B. 'Saudi Crusade Over "Infidel" Love Padlocks'. *The Times* (1 March 2017): https://www.the times.co.uk/article/lovers-locks-upset-saudi-traditionalists-k2q2mqhrc [Accessed 20/03/2019].

Tuchman-Rosta, C. 'From Ritual Form to Tourist Attraction: Negotiating the Transformation of Classical Cambodian Dance in a Changing World'. *Asian Theatre Journal* 31(2) (2014), 524–44.

Tuleja, T. 'The Tooth Fairy: Perspectives on Money and Magic', in P. Narváez (ed.), *The Good People: New Fairylore Essays* (New York: Garland Publishing, 1991), 406–25.

Turner, A.K. *The History of Hell*. New York: Mariner Books, 1993.

Turner, L., and J. Ash, *The Golden Hordes: International Tourism and the Pleasure Periphery*. London: Constable, 1975.

Turner, V. *From Ritual to Theatre: The Human Seriousness of Play*. New York: PAJ Books, 1982.

Turner, V., and E. Turner. *Image and Pilgrimage in Christian Culture: Anthropological Perspectives*. New York: Columbia University Press, 1978.

Tussyadiah, I.P., and D.R. Fesenmaier. 'Mediating Tourist Experiences: Access to Places via Shared Videos'. *Annals of Tourism Research* 36(1) (2009), 24–40.

UNESCO. 'Convention for the Protection of Cultural Property in the Event of Armed Conflict with Regulations for the Execution of the Convention 1954'. *UNESCO.org* (1954): http://portal.unesco.org/en/ev.php-URL_ID=13637&URL_DO=DO_TOPIC&URL_SECTION=201.html [Accessed 20/08/2018].

———. 'Convention Concerning the Protection of the World Cultural and Natural Heritage: World Heritage Committee, Twenty-fifth Session. Helsinki, 11–16 December 2001', WHC-01/CONF.208/23, 2001.

———. *Convention for the Safeguarding of the Intangible Cultural Heritage.* Paris: UNESCO, 2003.

———. 'Films and Videos': https://digital.archives.unesco.org/en/collection/films-and-videos/ [Accessed 24/03/2019].

———. 'Global Strategy': https://whc.unesco.org/en/globalstrategy/ [Accessed 03/03/2019].

———. 'Policies Regarding CREDIBILITY of the World Heritage List'. *World Heritage Policy Compendium* (2019).

———. 'Videos'. *YouTube*: https://www.youtube.com/user/unesco/videos [Accessed 24/03/2019].

Urry, J. *The Tourist Gaze.* London: SAGE, 2002.

Van de Port, M. 'Visualizing the Sacred: Video Technology, "Televisual" Style, and the Religion Imagination in Bahian Candomblé'. *American Ethnologist* 33(3) (2006), 444–61.

Van der Merwe, L. 'Bridge of Love Locks in Pretoria'. Interview on SABC (19 August 2014): https://www.youtube.com/watch?v=IToTDtDfxQA [Accessed 14/06/2019].

Van Gennep, A. *The Rites of Passage.* Chicago: University of Chicago Press, 1960.

'Venice Launches New Campaign against "Love Locks"'. *Gazzetta del Sud* (26 August 2014): https://gazzettadelsud.it/speciali/english/2014/08/26/venice-launches-new-campaign-against-love-locks--f5c31bb9-1d6d-4d70-b1c6-9678e655b52c/ [Accessed 03/07/2019].

Vente aux Enchères. *Vente Solidaire des Cadenas d'Armour de la Ville de Paris.* Paris: Crédit Municipal de Paris, 2017.

'Videos'. *Lovers Lock*: http://loverslock.com/videos/ [Accessed 13/02/2019].

VikingCruises [Twitter post]: https://twitter.com/VikingCruises/status/1083092769466249217 [Accessed 22/07/2019].

Vlaskina, N. 'The Types of Divination Used by the Don Cossacks: Highlighting Areas of Distribution', in T. Minniyakhmetova and K. Velkoborská (eds), *The Ritual Year 10: Magic in Rituals and Rituals in Magic* (Innsbruck and Tartu: ELM Scholarly Press, 2015), 303–10.

Vrnjačka Banja Tourist Organization, *Guide* (Nd.).

Walhouse, J. 'Rag-Bushes and Kindred Observances'. *The Journal of Anthropological Institute of Great Britain and Ireland* 9 (1880), 97–106.

Wallgren, M. 'Love Locks Tradition Spreads to Utah County'. *Serve Daily* (1 February 2018): https://servedaily.com/around-town/love-locks-tradition-spreads-utah-county/ [Accessed 14/02/2019].

Wallis, R.J., and J. Blain. 'Sites, Sacredness, and Stories: Interactions of Archaeology and Contemporary Paganism'. *Folklore* 114(3) (2003), 307–21.

Walloth, C. 'Emergence in Complex Urban Systems: Blessing or Curse of Planning Efforts?', in C. Walloth, J.M. Gurr and J.A. Schmidt (eds), *Understanding Complex Urban Systems: Multidisciplinary Approaches to Modeling* (New York: Springer, 2014), 121–32.

Walsham, A. *The Reformation of the Landscape: Religion, Identity, and Memory in Early Modern Britain and Ireland.* Oxford: Oxford University Press, 2011.

———. 'Sacred Topography and Social Memory: Religious Change and the Landscape in Early Modern Britain'. *Journal of Religious History* 36(1) (2012), 31–51.

Waterfall, C. 'The Padlocks of Paris: Love Incarcerated'. *Bonjour Paris* (2010): https://bonjourparis.com/archives/padlocks-paris-love-incarcerated/ [Accessed 04/12/2018].

Waterton, E., and S. Watson (eds). *Culture, Heritage and Representation: Perspectives on Visuality and the Past.* Farnham: Ashgate Publishing, 2010.

Watson, S., A.J. Barnes and K. Bunning (eds). *A Museum Studies Approach to Heritage*. Abingdon: Routledge, 2009.

'Wedding Gallery'. *Statham Lodge*: https://stathamlodge.com/wedding-gallery/ [Accessed 14/02/2019].

Weiner, A.B. *Inalienable Possessions: The Paradox of Keeping-While-Giving*. Berkeley: University of California Press, 1992.

Werner, E.T.C. 1890. 'Chinese Superstitions'. *British Periodicals*, September 1890, 955–60.

Wertime, J.W. 'Metalwork', in J. Gluck and S.H. Gluck (eds), *A Survey of Persian Handicraft: A Pictorial Introduction to the Contemporary Folk Arts and Art Crafts of Modern Iran* (Tehran: Bank Melli, 1977), 113–60.

Wight, M. 'Peasant Art in Britain'. *Design* 48(2) (1946), 18.

Williams, F.C. 'Revoking Vows'. *FLS Newsletter* 88 (2019), 9.

Williams, H. (ed.). *Archaeologies of Remembrance: Death and Memory in Past Societies*. New York: Kluwer Academic/Plenum Publishers, 2003.

Williams, J. 'The Coins and the Helmet'. *Current Archaeology* 188 (2003), 361–62.

Wood, J. 'Filming Fairies: Popular Film, Audience Response and Meaning in Contemporary Fairy Lore'. *Folklore* 117(3) (2006), 279–96.

Yolen, J. 'Folklore vs. Fakelore, the Epic Battle'. *The Horn Book Magazine* (September/October 2014), 55–57.

www.ingramcontent.com/pod-product-compliance
Lightning Source LLC
Chambersburg PA
CBHW051447050726

47593CB00005B/1967